tear here

The Top Cooking Tips of All Time

This tear-out card has handy little tips you can refer to when you cook.

➤ To put out a fat fire, throw baking soda on the fire. Do not use water!

➤ To get rid of cooking odors in your house, prepare a potpourri using an assortment of spices such as cinnamon sticks, cloves, whole allspice, and some citrus peel. Place these in a small amount of water and cook the ingredients over low heat. Replenish water as it evaporates.

➤ Always preheat your oven unless a recipe tells you otherwise.

➤ To make cake layers come out flat rather than rounded at the top, wet a sheet of newspaper and fold it to match the circumference of the baking pan. Wrap the wet paper around the outside edges of the pan and secure it with kitchen string. Then pour in the batter and bake the cake.

➤ When a recipe gives a range in the amounts of salt, herbs, condiments, and such to be used in a recipe, use the minimum amount first, and then taste the recipe to see if it needs more.

➤ To get the greatest volume when whipping cream, chill the bowl and beaters first.

➤ To get the greatest volume when whipping egg whites, let the egg whites come to room temperature first.

➤ You can slice raw meat more easily (for example, to use for stir-frying) if you put it in the freezer for 30 minutes first.

➤ To peel a clove of garlic, place it on a cutting board and hit it gently with the flat side of a cleaver, large knife, or pot bottom. The paper casing slips away.

➤ To peel a tomato, drop it into boiling water for 20 seconds, and then rinse it with cold water. Make a small X cut with the tip of a sharp knife at the stem end and peel the skin back; it should come off easily. If it doesn't, immerse the tomato for another 10 seconds and proceed with peeling.

➤ To measure flour, always spoon the flour into a measuring cup (not a measuring pitcher) and level off the top with the flat side of a knife. Do not scoop the flour with the cup.

➤ Before you fry breaded foods, let them stand for 15 to 30 minutes so the coating will stick better.

➤ Always slice bread with a serrated knife.

➤ Always use a rack when you roast poultry so the bird doesn't sit in its own rendering fat.

➤ If you need a warm place for yeast dough to rise, turn the oven on to 450 degrees, wait 2 minutes, turn the oven off, and place the dough inside.

➤ When you substitute vanilla extract for vanilla bean, add the extract after the ingredients have cooled.

➤ If brown sugar gets lumpy, put an apple wedge in it and microwave it on high for 20 seconds, or put the apple and sugar in an airtight container; within a few hours, the sugar will be fine.

➤ If you are cooking for company, don't decide to clean out your closet the same day. You'll enjoy the experience more if you relax and take all the time you need to prepare the meal.

alpha
books

Commonly Used Measurement Equivalents You Need to Know

1 TB.	=	3 tsp.	1 medium garlic clove	=	½ tsp. minced garlic (approx.)
2 TB.	=	⅛ cup	8 oz. hard/firm cheese	=	2 cups grated cheese
5 TB. plus 1 tsp.	=	⅓ cup	6 oz. chocolate chips	=	1 cup
12 TB.	=	¾ cup	2 slices bread	=	1 cup bread crumbs
1 cup	=	8 fluid oz.	1 lb. all-purpose flour	=	3½–4 cups
2 TB. butter	=	1 oz.	1 lb. granulated sugar	=	2 cups
1 medium lemon	=	3–4 TB. juice and 2–3 tsp. grated peel (approx.)			

Substitutions for When You Run Out of an Ingredient in a Recipe

1 tsp. baking powder	=	¼ tsp. baking soda plus ½ tsp. cream of tartar	1 clove garlic	=	⅛ tsp. garlic powder
1 cup broth or stock	=	1 bouillon cube dissolved in 1 cup boiling water	1 tsp. dried herbs	=	1 TB. fresh herbs
			1 TB. prepared mustard	=	1 tsp. dried mustard
			1 cup sour cream	=	1 cup yogurt
1 cup buttermilk	=	1 cup yogurt, or 1 cup (minus 1 TB.) warm milk plus 1 TB. vinegar or lemon juice. Let stand 5 minutes.	1 cup brown sugar	=	1 cup white sugar plus 1½ TB. molasses or 1 cup honey plus ½ tsp. baking soda
¾ cup cracker crumbs	=	1 cup dry bread crumbs	2 cups canned tomatoes	=	2½ cups peeled fresh cooked tomatoes
1 cup cream	=	⅓ cup melted butter plus ¾ cup milk	1 2" piece vanilla bean	=	1 tsp. pure vanilla extract

Cooking Abbreviations to Keep in Mind

t., tsp.	=	teaspoon
T., TB., Tbl., Tblsp.	=	tablespoon
C., c.	=	cup
pt.	=	pint
oz.	=	ounce
lb.	=	pound
min.	=	minutes
hr.	=	hours
g	=	gram
L	=	liter
mL	=	milliliter

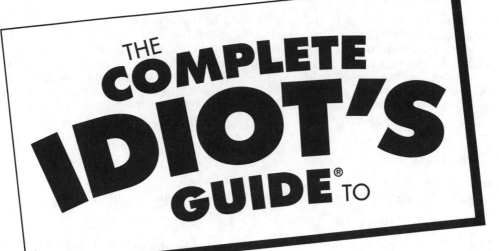

THE COMPLETE IDIOT'S GUIDE® TO

Cooking Basics

Third Edition

by Ronnie Fein

alpha books

Macmillan USA, Inc.
201 West 103rd Street
Indianapolis, IN 46290

A Pearson Education Company

Publisher
Marie Butler-Knight

Product Manager
Phil Kitchel

Managing Editor
Cari Luna

Senior Acquisitions Editor
Renee Wilmeth

Development Editor
Jennifer Williams

Production Editor
JoAnna Kremer

Copy Editor
Amy Borelli

Illustrator
Jody P. Schaeffer

Cover Designers
Mike Freeland
Kevin Spear

Book Designers
Scott Cook and Amy Adams of DesignLab

Indexer
Angie Bess

Layout/Proofreading
Svetlana Dominguez
Bob LaRoche
Gloria Schurick

Contents at a Glance

Contents

9 A Trip to the Dairy Barn and Down the Grocery Aisles   101

Part 4: Getting Ready to Cook   115

10 Making a Game Plan   117

Foreword

I learned to cook at my mother's knee. I was the eldest daughter in a family of eight children, and it was simply a matter of course that I pitched in and cooked a meal or part of a meal with some regularity. Lucky for me, my mother enjoyed time in the kitchen and passed on her enthusiasm. Consequently, I was excited when my first apartment brought with it my first kitchen—and ever since I have preferred the kitchen to all other rooms, no matter where I have lived. However, despite my youthful confidence, I could have used Ronnie Fein's sure hand and practical advice back in those days when I was organizing and enjoying my first kitchen.

I can only imagine how delighted and *relieved* beginning cooks, as well as those who have already logged some kitchen hours, will feel when they read this book. Relieved because here, at last, is a book so packed with straightforward, sensible advice that even the most terrified novice will feel as though a trusted friend has walked into the room with the sole purpose of helping. From organizing kitchen countertops, cupboards, and drawers to success with your first dinner party, Ronnie is there. Her measured advice never wavers: Be sensible, follow your own style, read the recipe several times, keep it simple, use good equipment, trust yourself, and plan ahead.

This advice is not doled out like cheese and stale crackers at a political fund-raiser. It is carefully and thoroughly presented. She discusses such details as where to keep the measuring spoons, store the nutmeg, and put the fish. She emphasizes such major points as the importance of good organization for good cooking, telling readers (among other things) to clean up as they go along, to measure accurately, and to put things back where they belong. As Ronnie explains, a kitchen can be sleek or cluttered, depending on the taste of the cook, but regardless of its appearance, the kitchen should be organized as a serious work center. This means you will be able to find the long-handled spatula, the baking sheet, or the balsamic vinegar when it's needed, and will have ample space to roll the pastry, chop the onions, and drain the pasta.

In her friendly manner, Ronnie teaches beginning cooks how to stock the kitchen and buy cookware, how to buy meat and vegetables, when to buy food in bulk and when not to, what tastes fine if bought frozen and what should only be purchased fresh. She includes extensive glossaries for meats, poultry, fish, dairy products, vegetables, fruits, and herbs and spices. In addition, there is a glossary of kitchen procedures in which Ronnie defines not only common cooking terms, but everything from *bind* and *coddle* to *stud* and *truss*.

More experienced cooks can benefit by brushing up on skills and picking up tips and kitchen wisdom generously served by the author. Or, such readers might just skip to the end of each chapter, where Ronnie summarizes the chapter's information in a handy section titled "The Least You Need to Know." Just skimming these boxes is a refresher course in good kitchen sense.

One of the sections I most appreciated was the one on reading a recipe. Few cookbook authors dare broach this subject because (I suspect) it strikes too close to home. But with obvious regard for the intelligence of the reader, Ronnie explains her ideas of a good recipe: "A good recipe tells all. A well-planned recipe lists all ingredients in the order they are used." As would any conscientious recipe writer, she urges readers to read the recipe at least once to determine its appeal, its level of difficulty, and its usefulness. Consider such things as: Are all the ingredients listed used? Do you have a 5-quart Dutch oven or the equivalent? She then suggests that the reader read the recipe at least one more time for familiarity. Excellent advice!

Page after page of helpful advice builds in a crescendo that leads to the recipes. The actual recipes in this book are simply written and tend to be on the easy side. However, the author goes way beyond meatloaf and apple pie. The recipes are meant to inspire the beginner as well as the more adept cook to enter the kitchen with enthusiasm, tie on an apron, and *cook!* In other words, just because the book is directed toward the novice, the author never assumes the novice is not interested in eating well.

This is a book all parents will want to give grown children starting out on their own. However, its not just for newlyweds and single people—it's for everyone who is the least bit doubtful about his or her cooking skills. With Ronnie Fein's assurance and helpful hand at every step of the way, an entire generation of beginning cooks will come to experience the sheer joy of time spent in the kitchen.

—Mary Goodbody

Mary Goodbody is a senior editor for *Chocolatier* magazine and *Pastry Art and Design* magazine, author of *The Best of Chocolate*, and co-author of *Sunday Dinners*.

Introduction

People have been cooking food since Neanderthal man discovered fire hundreds of thousands of years ago. We humans have been at it for so long that many people believe they are supposed to grow up *knowing* how to cook. Some feel like idiots if they don't.

But let's not confuse lack of intelligence with lack of knowledge. You might not have lots of confidence and you might feel intimidated about cooking. You might think you could never get a meal to come out right. But no one who buys a book about cooking could possibly be an idiot. In fact, the people who buy cookbooks typically are men and women who are capable in many other areas; they just feel they should be more competent in the kitchen.

This book was designed to let you be just that: competent in the kitchen. It will help you understand that cooking skills are something you can learn easily.

What You'll Learn in This Book

This book is divided into six parts that take you through the cooking process, from your first look at the empty kitchen of your abode to the recipe masterpieces you will prepare in it. You will see that learning to cook means learning to organize your space and your time, as well as knowing how to shop and what to buy. It involves reading food labels and recipes. It includes a basic knowledge of cooking methods and culinary terms and some awareness of the appropriate tools you will use when you cook. With this step-by-step approach, you will build your confidence as well as your competence.

Here's what the six parts cover:

Part 1, "Organizing Your Kitchen," mentally plants you in your empty kitchen and describes what you are likely to see. It focuses on the most convenient places to put food and kitchen tools, and also gives tips on how to organize recipes.

Part 2, "You've Gotta Have Them: Kitchen Staples," talks about filling bare cupboards with the staple foods, pots and pans, cutlery, and appliances you'll probably need, and explains why you need these items.

Part 3, "Did Anyone ever Give You a Shopping Lesson?" begins by discussing when and where you can shop for food and food products. The chapters then turn to buying decisions (such as whether to buy brand names or generic products). If you want your meals to taste terrific, you've got to know how to choose quality ingredients. This part will guide you through the selection process, give some information on how to use the ingredients (round steak versus sirloin steak, for example), and offer tips on how to store your staples.

Part 4, "Getting Ready to Cook," helps you make the transition from shopper to cook. It begins by explaining how to read a recipe so that you will be fully prepared when you start cooking, and then focuses on how to tell whether or not a recipe is a good one. This section also tells you in detail how to measure and substitute ingredients, and provides information on the meaning of many cooking terms. The "Compendium of the Top 100+ Cooking Terms," a super-glossary, defines more than 100 of the most common cooking terms—procedures you must follow or things you must do to food as you cook it (*whip* or *knead*, for example). In appropriate cases, it also explains how these procedures work or why they are important. This part also has a "Compendium of Catchwords Used in Recipes" (a second super-glossary) that explains food terms (so that you'll know what words such as *al dente* mean) and equipment terms (so that you'll know a *bain-marie* from a *double boiler*). Finally, this part describes fundamental cooking methods so that you can easily distinguish the difference between stir-frying and sautéing.

Part 5, "Now You're Cooking," helps you create your first dinner—not just cooking it, but getting all the different parts of the meal to come out on time and doing all the noncooking tasks such as setting the table. If you've made a mistake, don't worry: There's a chapter here that will help you determine whether or not the mistake is fixable and, if possible, how to fix it. There's also a bit on beverages to serve before, with, and after dinner. And if you feel like you're an accomplished cook at this point, it's time to invite company. A chapter here, complete with menus, will help you plan a few simple get-togethers.

Part 6, "Recipes," is simply that. The recipes (all kitchen-tested) cover everything from hors d'oeuvres to desserts. Most are easy, easy, *easy* to prepare—even though some may contain ingredients you may not have used before. (These easy recipes are marked, appropriately enough, "Easy.") There also are a few more involved recipes (marked "Intermediate") for when you gain some confidence, and a few even more advanced ones (marked "Challenging") for you to tackle when you are ready—and you will be.

By the time you finish the book and have honed your skills preparing some of the recipes, you will find that you feel smarter and more sophisticated about food. It is simply a matter of learning something easily learnable, having the courage to test your abilities, and being a bit adventurous.

Extras

Besides all the explanation and advice, this book has lots of tidbits of useful or interesting information strewn here and there in sidebars throughout the chapters. The following sidebars set these tidbits apart.

Fein on Food

These boxes contain fascinating morsels of history and folklore about a particular food or ingredient. You don't need this information to be a good cook, but it makes great dinner conversation.

Something Simple

These boxes present simple, tasty, almost-recipes anybody can throw together.

Kitchen Clue

These boxes contain hints that make cooking more organized, more accurate, more fun, and more easily understandable.

What Is It?

These sidebars define cooking terms that might be unfamiliar. Some of these words can also be found in the super-glossary sections.

Warnings

These boxes caution you of circumstances or practices that could mean trouble in the kitchen, such as slicing hot peppers without protecting your skin.

Second Thoughts

These sidebars tell you how to change the recipe a bit so that you can wind up with two, three, or more recipes in one.

Acknowledgments

I would like to express a debt of gratitude to Renee Wilmeth, whose professionalism, insight, and tenacity are extraordinary, but mostly for listening and for following through. Thanks also go to Jennifer Williams for her thoughtful comments, suggestions, encouragement, and good humor. I also appreciate the efforts of JoAnna Kremer, Phil Kitchel, Angie Bess, Jody Schaeffer, and everyone else on the hardworking Macmillan team who helped make this third edition a reality.

Trademarks

All terms mentioned in this book that are known to be or are suspected of being trademarks or service marks have been appropriately capitalized. Alpha Books and Macmillan USA, Inc., cannot attest to the accuracy of this information. Use of a term in this book should not be regarded as affecting the validity of any trademark or service mark.

Part 1
Organizing Your Kitchen

Here you are in your new living quarters. You're newly married, newly divorced, newly graduated, newly widowed, whatever. It's your own place and that's great, but facing an empty kitchen can be a daunting proposition. You may have a bed to sleep in, a couch to sit on, and a TV to watch, but the kitchen cupboards are BARE! The refrigerator might not be turned on. You haven't got a plate to put a sandwich on. How are you going to feed yourself?

Relax and read on. The next two chapters will introduce you to the logic of your kitchen. I'll show you where things belong and how to take advantage of counter space, cabinet space, and refrigerator space so that you can be prepared to buy what you need. Ready? Let's begin.

Chapter 1

Staking Your Claim to Your Kitchen

> **In This Chapter**
>
> ➤ Sizing up your kitchen to see where you want things
>
> ➤ Using the "outer space" of your kitchen and deciding how you want it to look
>
> ➤ Determining what goes on the countertops

You've been in a kitchen before—but maybe not your *own* kitchen. Perhaps you've moved, or redesigned your kitchen. Or maybe you simply want to change your cooking style, learn new ideas, and develop better culinary habits. This chapter explains how to size up your space so that you can make your kitchen convenient and fun to cook in.

Taking Charge of Your Kitchen Space

Unless you are redesigning your entire kitchen, you can't rearrange the refrigerator, oven, sink, and cabinets. But the rest of the space is yours to rule. Arrange it so that you will *enjoy* cooking in it.

Don't worry if your kitchen is small. Big kitchens aren't the key to great meals. If you use your space efficiently, you can prepare everything from simple snacks to sumptuous feasts.

Take a Good Look Around

Walk through your kitchen to get a feel for the layout. Determine where your countertop work area will be. The part nearest the sink is usually the most convenient, especially when you prepare vegetables or other foods that require quick and easy access to running water.

Open the drawers and cabinets. You probably will form an initial impression about what belongs where. But before you start putting things away, think about the kind of kitchen that makes you happy.

Kitchen Clue

Many people keep blenders on the counter simply out of habit. Blenders are superb for mixing liquid ingredients and blending beverages. But they are compact enough to fit in a cabinet. If you use a blender only occasionally, why not store it?

What Is It?

Skimmers are long-handled tools that you use to remove unwanted pieces of food, soup scum, or fat from the surface of soup, stew, and so on.

Your Kitchen Style: The Homey Kitchen or the Stark Look

One of the first particulars to consider is whether you'll feel calmer in a kitchen that's clear of clutter or whether the sight of hanging pots and pans, herb crocks, and books and magazines will make you happier.

Suit yourself, with this one caveat: Leave plenty of room to work so that the extra stuff doesn't get in your way while you're cooking and cause more work.

What Goes on the Countertop

Whether you're neat or comfortable with clutter, there are a few simple guidelines to follow when deciding what to keep on the countertop.

If you use an item with regularity, keep it out.

An item that is too large or heavy to store and lift out—a knife block or stand mixer, for example—should also be on the countertop.

In kitchens with minimal drawer space, you may need a tall, durable urn or jug on the countertop to hold long-handled tools such as whisks, wooden spoons, *skimmers*, spaghetti forks, and ladles. Plastic-covered boxes or pretty baskets that hold small gadgets may also come in handy if you're short on drawer space.

Decorative items that are also practical (such as cookie jars, bread boxes, paper towel holders, spice racks, and canisters) can go on the countertop. Canister foods such as flour and sugar, however, can be stored in a cabinet.

If you don't have much cabinet space, consider mounting shelves or hooks on the wall (for spices, potholders, dishtowels, and mugs) or hanging racks from the ceiling (for pots and pans and so on). Shelf dividers and inside-the-cabinet door racks are useful if you prefer to keep these items hidden.

If you don't have enough room or counter space for all your stuff, think about buying space-saving appliances that you can mount under the cabinets.

The Least You Need to Know

➤ Keep items you use regularly on the countertop.

➤ Bulky, heavy items belong on the countertop.

Chapter 2

What to Do with All Your Stuff

In This Chapter

➤ Deciding where to put food and nonfood items

➤ Capitalizing on refrigerator space

➤ Organizing your recipes

Now that you've decided which items to keep on the counter, you have to figure out where to put everything else: food, cookware, dishes, and so on. This chapter helps you find the best places for these items so that cooking will be hassle-free. The chapter also includes some suggestions about where to put your cleaning supplies, even though you might not want to think about the cleaning-up part of cooking. And, don't forget, you've got to keep your recipes somewhere. What's the best place? You'll find that here, too.

Do You Have to Line Your Drawers and Cabinets?

Some people line cabinets and/or drawers before storing things in them. There are pros and cons to this trick. Lined shelves and drawers are easier to keep clean, but the process takes a lot of time. Is it worth it? That's up to you.

What Type of Drawers and Cabinets Are Best for What?

There's a logic to using your kitchen's inner spaces. Obviously, no one would put dish detergent in the high cabinet over the refrigerator. It's more convenient to keep it under the sink. High, out-of-reach places are best for the paella pans, French-onion soup crocks, and other wedding cookware gifts you never returned, as well as the electric juice extractor you once swore you needed.

Wide drawers are better for items that usually go together: flatware, serving spoons, cooking utensils, and so on. Sometimes these drawers have dividers that separate spoons from forks and the like. Or you can buy flatware trays or drawer separators. Deep drawers accommodate paper goods, plastic storage containers, dish towels and aprons, and other stackable items; some are wide enough to fit pots and pans or bowls.

What to Do with All the Stuff That Isn't Food

You'll find cooking, serving, and cleaning up more convenient if you store your dishes, glassware, and cups and saucers near the sink or dishwasher. Pot holders and *trivets* must be within easy reach when you're cooking, so place them near the stove or oven—either on a hook or in a nearby drawer. Pots and pans are handier if you put them in a large cabinet where you can stack them. Unless you have a special cabinet for trays and cookie sheets, the pot cabinet is useful for these, as well as for cutting boards.

What Is It?

You use a **trivet** under hot pots and casseroles to protect your table. Trivets can be made of metal, marble, ceramic, or thick fabric.

Birds of a Feather

If you keep similar items together, you only need to go to one place to find them. For example, you might keep cake pans, pie pans, measuring cups, and perhaps even measuring spoons (tucked in a bowl or jar), on one cabinet shelf.

You'll find it saves time to store items that you use regularly—wooden spoons, vegetable peelers, spatulas, tongs, and such—in a drawer near your work area. Gadgets such as the melon-baller and butter-curler that you got practically brand-new from your cousin can go in a drawer that's further away, and which you rarely open.

It's a good idea to have a separate drawer for noncookware tools: screwdrivers, scissors, and twine, for example. This drawer might also be a good place for all those cords from electric appliances.

If you can't live without a junk drawer, use the smallest possible drawer for stuff like the deck of cards you use to play solitaire while waiting for the scones to brown, as well as labels, note pads, cake candles, pennies, your extra keys, the plastic-bag ties you removed from the plastic-bag carton, your recent sales receipts, and all the other little stuff that collects. Plastic drawer organizers will help here. Clean your junk drawer every two to three months. You'll be amazed at how many pennies you'll find.

Most people find it convenient to store cleaning supplies and tools under the sink. This spot might also be handy for a dish rack and drain board and, if you have room and prefer not to leave it exposed, a garbage pail lined with a plastic trash bag. You can mount shelves on the inside door of this cabinet to hold your soap and soap dish, sponge, or dish scrubber if you don't want to keep them at the sink.

Kitchen Clue

Potholders get dirty! Wash them occasionally with your regular laundry and you'll find they'll last longer and look better.

Put Things Back in the Same Place

Although it's important to be an individual and arrange your kitchen to suit your needs, follow one important rule: Always put things back in the same place. The refrigerator has its place. The sink has its place. So should your wooden spoons and spaghetti fork. If you put things back where they belong, you'll never have to ask, "Where did I put that thing?"

Kitchen Clue

It's a good idea to keep a small fire extinguisher or some baking soda under the sink. In the event of a small fire, you might be able to control it quickly with one of these items. If you use a fire extinguisher, know exactly where it is and how to use it. Of course, if the fire is large or out of control, call the fire department.

Make a list that notes where you've stored items that you don't use regularly. If you forget where you put the snail shells, you can simply refer to the list. (By the way, make sure you put the *list* in a place you'll remember. What's the use of a list if you can't find it?)

Where to Put the Food

Storing groceries follows the same logic as storing nonfood items; that is, put like items together. For instance, you could stock canned tomatoes, tomato paste, and pasta on one shelf, and all sweet items, such as sugar, jam, honey, and molasses, on another. It's handy to store salad-dressing ingredients such as oil, vinegar, dried herbs,

salt and pepper, and spices together and to store baking goods such as baking powder, baking soda, yeast, and chocolate chips together.

This may sound nutty, but you might want to keep dried herbs and spices in alphabetical order. Wait until you need the dried rosemary in a hurry. If it's always between the paprika and the sage, you don't have to move every bottle to find it. Why not separate the herbs and spices you use for cooking from the spices you use for baking? Cinnamon, nutmeg, and other seasonings used for baked goods belong with ingredients such as vanilla extract and baking chocolate.

How to Organize and Capitalize on Refrigerator Space

You will be happier and richer if you use your refrigerator shelves efficiently. Some of the drawers, sometimes called crispers, are specially humidified to keep certain produce moist and fresh, so use them for the fruits and vegetables that require moisture for storage. (Some refrigerators also have specially marked meat drawers, and some have basket drawers for produce that doesn't require moisture.)

Everything that doesn't have a designated holder goes on a shelf. Foods that are piled on top of one another deteriorate faster. You also tend to forget about them, and they become hideous-looking mold experiments after awhile. If you keep foods unstacked, they will stay fresher longer and you are more likely to use them, which saves money. The door is the perfect place for storing ingredients with a long shelf life: jarred olives, ketchup, jelly, and so on.

You also can save money if you don't open the refrigerator door frequently and don't hold it open to take inventory while you decide what you want. Keeping the door open lets warm air in, wastes energy, and makes food deteriorate faster.

How to Organize Your Recipes (Or, No More BIG BOX)

If you think it's silly to spend time organizing recipes, consider this scenario: You have photographs of all your friends: childhood friends, high school friends, college friends, and married friends. You collect all these photos in a box and label it "Friends." After several years, the box is crammed with pictures, and you have to spend hours finding the baby photo of your friend Jim, which you want to have enlarged for a special birthday. If you had organized the photos in some logical way—"Baby Pictures," or "Pictures of Jim," or even "Photos, 1974"—it would be easier to find the one you wanted.

It's the same with recipes. If you throw all your recipes into a BIG BOX, 30 years from now when you finally sort through them, you will find that recipe for Chocolate Decadence Cake that you always wanted to make but didn't because you couldn't find the recipe. Only by then you won't be able to make it because you have to watch your weight.

Discard Those Dumb Recipes

Before you begin to organize your recipes, you must do something first: *Discard*.

Discard duplicate recipes, or recipes that are so similar they might as well be. You don't need four recipes for applesauce. If you have a good one, keep it. When you gain experience, you will know you can use brown sugar in place of white or add lemon peel, cinnamon, and raisins without a recipe telling you so.

Discard recipes that are so complicated you know you'll never cook them.

Discard recipes that are so simple you don't need a recipe. Do you really need instructions for an ice cream sundae?

Discard recipes that say "Continued on the next page" if you don't have the next page.

Just Say "No" to Some Popular Methods of Storing Recipes

There are several ways to organize recipes. Some, despite being popular, don't work well because they are inefficient, time-consuming, or perishable.

Just say "no" to cute accordion files. These are better than the BIG BOX—but just barely. These files do have separate sections, but the categories are too broad, and when one or two sections become overburdened, the flimsy cardboard compartments will tear. Besides, in order to find a recipe, you have to stick your hand into the compartment, lift out all the recipes, and finger through them to find the one you're looking for.

Say no to index cards/file boxes. These require you to rewrite recipes by hand on small pieces of cardboard or clip only those recipes that will fit on the file card!

Say no to notebooks. These don't allow for expansion beyond the confines of the book, and you can't remove a page when preparing a recipe.

The Most Convenient Way to Store Recipes

Three methods work well for recipe organization. One easy-to-manage method is the loose-leaf binder, with recipes taped to the loose-leaf pages. It's ideal for several reasons: It's easy to store, it's portable, and it allows for expansion; all you have to do is open the center ring and add paper. An added plus is that the pages lay flat, so it's easy to see the recipe and you can take out a single page if you like. For this reason, you should tape only one recipe per page. If you have lots of recipes, you can divide them into categories by separating the sections with tabs that indicate food categories. Loose-leaf binders rarely become overburdened. If yours is filling up, start a second one just for desserts, ethnic specialties, or some other category that appeals to you.

Kitchen Clue

You might want to keep a running index of your recipes, either on a loose-leaf page or in a computer file. Add the recipe title to your list each time you add a recipe file to your collection.

A cabinet and file folders work the same way as loose-leaf binders, but you place the recipes inside file folders instead of taping them onto loose-leaf pages. This is a handy system if you have a deep desk drawer in your kitchen. As with loose-leaf binders, you can separate foods into categories and file them alphabetically. It's smarter to break down categories somewhat; file "chicken" and "turkey" separately rather than as poultry, for example, because file folders on general subjects can become overburdened and tear apart—just like accordion files. Your file folder categories can become quite specific. You can divide them by event (e.g., picnics), holiday (the Super Bowl), ethnic or regional specialty (Cajun or Caribbean), ingredient (dishes with mustard), and so on.

Computer files work like cabinet files, only you have to type the recipes. If you use this method, arrange the recipes in separate files as you would for a loose-leaf binder or cabinet.

The Least You Need to Know

➤ Arrange cabinets and drawers so that the most-used gadgets and utensils are near your work area and infrequently used items are farther away.

➤ Don't stack food in the fridge, and try not to keep the door open too long.

➤ Organize recipes in a loose-leaf binder or file folders.

Part 2

You've Gotta Have Them: Kitchen Staples

Now that you've got a handle on how the kitchen works, it's time to focus on "filling in." I mean shopping. That's no simple task. To make the matter a little less overwhelming, the next two chapters offer suggestions on the basics you'll need: staple foods, paper goods, and (ugh) cleaning supplies, as well as cookware, appliances, and table items. I also offer a few ideas on what not to buy. Let's start "filling in."

Chapter 3

The Bare Essentials: Supermarket Staples

In This Chapter

➤ Buying the essential groceries

➤ Knowing the necessary refrigerator and freezer items

➤ Purchasing cleaning supplies and paper goods

By now you're familiar with your kitchen and have an idea where you want to store things. What's next? Shopping. For this you need three things: ample time, a wad of money, and a list.

Before you even begin to think about cooking, you have to buy some basic ingredients for your house. We all know people who don't have anything but a beer and an orange in the fridge, or those takeout types who regularly buy costly prepackaged dinners. But if you're going to be cooking for *real*, you have to stock up accordingly.

No matter what you cook, how often you cook, or how well you cook, some staple items are a must for every household. In this chapter, we will discuss the essential grocery items you need on hand in order to cook properly.

Filling Those Bare Cupboards

Practically everyone you know will have a different list of staples needed for cooking, but these lists usually have a lot of overlap. Start with the items mentioned next. They are broken into categories to avoid confusion.

Kitchen Clue

Dried herbs have a more intense taste than fresh ones. A general rule of thumb is to use one-third the amount of dried herbs as fresh (for example, 1 tablespoon chopped fresh rosemary or 1 teaspoon dried rosemary). For optimum flavor, crush dried herbs slightly between your fingers before you add them in a recipe.

Kitchen Clue

Don't use dried parsley in a marinade, in recipes that take a short time to cook, or as a garnish for food. Only fresh parsley offers the flavor and color you need for these purposes. Don't use dried ginger or dried coriander as a substitute for the fresh varieties—the fresh and dried varieties do not taste alike.

The Whys and Wherefores of Herbs and Spices

Herbs and spices enhance the taste and aroma of food and offer variety by providing subtle or robust flavors. They also encourage creativity in cooking. Both come from aromatic plants. Herbs come from the plants' leaves and stems, while spices generally come from the plants' seeds, roots, bark, and flower buds or berries. Herbs can be used either fresh or in dried form. Fresh herbs usually taste better than dried ones and they have become more widely available in recent years. But dried herbs suffice for many dishes. Experiment with different ones to discover those you enjoy. (See Chapter 7, "You Only Think You Hate Vegetables," for more on fresh herbs, including an herb-use chart.)

To keep dried seasonings from deteriorating too quickly, keep them in tightly closed bottles or plastic containers. Buy herbs and spices in small quantities and store them in a cupboard away from the oven's heat. Except for salt, pepper, garlic or onion salt, and whole spices (such as nutmegs or whole allspice), discard herbs and spices after a year. For optimum flavor, grind your own peppercorns and nutmegs instead of buying the preground kind.

You needn't buy items such as apple pie spice, pumpkin pie spice, or poultry seasoning. These blends of seasonings limit your culinary creativity. For example, a typical blend of poultry seasoning contains thyme, marjoram, sage, rosemary, pepper, and nutmeg. If you season the chicken with herbs of your own choosing, it will taste the way you want. Even better, if you change the seasoning each time you make chicken, rather than using the same old blend, your meals will be more interesting.

Fein on Food

Peppercorns were the only ingredient ever enticing enough to make men risk their lives or kings and queens risk their fortunes. If it weren't for peppercorns, there may never have been a famous Columbus, a European settlement in America, Thanksgiving with turkey and all the trimmings, and so on. Pepper is the spice that changed history. You've got to respect it. Grind fresh whole peppercorns in a pepper mill, and you will notice how their flavor brings vitality to food.

Shopping List: Essential Herbs and Spices

- ❏ basil
- ❏ bay leaf
- ❏ cayenne (ground red pepper)
- ❏ chili powder
- ❏ cinnamon (ground)
- ❏ cloves (whole and ground)
- ❏ cumin (ground)
- ❏ curry powder
- ❏ dill weed
- ❏ ginger (ground)
- ❏ mustard (powdered)
- ❏ nutmegs (whole)
- ❏ oregano
- ❏ paprika
- ❏ peppercorns
- ❏ rosemary
- ❏ salt
- ❏ thyme

Spice Chart

Spice	Use with ...
allspice	spice cake, barbecue sauce, relishes
cardamom	baked goods, curries, sweet potatoes
cayenne	any dish in which heat is needed, especially egg, cheese, and chicken dishes
chili powder (mixed ground chili pepper, cumin, oregano, and other seasonings)	casseroles, soups, stews

continues

Spice Chart (continued)

Spice	Use with ...
cinnamon	baked goods, applesauce, sweet potatoes, lamb, casseroles
cloves	baked goods, sweet potatoes, ham, stock
coriander	baked goods, pickles, marinades
cumin	curries, chili, chutney
curry powder (mixed seasonings such as turmeric, chili pepper, and nutmeg)	curried dishes of all kinds
ginger (ground)	baked goods; marinades; pork, poultry, and ham dishes
mace	baked goods, fruit desserts
nutmeg	baked goods, cream sauces, spinach, carrots, pumpkin, eggnog
paprika (hot and mild versions)	stews, roasted meats and poultry, garnishes
peppercorns	any dish in which heat and pungency are needed, such as fresh salad, grilled steak, or scrambled eggs
saffron	paella, bouillabaisse, rice, tomato dishes, baked goods
turmeric	curries, chili, pickles, relishes, rice

Oils, Vinegars, and Condiments

Oils, vinegars, and condiments are used for salad dressings, marinades, and lots of other recipes. Oils are also used to help keep foods from sticking to pans and to add a rich quality to dishes. The word "fat" has taken on a sinister reputation in recent years. No one wants to have too much of it, but sometimes you need fats in recipes. Vegetable shortening, for example, makes pie crust flaky. It also is useful for greasing pans for baking cakes and cookies.

Olive oil is a must on the basic-buy list. Not only is it considered one of the healthier oils, but it also is rich and full-bodied, and has numerous uses. You can't use it to deep fry foods, though, because it smokes at low temperatures, which can ruin your food and create a foul kitchen odor.

Because a gazillion olive oil varieties are available, picking one can be confusing. First things first: Just because it's expensive doesn't mean it's better. There are three main types of olive oil: *extra-virgin, virgin,* and *pure.* The grades are based on levels of acidity (oleic acid content). The highest grade, extra-virgin, is the least acidic. It also has the most appealing fragrance and richest taste. Extra-virgin olive oil is best for salads and subtle dishes; the others, for heartier foods. Virgin is the next best grade, and then comes pure. While all these olive oils are made from the first pressing of olives, pure may also come from second and third pressings. Some pure olive oils are blended with virgin or extra-virgin oils to give them better flavor. *Light* olive oil is specially re-fined to have a mild flavor and light color; keep in mind that it has the same number of calories and fat grams as regular olive oil.

You may see *infused* or *flavored* olive oils in the mar-ket. These contain essences of herbs, spices, vegeta-bles, or fruit. They can add pizzazz to food, but tend to be costly.

The words "vegetable oil" usually mean soybean oil, although manufacturers are reluctant to say so. Years ago everyone thought the word *soybean* would scare people off, and the prejudice stuck. There are other types of vegetable oil, too, all specifically labeled. They include canola, corn, peanut, safflower, and sunflower oils. You can use them interchangeably in recipes. However, they taste different, so sample all of them at some point to see which you like best. You can use vegetable oil for deep-frying, panfrying, and stir-frying, as well as for salad dressing.

Kitchen Clue

You can create your own infused oils by steeping olive oil with such ingredients as peeled, cut garlic, chili peppers, sliced fresh ginger, and so on.

Vegetable oil, whatever type or variety, contains fat, but not cholesterol. Cholesterol is present only in animal products. Your body can manufacture cholesterol from the fats you eat, however, so you're not necessarily cholesterol-free if you use vegetable oils. There are several different kinds of dietary fat. Most doctors recommend cutting down on saturated fats such as coconut and palm oils, and using more monounsatu-rated fats (olive oil) and polyunsaturated fats (safflower oil, for example).

Wine vinegar is used for salad dressings and marinades. Many kinds are available, in-cluding those made from sherry, champagne, and rice wine. Try a good brand of red-wine vinegar first, then sample others to see which you like best for particular foods. Sherry vinegar, for example, has a rich, intense taste, while rice-wine vinegar is milder. You may prefer the more robust variety in a marinade for meat, and the other in a dressing for shellfish salad.

White vinegar and cider vinegar are used to make certain dishes taste tangy (particu-larly chutneys, pickles, and other relishes).

Balsamic vinegar is worthy. It is a dark, sweet, nectar-like liquid made from ripe Trebbiano grapes. The best varieties are aged, and, like fine wine, can be very expen-sive. This is not the kind of balsamic vinegar you pour freely into salad dressing—you would use this kind sparingly over greens or fresh fruit. It is also delicious as a condi-ment over grilled meats and vegetables. The commercial varieties of balsamic that are

21

available in supermarkets are fine for salad dressing and marinades. Because balsamic vinegar tends to be sweet and strong, you may want to combine it with other types of vinegar and adjust recipe proportions to your taste.

You may also find "infused" vinegars at the store. If you have the room and don't mind spending extra money, these vinegars can come in handy to give a boost of flavor to food. (You can easily make your own, though: Cover a few sprigs of fresh herbs or some spices or other flavoring with wine vinegar and let the mixture steep for a few days.)

Condiments enhance food's flavor. Use them in salad dressings, barbecue sauce, soups, casseroles, and so on.

Shopping List: Oils, Vinegars, and Condiments

- ❏ balsamic vinegar
- ❏ bottled salsa
- ❏ Dijon mustard
- ❏ extra-virgin olive oil
- ❏ hoisin sauce
- ❏ hot pepper sauce
- ❏ ketchup
- ❏ mango chutney
- ❏ mayonnaise
- ❏ prepared white horseradish
- ❏ pure olive oil
- ❏ red-wine vinegar
- ❏ shortening (small can)
- ❏ soy sauce
- ❏ vegetable oil
- ❏ white vinegar
- ❏ Worcestershire sauce

If You Want to Bake, You Need These

The following items are a must if you plan to bake even a minimum amount of cookies, pies, and cakes. This list includes the obvious—flour and sugar—as well as more specialized items, such as unsweetened cocoa powder, that you'll use for baking *and* for making hot chocolate.

Shopping List: Baking Staples

- ❏ baking powder
- ❏ baking soda
- ❏ brown sugar (light or dark)
- ❏ chocolate (squares of semi-sweet and unsweetened)
- ❏ chocolate chips
- ❏ confectioner's sugar
- ❏ corn meal
- ❏ cream of tartar
- ❏ flour, all-purpose
- ❏ granulated sugar
- ❏ honey
- ❏ unflavored gelatin

The Miscellaneous Staples You Need

You need several miscellaneous staples. Notice that this shopping list does not include bouillon cubes (or paste). These can be loaded with salt and additives, so you might consider substituting homemade or canned stock instead. (See "Soups and Salads," Section 2, for a recipe.)

You needn't buy bread crumbs, either. You can easily make your own, using stale bread. Tear the bread into pieces and whirl them in a food processor or blender. To make dry bread crumbs, toast crumbs in the oven at 350°F for a few minutes until they turn light brown. Store homemade bread crumbs in plastic bags in the freezer.

Consider keeping sun-dried tomatoes on hand. They aren't essential, but they do have an intense, tangy tomato flavor that livens up a variety of dishes, particularly pasta. They come either packed in oil or in dry packages. The dry ones must be reconstituted in oil or hot water. Store sun-dried tomatoes in an airtight container; they last for six to eight months.

Fresh Parmesan cheese is a big bonus in the kitchen. Keep a chunk of it (preferably Reggiano) in the fridge to grind as needed.

One item to keep off your shopping list is cooking wine. It doesn't taste like wine and can ruin a good recipe. When cooking with wine, follow this simple rule: If you wouldn't drink it, don't cook with it.

Kitchen Clue

Don't buy imitation vanilla extract. It seems cheaper, but it isn't. Its flavor has no depth, and you need twice as much of it as you need of pure extract. Even then, the recipe doesn't taste right.

Kitchen Clue

You needn't buy bottled salad dressings, which are expensive and often contain lots of salt, fat, or additives. Homemade vinaigrette is easy (see the recipe in Section 7, "Sauces and Gravies"), and you can make it in bulk to last a week or more.

Shopping List: Miscellaneous Must-Haves

- ❏ canned beans (such as garbanzo and kidney beans)
- ❏ canned chicken and beef broths
- ❏ canned tomatoes
- ❏ canned tuna
- ❏ coffee
- ❏ cold cereal
- ❏ corn syrup (light or dark)
- ❏ crackers
- ❏ dried white beans

❑ jelly
❑ maple syrup
❑ oatmeal
❑ pasta
❑ peanut butter
❑ pure vanilla extract
❑ popcorn kernels

❑ raisins
❑ rice
❑ your favorite snacks
❑ tea
❑ tomato paste
❑ unsweetened cocoa powder

Kitchen Clue

Baking soda is versatile! It is used to leaven baked goods, douse fat fires and keep your fridge and freezer smelling fresh. That's why you need four boxes.

Also suggested: sun-dried tomatoes, cranberry sauce, capers, green and black olives, jarred roasted red peppers, brownie mix, white wine, a bottle of brandy.

The Staples You Need for Your Fridge and Freezer

You'll also need some refrigerator staples. Notice that the refrigerator items include onions, potatoes, and garlic. Most people will tell you not to store these items in the fridge, but you can safely keep them in the baskets or on the shelves—just not in the moisture drawers.

Shopping List: Cold Essentials

❑ apples
❑ butter, unsalted
❑ carrots
❑ celery
❑ eggs
❑ garlic cloves
❑ ice cream or frozen yogurt

❑ lemons
❑ milk
❑ onions
❑ Parmesan cheese
❑ parsley
❑ plain yogurt
❑ potatoes

Also suggested: mozzarella and cheddar cheeses, cream cheese, frozen pie shells, frozen orange juice concentrate, frozen waffles.

Paper Products and Cleaning Supplies

Finally, you'll need several nonfood items for your kitchen. This shopping list includes paper goods, cleaning supplies, and emergency items.

Shopping List: Paper and Cleaning Items

- ❏ all-purpose cleaning spray
- ❏ aluminum foil
- ❏ baking soda (four boxes)
- ❏ bandages
- ❏ candles
- ❏ cheesecloth
- ❏ coffee filters
- ❏ dish/pot scrubbing pads
- ❏ dishwasher detergent
- ❏ flashlight
- ❏ food storage bags
- ❏ glass spray
- ❏ liquid detergent
- ❏ matches
- ❏ napkins
- ❏ nonperfumed soap
- ❏ oven cleaner
- ❏ paper towels
- ❏ parchment paper
- ❏ plastic wrap
- ❏ rubber gloves
- ❏ sink cleanser
- ❏ small fire extinguisher
- ❏ sponges
- ❏ steel-wool pads
- ❏ toothpicks
- ❏ trash bags
- ❏ waxed paper

Warnings

Never use water on a fat fire. You can easily extinguish flames from burning fat by throwing baking soda on them.

Kitchen Clue

Throw away sponges every two to three weeks or when they start to smell bad, whichever comes first. You can wash sponges in the dishwasher or with the laundry if you prefer.

The Least You Need to Know

➤ Buy whole peppercorns and nutmegs and grind them fresh into your dishes.

➤ Use fresh parsley, Parmesan cheese, and pure vanilla extract.

➤ You can store onions, potatoes, and garlic in the wire basket of the refrigerator.

Chapter 4

The Bare Essentials Part Deux: Equipment Staples

In This Chapter

➤ All about pots and pans

➤ Cutlery basics

➤ Must-have appliances

➤ Gadgets and miscellaneous kitchenware that will make your life easier

---

You may never need fancy cookware in a multitude of shapes and sizes, a pasta-making machine, or a device for pitting cherries, but you can't cook without pots and pans, knives, mixing utensils, and the like. A labor-saving appliance or two also comes in handy, as can some interesting little gizmos such as a lemon-juice squeezer. This chapter describes the items you should consider buying.

All About Pots and Pans

A hundred years ago, home cooks used a cast-iron skillet for everything. Today, the variety of cookware is almost bewildering, even to experienced cooks. Here's some information that will help you start buying what you need.

You Could Buy a Television for What These Pots and Pans Cost

Cookware today is unbelievably expensive! Multi-piece cookware sets can save you a lot of money. However, large sets may have pieces you don't really need. And you may not have room to store all those pieces, plus others you can't live without.

Besides, no single kind of cookware is best for every kind of cooking. It's better to buy a small set (seven or eight pieces, including lids) of general-purpose cookware and "fill in" with other pans that may be more suitable for specific types of cooking. High-quality stainless-steel cookware offers the most versatility.

Most important is this: Buy the best cookware you can afford. It needn't be the most expensive stuff in the store, but buy for value, not merely price. Cheap cookware is flimsy, and it often has hot spots, which can result in unevenly cooked food—or ruined recipes. Cheap pots are also dangerous. They tend to wobble and warp, and their handles often fall off. In the end, if you wind up replacing them, you haven't saved any money.

Kitchen Clue

If you are strapped for money, buy fewer pieces of good cookware and make do with what you have for a while. Look for sales. With so many brands of cookware on the market, prices can be competitive. Check cookware catalogs, as well.

The Virtues and Vices of Different Types of Cookware

Good cooks use the pot that does the best job for a particular purpose. Here's a brief rundown of the pots and pans you may need and how to use them properly.

Cast-Iron Cookware

The pan that great-grandma used holds its heat really well, so it is wonderful for frying and "blackening" foods. But it isn't good for delicate dishes or sauces, and the metal reacts with acidic ingredients. Some cast-iron cookware comes with a protective surface coating; others must be seasoned periodically. After washing cast-iron cookware, wipe it dry thoroughly to prevent rusting.

Enameled cast iron will not corrode. It heats slowly and holds heat well, making it perfect for long-simmering sauces, stews, pot roasts, casseroles, and soups.

Warnings

Cast-iron cookware handles get HOT! Be careful.

Copper Cookware

Professional chefs like copper cookware because it heats rapidly and cools down just as quickly. This kind of sensitivity to heat makes copper the best choice for delicate sauces and sautéed dishes. But it is extremely expensive and high maintenance. Tin linings found in some copper cookware must be replaced periodically. Some copper pans are lined with stainless steel; these should last a lifetime.

Warnings

Copper can be toxic. If you own copper cookware, and its lining wears off to the point that you can see the copper underneath, do not use the pan until you can have it relined.

Aluminum Cookware

Aluminum also is exceptionally responsive to heat and browns foods well, so it is a good choice for frying and braising. But the metal "reacts" with acidic ingredients—that is, it corrodes if you use wine, tomatoes, lemon juice, vinegar, and so on. Aluminum cookware discolors and gives a metallic taste to dishes made with these ingredients. You can't use an aluminum pan to make pot roast with wine or tomato sauce, either.

Enameled aluminum is noncorrosive. It is fine for sauces, vegetables, pasta, and soups. However, the enamel cuts down considerably on the heat response, so it won't brown foods well.

Anodized aluminum is aluminum that has been changed chemically during manufacture. It has all the virtues of regular aluminum but it isn't "reactive," which makes it versatile. However, it will darken certain foods, such as artichokes. And you can't put anodized aluminum cookware in the dishwasher.

Nonstick pressure-cast aluminum cookware is safe for use with all ingredients. It is easy to clean and browns food well.

Stainless Steel

Stainless steel has many benefits: It doesn't react with any ingredient, it is durable and easy to clean, and you can put it in the dishwasher. Unfortunately, it doesn't conduct heat very well and must be combined with better heat-conducting metals. Some stainless-steel pots are clad on the bottom with disks made of copper or aluminum. To be effective for cooking, these disks must be thick and should cover the entire bottom surface. In the best stainless-steel cookware, the entire core of the pan (not simply the bottom) is made of aluminum or copper, while the surfaces are completely coated with stainless steel. Another outstanding stainless steel cookware choice is aluminum at the core, a stainless steel coat inside, and an outside that is sheathed in anodized aluminum or copper. All of these coated, copper or aluminum core pots and pans are known as "tri-ply" and "five-ply." If you buy good stainless-steel pots and pans, you can use them for every type of cooking.

Ceramic Glass and Porcelain Cookware

You can cook almost any kind of food in glass or porcelain cookware because it isn't "reactive," doesn't rust, and is easy to clean. It retains heat well so it is particularly useful for casseroles. You can pop it into a microwave and serve the food straight from the pan. However, glass and porcelain don't conduct heat well and can't brown foods adequately. They also are extremely fragile.

What About Nonstick Cookware?

Most cookware sold today is nonstick. It is easy to clean and it allows food to "release" from the surface with little or no fat. Avoid cheap nonstick pans: the surfaces wear off and scratch quickly and the underlying pan is usually thin and flimsy. Better brands have long-lasting nonstick capabilities, and some are guaranteed for a lifetime.

Nonstick cookware may be fine for steaming vegetables, simmering sauces, and cooking soups, rice, beans, and pasta. However, the surfaces cut down on heat so they don't brown foods as well as regular cookware.

Most, but not all, manufacturers warn you not to use metal utensils with nonstick cookware and not to put the pans in the dishwasher.

What Else to Look For When Buying Pots and Pans

Whatever cookware you choose, be sure that it is well designed, safe to use, and long-lasting. Look for these hallmarks:

Kitchen Clue

Be sure you read the manufacturer's instructions on whether or not you can use metal utensils with the nonstick cookware you choose.

➤ Pans that are well balanced and heavy enough to resist wobbling or warping.

➤ Handles that are comfortable and help you maneuver the pan.

➤ Handles that are securely fastened, either with rivets, sturdy screws, or solid-looking welding.

➤ Handles that stay cool. Wooden and plastic handles stay cooler than metal ones, but you can't put wooden-handled pots in the dishwasher or oven. Metal handles stay cooler if they are hollowed or if they are made of a material different from the pot.

➤ Lids that fit snugly.

➤ Handles or knobs that are easy to grip and roomy enough to keep your fingers from touching the hot lid.

The Indispensable Pots and Pans

A beginner's kitchen should include pots and pans that will give you the most use with the least equipment. Following is a list of the essential cookware, including suggestions for best choices:

➤ Two saucepans with covers: a 1½- to 2-quart and a 3-quart (stainless steel or anodized aluminum). One pan can be nonstick.

➤ Two skillets/sauté pans/frying pans: a 7- to 8-inch slope-sided pan (you can use it as an omelet pan), and a 10- to 12-inch straight-sided pan with a lid (stainless steel or anodized aluminum). One pan can be nonstick.

➤ 8-quart soup/stock pot (which can double as a pasta pot) with a lid. The most useful ones come with steamer baskets and/or pasta inserts (stainless steel, aluminum, or enamel).

➤ Roasting pan (stainless steel, enamel, or anodized aluminum).

If you have some extra money and space, add one or more of the following items as you build your supply:

➤ 10-inch nonstick *skillet* (if others are not nonstick).

➤ Wok or stir-fry pan.

➤ Fait-tout pan (sometimes called "chef's pan"). The name of this pan means "does everything," and you can use it to sauté or to make risotto, sauce, and various other dishes.

➤ 3- to 5-quart enameled casserole (for casserole dishes, tomato sauce, stew, soup).

➤ Dutch oven or braising pan with cover (stainless steel, anodized aluminum, cast-aluminum, or copper).

➤ Double-boiler insert.

➤ Shallow "au gratin" pan (stainless steel or enamel) that doubles as a casserole dish and small roasting pan.

➤ 1-quart saucepan with cover.

➤ Cast-iron skillet.

➤ Griddle.

What Is It?

Skillet means "frying pan," but the term usually refers to a frying pan with sloped sides that may or may not come with a lid. A sauté pan has a more specific meaning: a deep, straight-sided pan that usually comes with a lid. You can sauté foods in either kind of pan, but the sauté pan holds more, so it's handier for dishes that have lots of sauce, vegetables, or other ingredients.

Cutlery Basics

Experienced cooks may tell you that the only tools you'll ever need are a few good knives. Well, this may be true, but a few good appliances (as you will see below) don't hurt, either. You'll probably be using a knife every time you cook, however, so buy good ones. They are worth the expense because cheap knives don't hold a sharp edge and can be frustrating to use. Worse still, they can be dangerous: Dull knives force you to push down hard when you're chopping or slicing, and that increases the risk that your hand will slip and cause an accident.

No knife stays sharp forever, so forget what you've heard on TV. Serrated knives may hold an edge longer, but these should be used only for bread or tomatoes—never for meat (the blades "saw" the flesh). Buy knives with high carbon-steel alloy blades; these take and hold a sharp edge well and don't discolor or rust.

Look for forged (rather than stamped) knives; they are better balanced. The best knives, especially the larger ones, also have a full-length *tang*—a single piece of metal that extends from the blade to the back of the handle—that is the same length, width, and shape as the handle. The tang helps balance the knife and strengthen the handle. Smaller knives may have a rattail tang (a piece of metal that is the same length as the handle, but not as wide) or a half-tang (a piece of metal that is as wide as the handle but not as long). Avoid knives that have no tang at all.

Knife handles are made of wood or plastic and are riveted or molded onto the tang. There are fine knives in all these categories.

Which knives do you need? Here are some suggestions:

➤ Chef's knife, for chopping and slicing. It tapers from the bolster (the piece between the blade and the tang) to the tip of the blade.

➤ Utility knife, for chopping and slicing small vegetables and herbs. It is similar to a small chef's knife.

➤ Paring knife, for trimming vegetables, peeling fruit, and making garnishes.

➤ Serrated bread knife.

➤ Poultry shears.

Warnings

Never use a knife as a screwdriver, letter opener, or device to open packages. Not only can these actions ruin the blade, they can also maim you. Never put knives in the dishwasher, which loosens handles and dulls the edges of the blades.

Also suggested: steak knives, kitchen scissors.

Knives require maintenance. Keep them sharp. One way is to have them sharpened professionally in a nearby cookware store or butcher shop. Never use the knife-sharpening devices that come with can openers; these will ruin your knife blades. But a good electric knife sharpener is a valuable tool and worth a few extra ducats. To keep blades in prime condition, you can sharpen blades on a "knife steel," or, if you buy a first-rate electric knife sharpener, use its honing section instead.

It's tempting to throw knives into the dishwasher, but you're better off cleaning them by hand. The rattling around inside the dishwasher dulls the blade and the heat creates cracks in wooden handles. Your knives will stay sharper if you store them in a wood knife block or on magnetized strips mounted to a wall or in a drawer.

A knife block: The best way to keep your knives clean, sharp, and handy.

Chef's knife

Bread knife

Utility knife

Paring knife

Poultry knife

Different kinds of knives.

33

In addition to knives, you will need ...

➤ Cutting board

➤ Electric knife sharpener

➤ Wooden knife block or magnetized knife strips

The Essential Appliances

There is no denying that appliances can save you time and work. Avoid the trendy, silly ones and stick to tools that make cooking easier and more fun. This section discusses the most useful small electric appliances and what to look for when buying one.

Appliance-Buying Basics

Forget about what's fashionable; only buy an appliance that you need. Compare brands. You can see for yourself which models look and feel more durable. Ask salespeople which brands are returned most often and for what reason. Ask in several stores because salespeople are apt to promote the ones they sell. Look for suggestions in consumer magazines.

Buy brands from manufacturers with a good track record for products and service. But remember that one particular manufacturer doesn't always make the best of every product.

While price is important, it isn't everything. If the product is poorly made, it isn't worth *any* money. Look for UL symbols and good warranties; these are signs of safety and manufacturer confidence. Sometimes stores sell discontinued items at terrific prices. That's good if the item was dropped because of style changes or because more updated versions have more bells and whistles, but not if there were problems with the product. Ask a salesperson why the item is no longer in the line.

The upcoming sections describe some of the more useful kitchen appliances and explain their advantages and disadvantages.

Are Food Processors for Everyone?

Food processors are the workhorses of the kitchen. They chop, shred, and slice foods quickly and efficiently. The more powerful ones also knead dough. They are all similar; each one has a work bowl, cover, and cutting blades.

You can buy food processors in several sizes. Some small ones have a "continuous feed" chute through which food can be processed continuously into a waiting bowl—great if you're really short on space.

When you buy a food processor, look for one that's heavy and stable. The work bowl should be thick and durable-looking, the blades razor-sharp.

"High" and "low" speeds and a pulse setting are all that's needed, and a wide feed-tube makes processing tasks easier. Don't bother buying special attachments for beating egg whites or whipping cream; mixers are better for these jobs.

How to Choose a Handheld Mixer

A handheld mixer is useful even if you bake only occasionally. It doesn't take up much space and doesn't cost as much as a heavy-duty stand-mixer, but it performs some of the same functions (mixing cake batter and whipping egg whites and cream).

Kitchen Clue

If any kitchen appliance can help you make the leap from a know-nothing to a world-class cook, it's a food processor. It eliminates some of the drudgery and the boredom of getting through noncreative tasks such as chopping onions and slicing mushrooms.

You can find inexpensive handheld mixers that don't have much power and come with flat-edged beaters. But it pays to spend a little more money on a model with higher wattage and beaters that are curvy looking, without center posts. These are sturdier, aerate ingredients better, and are easy to clean.

Multiple speeds are practical, especially an extra-slow speed. This lets you mix dry ingredients such as flour without dust flying out of the bowl. Some handheld mixers are so powerful you can mix cookie dough with them. Always choose a mixer that's comfortable and isn't too heavy for your arm.

Being Savvy About Stand-Mixers

Stand-mixers are for people who bake with some regularity. The best ones have powerful motors that outperform even the top handheld mixers. One of the most important features to consider is the mixer's weight; it should be heavy and stay still, not creep along the counter when it is in use. The best ones feature "all-metal construction."

Equally important is the way in which the beaters and bowl work together. Those that offer "planetary action" (the beater moves around a stationary bowl) do a better job than mixers that operate with moving bowls and beaters that stay still.

Blender Basics

Blenders are the best tools for whirling beverages and liquid ingredients such as soups and sauce. Several types are available with pushbuttons, levers, switches, or touch-pad controls. Two blender speeds are enough for most purposes (and more than eight seems useless), but a pulse feature is desirable because it gives you more control. Glass jars are more costly than plastic ones, but they are sturdier and don't get as scratched and cloudy. Some blenders crush ice without using water, some need water, and some don't crush ice at all.

The three most important things to consider when buying a blender are a base that's heavy, so the blender won't topple over; a jar that fits securely onto the motor base, so it won't fall off when the machine is on; and a lid that fits snugly, so that it won't pop off the jar during blending.

Immersion blenders are tall, handheld rods that have a cutting/blending blade at the bottom. They process and puree ingredients right inside the pot or bowl you are using. They are a cinch to clean and safe to use because you don't have to transfer hot ingredients to a blender jar or food processor in order to use it. If you buy one of these blenders, look for a model that's comfortable to hold and that has a well-placed on/off button.

You Can't Get Along Without These Gadgets

There are loads of gadgets, utensils, and other sorts of paraphernalia needed to equip your kitchen, and shopping for them could put a serious dent in your budget. Collect them gradually, but consider the items noted in the following sections.

Bakeware Basics

Here are some of the tools you need for baking:

➤ Measuring cups and spoons

➤ Glass measuring pitcher

➤ Three mixing bowls (different sizes)

➤ Two 9-inch cake pans

➤ 8- or 9-inch-square cake pan

➤ 9 × 5 × 3-inch loaf pan

➤ Two cooling racks for cakes and cookies

➤ 9-inch pie pan

➤ Two cookie sheets (one can be a *jelly roll pan*)

➤ Cake tester

➤ Rolling pin

➤ Pastry board—a wooden, marble, or granite slab on which you roll pastries

What Is It?

A **jelly roll pan** is a cookie sheet with a rim around it.

Mixing, Stirring, and Turning Tools You'll Need

You can't get along without implements to help you mix, stir, and turn food:

➤ Several wooden spoons

➤ Long-handled slotted spoon

➤ Medium-size rubber spatula

➤ Small rubber spatula

➤ Rigid metal spatula

➤ Potato masher

➤ Two whisks: a stiff one for blending sauces, a larger balloon whisk for whipping cream and egg whites

➤ Two-pronged long metal fork

➤ Tongs

➤ Spaghetti fork

➤ Soup ladle

Odds and Ends: Kitchen Necessities You Can't Forget

In addition to purchasing food-preparation tools, you'll also need to buy some rather unglamorous but indispensable little odds and ends. An apron, for instance, can save you cleaning bills and distress, so it pays to get at least one and actually *wear* it when you cook. Here are some other necessities:

➤ Plastic containers for storage

➤ Canisters (or large plastic containers)

➤ Four pot holders

➤ Four dishtowels

➤ Dish rack

➤ Drain board

➤ Salt and pepper shakers

➤ Garbage can

➤ Flatware tray (if you don't have drawer dividers)

➤ Step stool

➤ Microwaveable dishes (if you have a microwave oven)

➤ A soap dish for the sink

Also suggested: wall hooks, a paper-towel holder.

Kitchen Clue

Don't leave flour or sugar in your cabinet in the original bag once the bag is opened. Put the bag inside a plastic bag or, even better, in canisters or large covered containers. An open bag *is* an invitation to wildlife.

The Handiest Gadgets

Finally, here are several gadgets that will make your life a whole lot easier:

➤ Colander

➤ Pepper mill

➤ Vegetable peeler

➤ Manual can opener (for when there's a power outage)

➤ Bottle opener

➤ Meat thermometer (instant read or oven-proof)

➤ Garlic press

➤ Lemon-juice squeezer

➤ Nutmeg grater

➤ Salad spinner

➤ Bulb baster

➤ All-purpose grater (flat or four-sided)

➤ Corkscrew

➤ Funnel

➤ Kitchen timer (if you don't have one on the oven)

➤ Steamer insert for vegetables

➤ Ice cream scoop

➤ Two 1-inch brushes

➤ 8-inch strainer

➤ Small strainer

A salad spinner.

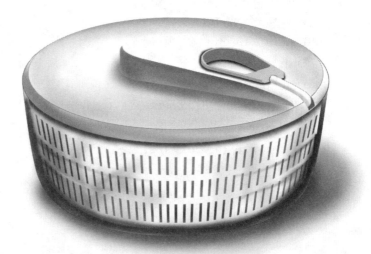

You Don't Need These Gadgets, But They Sure Would Help

If you have any money left, a few other nonessential gadgets come in handy in most kitchens. Consider splurging for these:

➤ Muffin pan

➤ 9 × 13-inch cake pan

➤ 10-inch tart pan with removable bottom

➤ 6- to 8-cup soufflé dish

➤ 9- to 10-inch springform pan

➤ Small serrated knife for tomatoes

➤ Skimmer

➤ Chopsticks

➤ Wooden skewers

➤ Citrus zester

➤ Meat mallet

➤ Cheese plane

➤ Egg separator

➤ Strawberry huller

➤ Microwave leak tester

What You Need for Serving

After you've bought the ingredients and cooked them, you'll need serving utensils and equipment. You may have some odds and ends to use, but if you are just starting out or wish to restock, you'll need four each of the following:

➤ Dinner plates

➤ Salad or dessert plates

➤ Cups and saucers or mugs

➤ Cereal/soup bowls

➤ Tumblers

➤ Juice glasses

➤ All-purpose wine glasses

➤ Knives

➤ Forks

➤ Teaspoons and tablespoons

... two of each of these items:

➤ Platters

➤ Vegetable serving bowls

➤ Serving spoons

➤ Serving forks

➤ Trivets

... and, finally ...

➤ Salad bowl and servers

➤ Cream pitcher

➤ Sugar bowl

➤ Pitcher

➤ Pie and cake servers

Although they aren't absolutely necessary, a tablecloth (or two or four place mats), candlestick holders, and an ice bucket add a gracious touch.

The Least You Need to Know

➤ Buy the best pots, pans, and knives you can afford.

➤ You can save money by buying cookware in sets, but pick individual pots for specific purposes.

➤ Store your knives in a wooden knife holder or on a magnetized knife strip.

➤ Never put your good knives in the dishwasher.

➤ Buy appliances from reputable brand-name manufacturers that have a good track record.

➤ Wear an apron when you cook.

Part 3

Did Anyone Ever Give You a Shopping Lesson?

You now have a list of the grocery staples and kitchen supplies you need, but the real nitty-gritty of daily meals means real food: meat, veggies, fruit, milk, and so on. For that, again, you have to shop.

Wait a second! You can't go out and shop, not just yet. Which is the most convenient place to go? Where can you get the best stuff for the best price? When you get there, how do you distinguish between cuts of meat or poultry parts so that you won't waste time and money cooking them improperly? You may wonder about some curious-looking produce you've never tried, or you may be unable to figure out how to choose even the most familiar lettuce or pears. You may want to know what kind of cheese or butter or coffee to buy, or how to select canned goods from among the dozens of brands facing you on the shelves.

In short, you want to be a smart shopper. Read on. The next several chapters will show you the way.

Chapter 5

Filling in the Spaces

In This Chapter

➤ Deciding when and where to shop

➤ Applying the basic principles of buying: understanding value, reading labels, choosing fresh or packaged, debating brand name or generic

---

Have you forgotten that you have to eat? You can't make a meal out of flour and olive oil, or any of the other staple items on the shopping list. You have to buy real food. Meat and vegetables. Fish and fruit. Stuff you can cook for dinner.

You don't have to buy all the food at once. In fact, if you have the time, buy during the week on mini-shopping trips. That way, foods that should be fresh, will be. Besides, it will make the shopping trips for staples shorter.

Where to Shop

There are several types of food retailers. Before you shop the first time, check them out to see what they're like and to determine which ones make your shopping experience a pleasant one, which ones give you the best value, and which ones give you a headache. In most areas, you will find one or more stores that fit each of these descriptions.

What You Can Expect at a Supermarket

You'll probably do most of your shopping at a supermarket. Prices vary so it pays to read store flyers and check the windows for postings of weekly specials. Some supermarkets offer lower prices on certain items to customers with special "member" cards (which are free). Comparison shopping is fine, but if you have to drive for miles to find better prices for just a few items, you've wasted time and gasoline money.

If you are shopping for one or two people, don't buy large packages of food. Individual servings and small quantities may cost more, but if you buy a family-size package and don't use up the item before it becomes stale, you waste money. However, you can save money if you buy staple items that stay fresh (such as ketchup) in big packages or containers.

Store managers come up with all sorts of ways to tempt you to buy, which is why everyone will tell you not to go to the supermarket when you're hungry. But even if you just finished eating, it is difficult to resist the fragrance of fresh-baked goods or other tantalizing foods in the store. To save money and cut calories, enjoy the smell but don't let your nose control your pocketbook. Be vigilant at the checkout counter, too—they keep the candy and gum there to tempt you while you're waiting in line. Instead of buying some, survey the magazines and newspapers. Without even buying a copy, you can find out which movie stars are getting divorced and where Elvis was last sighted.

Kitchen Clue

Some stores have the cost per ounces listed on shelf tags. Don't assume the bigger packages provide bigger savings. Compare sizes to see which is the better deal.

Kitchen Clue

When you first start to cook, you may not realize that quality differences in produce can determine whether or not a recipe will be successful. If you make gazpacho with hard, mealy, orange tomatoes, for example, the soup won't be good. It's not your fault—it's the tomatoes. You're better off choosing a different recipe than using an inferior ingredient.

Are Warehouse Clubs Worth Joining?

Warehouse clubs are mammoth-sized, no-frills places that sell grocery items as well as TVs, office supplies, and hundreds of other products. Some also sell fresh produce, meats, and frozen foods. Prices are generally the lowest of all retailers for *many* items, but not for *all* items—and you have to buy in bulk. Warehouse clubs charge a membership fee, and you have to bag your own groceries, so bring boxes and shopping bags.

Fun at Farmers' Markets, Farm Stands, and Greengrocers

Farmers' markets and farm stands are often the best places to buy locally grown, fresh produce. The prices are usually decent, too. Greengrocers also sell fruits and vegetables that may or may not be locally grown. Many have higher-quality produce than supermarkets, and they don't prepackage them. Prices may be higher but the produce is usually worth the extra cost.

Are Thrift Stores Worthwhile?

Thrift stores are operated by manufacturers as a way to dispose of overruns or goods that are slightly imperfect (for example, a cake on which the sugar glaze was thicker on one side than on the other). They can provide huge savings opportunities.

Shopping Takes Time

Some people enjoy the shopping experience, and others grow impatient quickly. Whichever you are, be sure you allow enough time to shop wisely. The following tips suggest several ways you can reduce shopping time and frustration:

➤ Make a shopping list and stick to it unless there is a great bargain on some fabulous seasonal fruit or other short-lived item.

➤ Organize coupons by type of item, by alphabetical order of manufacturer, or by expiration date. If you follow any logical procedure you will use, not lose, your coupons.

➤ Avoid shopping during hours when stores may be most crowded.

➤ Unless your shopping trip is urgent, don't shop if the weatherman predicts a major bad weather occurrence. That's when the stores become crammed with folks buying everything in sight in case the world comes to an end.

➤ Understand that some people will take advantage. You know how it is: They'll go to the express line with more than the limit. Relax, and leave yourself enough time.

How Often to Shop

How often you shop depends primarily on the demands of your schedule. But no one wants to spend more time shopping than necessary. To cut down on shopping time, stock up on staples and make frequent but short trips to the store to buy perishable items, such as meat, fish, produce, and other ingredients that demand freshness.

Intro to Buying

Now that you've decided which store to go to and how often to go, what do you buy? Before we get to actual products, there are some factors you must consider.

Brand Names or Generic Products?

Some generic foods taste as good as name brands, but compare them for yourself. The nutritional value is probably the same (read the label, which we'll discuss later), so if you like how the generic one tastes, buy it. It's probably cheaper. Generic paper products (paper towels and napkins) frequently don't fare as well. They're cheaper, but many are poor quality, and you wind up using twice as much so you're not really saving money.

Fresh, Frozen, or Canned?

Most people agree that fresh food tastes better than frozen or canned food. It's often a lot less expensive, too.

There are some notable exceptions to this axiom. Frozen peas, frozen winter squash, and canned beets taste substantially like their fresh equivalents. Frozen chopped spinach is ideal for soup or quiche. Canned broth, tuna, beans, and tomatoes are so useful that they're kitchen staples. And, of course, some frozen products, while not quite as good as fresh, are good enough and simply too convenient to pass up: waffles, juice concentrate, French fries, and pie shells.

Frozen entrées may be convenient, but they often have a lot of sodium and fat. If you learn to cook simple entrées that don't take much time, you will wind up with a tastier meal with less salt and fat—and you'll pay less, too.

Convenience Foods or the "from Scratch" Kind

Some people can't tell the difference between a cake from a mix and one baked from scratch, and others like them equally. Some people even prefer package-mix brownies to the homemade kind. These convenience items are fine, but it will probably be fun for you to make a real attempt at baking.

Expiration Dates Are Important

Expiration dates tell you when certain products cease to be fresh. Never buy a product past its expiration date. Look for these dates on perishables such as dairy products, breads, meats, and eggs. Some products, such as cold cereals, are dated to indicate that they are better tasting if eaten before that time (though not unsafe after the date).

What's on That Label?

Labels tell you important information: the manufacturer and a list of the ingredients in the order of quantity (which gives you an idea of how the product will taste). By comparing brands of jam, for example, you will see that some list fruit first, and some list corn syrup first. The first product will taste more fruity; the second one will be sweeter. Labels also give nutritional content per serving and they tell you to refrigerate after opening if necessary. Some have recipes.

Reading labels is especially important for people who have allergies and food sensitivities or are trying to avoid certain ingredients in their diets— if you are sensitive to gluten, for example, and need to avoid products with modified food starch.

Kitchen Clue

If you want to avoid sugar in your diet you'll have to look beyond the obvious on the label. Sucrose, glucose, fructose, dextrose, and lactose are all forms of sugar, as are corn syrup, maple syrup, and molasses.

Unfortunately, some labels give only general references to some ingredients. They may say "spices and flavorings added" without listing the specific spices and flavorings, so people with sensitivities to specific additives will find no help here. Some of the more common ingredients you may see on a label are listed by type in the table on the next page.

Nutrition Facts
Serving Size ¾ cup (30g)

Amount Per Serving

Calories 120 • Calories from Fat 20

	% Daily Value*
Total Fat 2g	3%
Saturated Fat 0g	0%
Cholesterol 0mg	0%
Sodium 140mg	6%
Potassium 20mg	1%
Total Carbohydrate 26g	9%
Sugars 12g	
Protein 1g	

Vitamin A	25% •	Vitamin C	25%
Calcium	2% •	Iron	25%
Vitamin D	10% •	Thiamin	25%
Riboflavin	25% •	Niacin	25%
Vitamin B₆	25% •	Folic Acid	25%

Not a significant source of dietary fiber.
*Percent Daily Values are based on a 2,000 calorie diet.

A typical nutrition label. You see them everywhere now.

Common Ingredients and Their Uses

Ingredients	Use
Sodium benzoate, sorbic acid, sodium nitrate, sulfur dioxide, potassium sorbate, calcium proprionate	Preservatives
Monosodium glutamate (MSG)	Flavor enhancer
Carob bean gum, modified food starch, fuar gum, xanthan gum, gum arabic	Thickening agents
Lecithin, mono- and diglycerides, polysorbate 60, polysorbate 80	Increase shelf life
BHA, BHT, ascorbic acid	Antioxidants
Dextrose, fructose, glucose	Preservatives

Comparing Cost and Value

Certain foods have a funny way of seeming to cost less, when they really cost more. For example, ground beef, which has a high percentage of fat, is less expensive per pound than ground round. However, if you make a hamburger, meatloaf, or chili with ground beef, you will notice how much it shrinks when you cook off the fat. You pay more for the ground round, but get more meat and less fat.

Past-its-prime produce also is inexpensive, but you must look it over carefully. If the produce is still in good condition, it's a bargain. If it's soft and has brown spots, any price is too high.

Certain foods cost less because they entail some work. For example, whole chickens are cheaper than cut-up parts. You can save money if you divide the bird yourself.

The Least You Need to Know

➤ Compare generic and brand-name products and buy the generic one if it tastes just as good. It's probably cheaper.

➤ With certain exceptions, fresh food is preferable to canned or frozen.

➤ Never buy food past its expiration date.

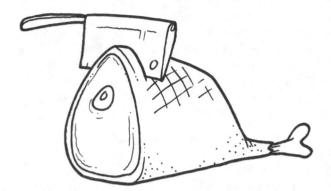

Chapter 6

The Meat Market

In This Chapter

➤ Learning what you need to know about beef, veal, pork, and lamb

➤ Discovering all about chicken and turkey

➤ Surfing a guide to seafood

➤ Using simple starter recipes that aren't really recipes

It's time to take your list to the store. Although many people have cut down on meat in recent years, it's still a major source of protein—and enjoyment—in our diets, so your list may include meat, poultry, or seafood. This chapter describes the more common cuts and varieties of these foods, and suggests the best uses for them. You will also learn how to select and store them. I've also included a few simple starter recipes that are so easy you really can't call them recipes.

Please! Gimme More Than Meatloaf!

Sure, meatloaf is great comfort food, but even beginner cooks and kitchen "idiots" may want something more glamorous once in a while.

Cooking meat can be incredibly easy, and it doesn't have to be expensive. You do have to understand the ingredients. You may have to rethink old, treasured recipes, too. If you've tried to cook your family favorites and failed, there's something you should know: Meat, particularly pork, is a lot leaner today than it used to be. Cooking times and temperatures may have to be adjusted, or liquids may be needed to prevent dishes from drying out.

A Minimanual on Meat

In the United States, meat typically means beef, veal, pork, and lamb, and—in recent years—buffalo meat, which is lean and tastes similar to beef. There are several grades for these meats, but most of what you will find in the stores is *choice*. *Prime* meats are usually reserved for specialty shops and restaurants. The difference between these two grades has to do with the marbling of fat within the flesh (prime has more, which makes the meat juicier) and sometimes with age (prime is aged longer where appropriate).

If you shop for meat in a supermarket rather than a butcher shop, you'll find precut meat in shrink-wrapped packages. Sometimes the market also has a special meat counter where you can get prime meats as well as more unusual or expensive meats such as sweetbreads, venison, game birds, crown roasts, and so on. A new offering is ostrich, which is lean, dark red, and tastes beefy, even though it is poultry. On the other hand, at some markets the "butcher counter" meat and the prepackaged stuff are exactly the same; the manager is simply accommodating the shopping preferences of two types of customer.

There are two general categories of meat: tender and tough. Tender portions are best when cooked by dry-heat methods (grilling, broiling, sautéing, stir-frying, baking, and roasting). Tougher portions require slow, moist-heat methods of cooking, such as stewing and braising, which softens fibrous tissue.

Check expiration dates before you buy meat, and store your purchases in the coldest part of the refrigerator. It's okay to refrigerate the meat in its original package. If the package should tear, place the meat on a plate and wrap it with fresh plastic wrap. To freeze meat, keep it in its original package and double-wrap it in freezer paper or aluminum foil, pressing the paper to exclude as much air as possible. Freezer burns are the white patches you may see on frozen meat, poultry, and fish. You can still use the food; just cut off the burnt part.

If you buy meat in bulk and want to freeze separate portions, wrap each portion first in fresh plastic wrap, then again with freezer paper or aluminum foil. Label

Kitchen Clue

Just because you don't buy meat at a butcher shop doesn't mean you can't get the cut and size you want. Although most of the meat may be packaged, you can ask the in-house butcher at your local supermarket for a particular cut, a smaller piece, a thicker steak, or whatever you want. Don't hesitate to assert yourself.

Warnings

To prevent food poisoning, always wash your hands before handling food—especially meat, poultry, and fish. After using a cutting board for raw meat, scrub the board (and any utensil you've used) and your hands with hot water and soap before working with other foods. Defrost meat in the refrigerator, not on the countertop. Bacteria grow wildly at room temperature.

and date the items. You'd be surprised how all the packages start to look the same; you really won't remember which package contains what or when you bought it.

The Bottom Line on Beef

Cuts of beef can be confusing. Tender portions include these steaks: *rib, Delmonico, club, porterhouse, T-bone, sirloin, shell, New York strip,* and *filet mignon*; and these roasts: *rib, top round, top sirloin,* and *tenderloin*. Tougher portions include *brisket, chuck, shoulder, cross-rib, rump, bottom round,* and *plate*.

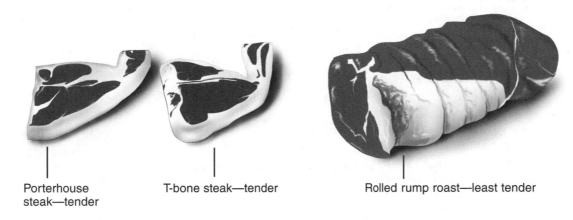

Porterhouse
steak—tender

T-bone steak—tender

Rolled rump roast—least tender

Although you usually cook tender meat with dry heat and tough meat with moist heat, there are exceptions. You can grill a flank steak and stir-fry skirt steak, even though these cuts are muscular, because cutting these meats across the grain makes them less chewy.

There are several ways to make meat tender. In addition to cutting it across the grain, you can pound it, as you do for minute steaks, or grind it—into hamburger, for instance. There are chemical tenderizers, too. In recent years there has been some controversy about whether acidic *marinades* tenderize meat. There is no question that acids break down fibrous tissue, but no one would suggest that marinades can penetrate a thick piece of meat, such as a pot roast, and turn it into a tender roast beef. In fact, if you marinate food too long, it will either toughen or become mushy. Use marinades for short periods of time for some tissue-softening. Of course, marinades have another purpose: They add lots of flavor to food.

What Is It?

If a recipe tells you to **marinate** meat, it means to let the food rest for a while in a mixture (usually an acidic liquid) that will make the meat more flavorful and sometimes more tender.

51

Always look for meat that's bright red, with tiny flecks of fat in the flesh and a small amount of fat around the edges. Pass up meat that has dark spots or discolored brownish streaks. Torn packages are another no-no.

The chart below is a quick guide to the best ways to cook and store various cuts of beef.

Beef Summary Chart

Cut of Beef	Texture	Best Way to Cook	How to Store
Steaks (T-bone, rib, Delmonico, club, porterhouse, sirloin, shell, New York strip, filet mignon, minute)	Tender	Grill, broil, sauté, stir-fry	2–3 days R 6 mos. F
Skirt steak	Tough	Grill, stir-fry, braise	2–3 days R 6 mos. F
Roasts (rib, top round, top sirloin, tenderloin)	Tender	Roast	3–4 days R 9 mos. F
Brisket, chuck, shoulder, cross-rib, rump, bottom round, plate, eye round (roasts)	Tough	Stew, braise	3–4 days R 9 mos. F
London broil	Tough	Grill/broil (marinate first)	2–3 days R 6 mos. F
Flank steak	Tough	Grill/broil marinate or score first)	2–3 days R 6 mos. F
Kebabs	Tender	Grill/broil	2–3 days R 4 mos. F
Stew meat	Tough	Stew	2–3 days R 4 mos. F
Ground beef	Tender	Most cooking methods	1 day R 3 mos. F

R = Refrigerator, F = Freezer

What You Need to Know About Veal

Veal is the delicately flavored meat of young calves. It lacks fat and can dry out easily. It is important to baste even the tender portions.

Milk-fed veal is from animals that weren't weaned and never ate grass. It is highly prized—pale, tender, and mildly flavored. It also is expensive.

Veal should be a light pinkish-cream color. If it has a deep, reddish hue, it is probably from an older animal, somewhere between a calf and cow, and lacks both the delicacy of veal and the richness of beef. However, some premium brands of veal have a darker flesh and are perfectly delicious.

The most tender veal portions include the *loin* and *rib. Boneless shoulder* is more tender than the corresponding portion in beef. Tougher veal sections include the *shank* and the *leg*. The best veal *cutlets* are carved from the leg and pounded to tenderness.

Kitchen Clue

Meats, poultry, and fish are safe to eat no matter how long you store them in the freezer because bacteria cannot grow in such a cold environment. Lengthy freezing, however, changes the quality and affects flavor, texture, color, and aroma. While the food may not poison you, it also may not taste very good.

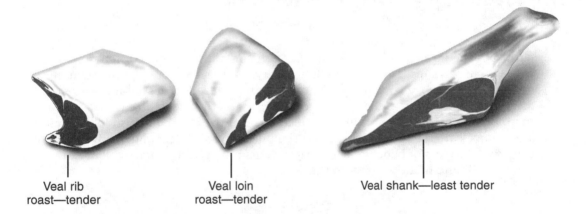

Veal rib roast—tender

Veal loin roast—tender

Veal shank—least tender

The chart below is a quick guide to the best ways to cook and store various cuts of veal.

Veal Summary Chart

Cut of Veal	Texture	Best Way to Cook	How to Store
Chops (loin, rib)	Tender	Broil, grill, sauté	1–3 days R 4–6 mos. F
Roasts (loin, rib)	Tender	Roast	3–4 days R 6 mos. F

continues

53

Veal Summary Chart   (continued)

Cut of Veal	Texture	Best Way to Cook	How to Store
Shoulder	Tough	Roast, braise, stew	3–4 days R 6 mos. F
Shank	Tough	Braise	2–3 days R 4–6 mos. F
Whole leg	Tough	Roast, braise	3–5 days R 6 mos. F
Cutlets	Tender	Sauté, grill	1–3 days R 3–4 mos. F
Stew	Tough	Stew	2–3 days R 6 mos. F
Ground veal	Tender methods	Most cooking	1 day R 3 mos. F

R = Refrigerator, F = Freezer

This Little Piggy—The Story on Pork

Pork has gone on a huge diet in recent years. Pigs are slimmer, and their meat is leaner. That's great for your health, but it creates a lot of problems when you cook. Less fat means the meat can dry out easily. Because pork must be cooked well-done to kill off possible parasites that cause trichinosis, dryness is even more of a problem. But too many people overcook pork. What they don't realize is that well-done doesn't mean *parched*. As long as the meat reaches 155 to 160°F, it's safe to eat. Use a meat thermometer to check (put it in the thickest part of the roast), but also look carefully at the juices when you carve the meat. The juices must be clear and yellow, not reddish. Pork has lots of benefits. The meat is rich and sweet. It contains plenty of Vitamin B1, and it adds variety to the diet.

Fein on Food

Pigs are among the most generous animals on earth. Every part of the animal is edible or otherwise useful—the meat for food, the skin for leather, and even the bristles for brushes. It's no wonder that pork has been a mainstay of civilization for centuries and is the most widely eaten meat in the world. Pigs are prolific, too: Some say that all the pigs in America are the descendants of the 13 hogs originally brought by the explorer DeSoto in the sixteenth century.

Pork should have a pale, pinkish-cream color, although shoulder sections may be slightly darker than the rib or loin. Look for meat that's marbled or grainy-looking.

Most pork portions are tender enough for baking, broiling, roasting, and other dry-heat methods. Because the meat is so lean, it's a good idea to cook pork slowly and at moderate temperatures so that the middle cooks through before the outside is parched. I also recommend that you baste the meat for added juiciness.

What Is It?

When you **parboil** food, you cook it partially in boiling water before cooking it completely by some other method.

Loin and *rib portions* may be cut into *chops* but are sometimes packaged as whole pieces (such as *pork loin roast* or *crown roast,* which is made up of two rib-loin portions tied together in a circle); in any case, these are tender cuts. *Country-style ribs*, which are carved from the bottom of the loin, are more tender than regular *spareribs. Fresh ham* is also called leg of pork; it is a large piece and comes as a whole ham, or as shank or butt portions. *Picnic roasts* (from the arm) and *Boston butt* (shoulder portion) are less tender than the leg. The most tender part of the pig is the *tenderloin.*

Ham is cured leg of pork. You can buy whole or half hams. Most hams offered in supermarkets are fully cooked and need only to be seasoned and heated through (about 10 minutes per pound), but read the label to be sure. The tastiest hams have the bone still intact. A *picnic ham* is smoked pork shoulder (also called Boston butt) and tastes like ham, although it contains more fat and, therefore, more waste. You can also buy fully cooked ham steaks. Refrigerate ham in its original wrapper.

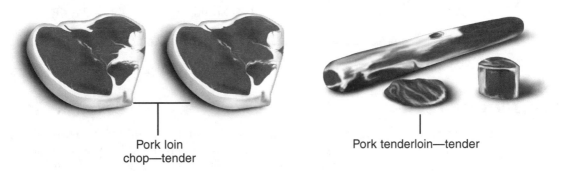

Pork loin chop—tender

Pork tenderloin—tender

The following table is a quick guide to the best ways to cook and store various cuts of pork and ham.

Pork Summary Chart

Cut of Pork	Texture	Best Way to Cook	How to Store
Chops (loin, rib)	Tender	Grill, broil, sauté	3 days R 4 mos. F
Roasts (loin, rib, crown)	Tender	Roast	3–4 days R 6 mos. F
Spareribs	Tender	Grill, broil, bake	3 days R 3 mos. F
Sausages	Tender	Grill, broil, bake	1–2 days R 2 mos. F
Country ribs	Tender	Grill, broil, bake	3 days R 3 mos. F
Fresh ham (shank, butt, or whole)	Tender	Roast, braise	3–4 days R 6 mos. F
Picnic roast, Boston butt	Tender	Roast, braise	3 days R 6 mos. F
Tenderloin	Tender	Roast, grill, sauté, stir-fry	1–2 days R 4 mos. F
Ground pork	Tender	Most cooking methods	1 day R 3 mos. F
Cured ham (whole, fully cooked)	Tender	Roast	2 weeks R 1 mo. F
Cured ham (half, fully cooked)	Tender	Roast	1 week R 1 mo. F
Ham steak	Tender	Grill, broil, bake	3 days R 1 mo. F

R = Refrigerator, F = Freezer

Lessons on Lamb

Lambs are benevolent, like pigs. The meat is used for food, the milk for cheese and other dairy products, the wool for clothing. Like pigs, lambs were among the first animals to be domesticated. Today, lambs are butchered when young, before they develop the strong taste that once characterized this meat. The meat is mild but the fat can be gamy, so cut away as much of it as possible, leaving just a thin film to provide succulence. Light, rosy-hued meat is younger and more delicately flavored than deep red meat. There's no real significance to the words "spring lamb" anymore. Years ago, lambs were raised through the winter to be slaughtered in time for spring holiday dinners among Christians, Jews, and Muslims. Now we can get young lamb any time.

Even the so-called tough sections of lamb are tender enough for dry-heat cooking, with the exception of *shoulder roast*, *shanks*, and *neck meat*. The most expensive and tender cuts are *loin* and *rib chops*. Loin and rib sections also can be made into a *crown roast*. *Leg of lamb* is a large cut sold either whole or in sections. A *butterflied leg of lamb* is boneless and flattened slightly.

Something Simple

This recipe for broiled lamb chops is so easy you can handle it right now, before you even get to the "real" recipes. Place loin or rib lamb chops (about 1½" thick) in a broiler pan and sprinkle them on both sides with salt or garlic salt and black pepper. If you want to make a grand effort, add a pinch or two of fresh or dried rosemary. Preheat the broiler and broil the chops about 3 to 5 minutes per side, depending on whether you like them rare, medium, or well done.

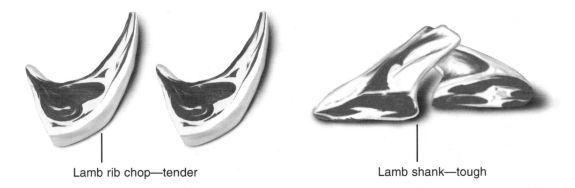

Lamb rib chop—tender   Lamb shank—tough

The following table is a quick guide to the best ways to cook and store various cuts of lamb.

Lamb Summary Chart

Cut of Lamb	Texture	Best Way to Cook	How to Store
Roast (loin, rib)	Tender	Roast	3–4 days R 8–9 mos. F
Chops (loin, rib, shoulder)	Tender	Broil, grill, sauté	2–3 days R 4–6 mos. F

continues

Lamb Summary Chart   (continued)

Cut of Lamb	Texture	Best Way to Cook	How to Store
Leg	Tender	Roast, grill	3–4 days R 8–9 mos. F
Boneless leg	Tender	Grill, broil	2–3 days R 4–6 mos. F
Shoulder, shanks, neck	Tough	Braise, stew	2–3 days R 4–6 mos. F
Breast, spareribs	Tender	Roast, braise	2–3 days R 4–6 mos. F
Kebabs	Tender	Grill, broil	2–3 days R 4–6 mos. F
Stew	Tough	Stew	2–3 days R 4–6 mos. F
Ground lamb	Tender	Most cooking methods	1 day R 3 mos. F

R = Refrigerator, F = Freezer

Kitchen Clue

When cleaning poultry, you might find a surprise inside: packaged giblets. More than a few home cooks didn't rinse the inside of the bird, cooked it, and to their embarrassment, came across plastic-packed giblets while carving at the dinner table. Once you take the giblets out of the bag, you can cook them along with the poultry or use them for stock, gravy, or stuffing.

A Primer on Poultry

Everyone loves a winner, and lately the big winner for dinner has been poultry, especially chicken and turkey. These barnyard birds have diet- and health-conscious folks to thank for their newly acquired culinary status. The meat provides high-quality protein with few calories, and it's low in fat and cholesterol—especially if you don't eat the skin.

All poultry is extremely perishable. Don't stop off to see a movie if you just went shopping and bought some. Take it home and put it in the fridge.

There's nothing glamorous about cleaning poultry, but you've gotta do it. Rinse the bird (or parts) under cold running water and cut off any excess fat. Rinse the cavity of the bird thoroughly and remove the package of giblets that's usually tucked inside (cook these separately or use them for stock or gravy). If you see any pinfeathers, take them out with a paring knife or tweezers. You can remove hairs by singeing them with a match.

Poultry-Handling Guidelines

Salmonella can be a serious problem, so be extremely careful when handling poultry. Not only do you have to wash your hands before you touch it, you also have to wash afterwards, to reduce the possibility of spreading bacteria to other foods. If you use a cutting board, knife, or other utensil, be sure to wash these implements carefully in lots of hot, sudsy water. (Plastic boards can go in the dishwasher.)

To defrost poultry, thaw it in the refrigerator (four to five hours per pound) or in several changes of cold water; never let it defrost on the countertop (bacteria multiply rapidly at room temperature). You can defrost birds by microwave, but if you do, be sure you cook the meat immediately after it has thawed.

Never cook poultry partially. If bacteria are present in the uncooked portions, they will flourish and contaminate the whole dish. Be sure you cook poultry completely to eliminate all bacteria. According to the USDA, the thigh meat should register 180°F on a meat thermometer inserted into the thickest part of the thigh. While some people may contend that the breast meat will be dry at this point, it needn't be if you baste the bird. Many cooking experts recommend cooking the chicken to 165°F (thigh temperature). You must decide whether to take the conservative route or not.

Stuffing Poultry

The subject of stuffing—what kind and even what you call it (in some parts of the United States it's called *dressing*)—can be the subject of great debate. The biggest argument is over whether to put the stuffing inside the bird or cook it separately. In days gone by, when chickens and turkeys took longer to cook, the debate was purely a culinary matter. But today's breeds of chickens and turkeys take a shorter time to cook so there's a potential health hazard: The meat may be fully cooked before the stuffing is cooked adequately enough to kill any bacteria present in the stuffing.

Current USDA guidelines recommend that you cook stuffing separately. However, if you absolutely insist on stuffing your chicken or turkey, be sure to follow these rules: Don't mix the stuffing until just before you use it and don't pack it into the bird until just before you roast it. Pack the stuffing loosely, and, after you have made certain that the bird is cooked completely (use a meat thermometer), check the internal temperature of the stuffing (it should reach 165°F.)

Chicken, the Champion

Of all poultry, chicken is champion in the kitchen. In addition to its nutritive value, chicken is among the world's most versatile foods. It pairs well with almost any herb, spice, or condiment. It lends itself to every cooking method. Cooking chicken means you never have a boring meal.

The color of a chicken's skin is irrelevant to flavor, quality, or cooking method. What matters is the freshness and condition of the chicken. Look for chickens with moist skin. Don't choose any that look like they've been in a barnyard fight and have bruises and blemishes. Avoid chickens with a lot of visible pinfeathers and long hairs. If the seller didn't take care enough to make his wares look good, how well could the bird have been treated? Look inside the package—if there's lots of runny red liquid, the bird has been frozen and defrosted.

Chicken parts are more perishable than whole birds.

Broiler-fryers are the most common type of chicken; they weigh 2½–4 pounds and serve three to four people. They may be cut into separate parts or sold whole. *Roasters* are larger, fatter birds, that weigh approximately 4½–8 pounds and serve about six people. *Stewing hens* are older, tougher chickens (3–7 pounds). *Capons* (6–9 pounds) are castrated male chickens whose meat is extraordinarily tender and sweet. They are large enough to serve approximately eight people. At the other end of the scale are *rock Cornish hens* and *poussins*, which are tiny chickens that weigh 1–1½ pounds and serve one or two people.

There's a lot of talk these days about *free-range* chicken. According to the USDA, free-range means only that the chicken has had some access out of its coop. It does not mean the bird spends its life basking in the sun, pecking here and there in the garden for good things to eat. And it doesn't mean the chicken has been given a diet free of pesticides, coloring agents, or antibiotics. Chickens that are allowed out of the coop may or may not be more tender than other birds. Should you buy it? Only if you try a particular brand and the flavor or some other factor appeals to you and you don't mind spending the extra money.

Sales of boneless, skinless chicken *breasts* have soared in recent years, and for good reason. The meat is lean and low-calorie and is versatile enough to combine with all sorts of flavorings. You can cook these breasts by almost any method, and because they are relatively thin, they cook quickly enough to satisfy even the busiest people. They also are incredibly easy to prepare.

Let's Talk Turkey

Turkey always used to be considered a feast bird, suitable for Thanksgiving and Christmas. Now you can buy small turkeys and turkey parts for everyday dinners. In addition, several other turkey products are available, including cutlets, breast tenderloins, ground turkey, turkey sausages, bacon, and luncheon meats. These are all tasty, lower-fat alternatives to more familiar items. You can substitute turkey cutlets for veal in any favorite recipe. Ground turkey is much drier than ground beef, though, so you can't just substitute one for the other in all recipes. To make a juicy burger or meatloaf using ground turkey, for example, you'll find it helpful to include a liquid such as stock or wine, or another moisture-laden ingredient such as egg, egg white, or water-rich vegetables such as spinach. Unlike beef burgers, turkey burgers must be cooked well-done.

Whole turkeys come fresh and frozen, plain and self-basting. Fresh turkey is infinitely more tasty and tender. Self-basting turkeys are a waste of money and loaded with calories. You pay extra for vegetable oil or broth that's injected into the meat, when you could just as easily baste the bird with some nonfat liquid such as orange juice or wine; or you could furnish your own fresh basting oil or chicken stock.

To figure out how much turkey you need when you roast a whole bird, consider the weight: 1 pound per person (including the bone) is about right. As for stuffing, the general rule is to use half as many cups of stuffing as the weight of the bird—5 cups of stuffing for a 10-pound turkey, for instance. (For more about stuffing, see the section "Stuffing Poultry" earlier in this chapter.)

The following table is a quick guide to the best ways to cook and store poultry.

Fein on Food

If Benjamin Franklin had had his way, the turkey—not the bald eagle—would have been America's symbol. Franklin believed the eagle was of "bad moral character," while the turkey was "a much more respectable bird."

Poultry Summary Chart

Type	Weight	Best Way to Cook	How to Store
Broiler/fryer chicken	2–4 lbs.	Grill, broil, sauté, deep-fry, poach	2–3 days R (whole) 1–2 days R (parts) 9 mos. F
Roaster chicken	4–8 lbs.	Roast, poach	2–3 days R 9 mos. F
Hen chicken	4+ lbs.	Stew, poach	2–3 days R 9 mos. F
Capon	6–9 lbs.	Roast	2–3 days R 9 mos. F
Rock Cornish hen	1+ lbs.	Roast, grill, sauté	2–3 days R 9 mos. F

continues

Poultry Summary Chart   (continued)

Type	Weight	Best Way to Cook	How to Store
Boneless chicken breasts	12–16 oz.	Most cooking methods	1–2 days R 3–4 mos. F
Whole turkey		Roast	1 week R 9 mos. F
Turkey cutlets		Grill, sauté	1–2 days R 3–4 mos. F
Turkey tenderloins		Grill, bake	1–2 days R 3–4 mos. F
Ground chicken/turkey		Grill, broil, bake	1 day R 3 mos. F
Chicken/turkey sausage		Grill, broil, sauté	2 days R 2 mos. F

R = Refrigerator, F = Freezer

The Subject Is Seafood

The first rule of fish is this: It must be fresh. The second rule is that fish shouldn't smell like fish. If that sounds like an oxymoron, here's what it really means: Fish shouldn't smell like something that's been left on the beach too long. Fresh fish—*really* fresh fish—has no odor. Neither does shellfish, except scallops, which have a distinctive, almost sweet, ocean scent, and mussels, which may have a salty aroma.

Going Fishing

Fish offers several advantages for the cook. Not only is it healthy and nutritious, it also is quick and easy to cook. And there are so many varieties of fish, with so many different flavors, textures, and even colors that it provides endless culinary possibilities.

Dozens of varieties of fish are for sale, but they fall into two general types: *lean* and *oily*. Lean fish have a mild, delicate flavor and firm, light-colored flesh. Because they are lean, their flesh can dry out easily, so these varieties are best when cooked with fats or liquids. You can poach, steam, deep-fry, sauté, bake, or broil them. The more common types include *flounder, sole, snapper, halibut, cod, grouper, orange roughy,* and *haddock*.

Oily fish are richer, with a more intense flavor, and they tend to have darker flesh. These varieties do best when grilled, broiled, and baked. Familiar varieties include *salmon, swordfish, mackerel, bluefish, catfish, tuna, monkfish,* and *trout*.

Oily fish don't usually fare well when poached or fried. The flesh is too rich. But there are notable exceptions. Poached salmon, for example, is moist and tender. Fried catfish is succulent, juicy, and satisfyingly crispy. And sautéed trout is a classic—light, delicate, and satisfying.

Before you buy fish, be sure it is odor-free. For whole fish, check the skin, which should be tight, and the scales, which should shimmer. The eyes should be clear and shiny. Fillets must look moist and lay flat; if the ends curl up like potato chips, the fillet is past its prime. Also, fish steaks should glisten with moisture and be uniformly colored. Try to avoid pre-wrapped fish; while it may *look* fine, you can't really tell if it is. When you buy fish, figure 6 to 8 ounces of fillet per person, 8 ounces of fish steak per person, or 12 ounces of whole fish per person.

You must cook fish the day you buy it or, at worst, the day after. Fish is highly perishable. Freezing can make it watery, but if you want fish at the ready, double wrap and freeze it. Keep fish in the freezer no longer than one month.

Old-fashioned cookbooks instructed readers to cook fish until it flakes. Frankly, by that point the flesh is so dried out it tastes like rubber bands. The other maxim—cook fish about 10 minutes per inch of thickness—doesn't work well either, especially for fillets. Thin fish fillets (less than an inch) cook differently than thick ones. The thin ones are done very quickly and you'll have to pay close attention so they don't over cook. Thicker fillets present a different problem: You want to be sure they are cooked sufficiently in the center. A better rule is to test the fish after about eight minutes per inch and look to see if it is done or not; thin fillets should look opaque and the very thinnest parts at the end should begin to flake. To look at thick fillets, you'll have to use the tip of a sharp knife to separate the flesh; it should be opaque.

Telling when fish steaks are done depends on the fish; they are all very different. Basically, though, you should be able to pierce the fish easily to the center with the tip of a sharp knife. Swordfish, salmon, and tuna are actually tastier when they appear to be undercooked—that is, pink or darker in the center and slightly resistant to the tip of a sharp knife.

As for whole fish, it should be cooked so that the thickest flesh is opaque and no longer adheres to the bone, but doesn't disintegrate. You should be able to part the flesh with a fork. An instant thermometer would be helpful here; the internal temperature of a cooked fish should be about 145°F. If you are poaching a whole fish to serve chilled, cook it only to within 10 minutes of expected completion time, remove the pan from the heat, and let the fish finish cooking in the liquid as it cools.

Remember that fish, like most other foods, continues to cook even after you remove it from the heat source. So, with all the above in mind, try to stop the cooking *before* the dish is done. It sounds difficult and you may not get it right the first time, but with experience, you will learn how to do it perfectly.

Some Info on Shellfish

Shellfish is evenmore perishable than fish and must be eaten within 24 hours of purchase. Like fish, it should have no odor. Keep all shellfish in the coldest part of the refrigerator, preferably with ice packs surrounding it. Freezing is not recommended except for king crab legs, lobster tail, and shrimp. Place these in double plastic bags and keep them frozen no longer than two months.

A number of sea items qualify as shellfish, and they are treated differently for culinary purposes. The most common are *shrimp, soft-shelled crab, king crab, lobster, clams, oysters, mussels,* and *scallops.*

Shrimp is the most popular shellfish in this country. It is sold by the size, but that can vary from place to place, so you are better off understanding the way shrimp cooks by the amount per pound (21 to 25 per pound, for example, means it takes that many shrimp, in their shells, to equal 1 pound). There are many varieties of shrimp; some look pink, others have stripes, and so on. Be sure the shells have no black marks (a sign of deterioration). You can cook shrimp by almost any cooking method, but first remove the shell and the gritty black vein on the outer curve of the back. To remove the vein, pierce the curve with a paring knife to reveal the vein, and then scoop it out. (See **devein** in Chapter 13, "A Compendium of the Top 100+ Cooking Terms," for an illustration.) Fishmongers may do this for you. But avoid shelled, frozen shrimp, since the shell protects the flesh from breaking down in the harsh freezer climate.

When you buy crab, be sure it is *alive* to assure yourself it's fresh. The merchant will kill the crab and remove inedible portions. Soft-shell crabs, which can be eaten in their entirety, shell and all, can be broiled, grilled, sautéed, stir-fried, or deep-fried. King crab legs (usually sold frozen) can be poached or steamed. You can also buy fresh or tinned crab meat to make crab cakes and salad. "Lump" and "claw" are larger pieces than "flake." You can freeze the meat for about one month.

Something Simple

Want something heavenly to eat that's also incredibly easy? Scrub some unshucked oysters and place them on a preheated grill. Let them sit on top of the heat until the shells pop open (usually this takes a few minutes). Discard any oysters whose shells haven't opened with the others. Serve the oysters with melted butter. Everyone will think you're an angel.

There are two types of lobster. Maine lobster has huge, meaty claws. Spiny lobster (lobster "tail," often sold frozen) has no claw meat. Except for frozen tail, lobster should be alive and thriving when you buy it. You can tell how vigorous a lobster is if you pick it up and the tail flaps back and forth like Flipper. You can poach, steam, grill, broil, bake, and stir-fry lobster.

There are several kinds of edible clams; hard-shells in sizes from tiny *littlenecks* to large *chowder clams* and soft-shell clams. All should be alive when you purchase them; be sure the hard-shells are tightly closed before you have the merchant open them for eating raw, on the half-shell. Many people love uncooked hard-shell clams and oysters. This creates some health risks (as do all uncooked proteins), and it is up to each individual to make the decision to eat them or not. Before you cook hard-shell clams and oysters, scrub the surfaces with a brush or clean sponge. Soft-shell clams usually have sand in them and should be soaked in a few changes of cold water before you cook them. As for cooking, clams and oysters may be grilled, baked, sautéed, steamed, and deep-fried. Mussels need a good scrubbing to remove dirt and the "beard" (unless you buy farmed mussels, which are much cleaner). These are never eaten raw, but may be steamed or grilled. Be sure to discard any clams, oysters, or mussels that don't open when cooked.

Scallops are usually sold out of the shell. There are many varieties, but stores usually sell either large sea scallops or smaller bay scallops. Both are vaguely sweet and fragrant. Look for scallops that are moist and shiny. One problem with scallops is that they become rubbery if you overcook them; they need only brief cooking, until they turn cream-white. Scallops can be steamed, grilled, sautéed, stir-fried, and deep-fried; they are also wonderful in chowders.

Fein on Food

An old wives' tale warned against eating oysters in any month that didn't have an "R" in it, as if by some magic, oysters that were okay on April 30 would suddenly become poisonous on May 1. No one pays attention to this "rule" anymore. It is true that oysters are the fattest and most succulent in cold months (those with "R"), but with quick transport, oysters from cold waters can be shipped anywhere, anytime, and you can get good oysters in June or December.

Fish Summary Chart

Type of Fish	Best Way to Cook
Lean: flounder, halibut, snapper, sole	Poach, steam, deep-fry, sauté, broil
cod, grouper, haddock	grill, bake
Oily: swordfish, mackerel, bluefish, tuna, monkfish	Broil, grill, bake
Salmon	Poach, broil, grill, bake
Catfish	Sauté, broil, grill, bake
Trout	Sauté, bake, broil, grill
Chilean sea bass	Broil, grill
Shrimp	Most cooking methods
Soft-shell crabs	Broil, grill, sauté, deep-fry, stir-fry
King crab	Poach, steam
Lobster	Poach, steam, broil, grill, bake, stir-fry
Clams, oysters	Eat raw, grill, steam, bake, sauté, deep-fry
Mussels	Steam, grill
Scallops	Steam, grill, sauté, deep-fry, stir-fry, in chowder

The Least You Need to Know

➤ Tender meats are usually cooked by dry heat methods, while tougher cuts require long, slow, moist heat methods.

➤ Wash your hands before and after handling meat, poultry, and seafood, and scrub any cutting boards and utensils you use.

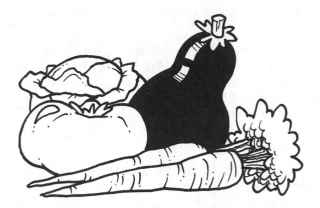

Chapter 7

You Only Think You Hate Vegetables

In This Chapter

➤ Learning all about vegetables

➤ Finding salad stuff

➤ Discovering all kinds of other little items in the produce section

➤ Trying simple starter recipes that aren't really recipes

Vegetables and salads have become much more important in our diets in recent years. For some people, vegetables, grains, legumes, and greens are the core of the daily menu. For others, these items are side dishes. In either case, many delicious choices are available. But vegetable selections can be confusing. This chapter discusses vegetable products in three categories: fresh vegetables, salad stuff, and miscellaneous fresh items (such as garlic and onions) that you use to enhance other foods. Information on dried beans, legumes, and grains appears in Chapter 9, "A Trip to the Dairy Barn and Down the Grocery Aisles." I've also included a few very easy recipes.

A General Overview of Vegetables

You may not have tried or even heard of some of the vegetables mentioned in this chapter. You may have passed them in the produce section and wondered what they were and how they tasted. This is your opportunity to learn about them. When you know a little about these ingredients, you may be more willing to try them and discover what you do and don't like. You may be surprised to find flavors you never knew could be so enticing.

Many vegetables and salad items are available all year, but some are seasonal. It is better to buy these in season when they taste fresher and more delicious. Always look for fresh-looking, unwithered leaves and stems. Avoid vegetables with obvious bruises and the overaged, woody look of fossils: giant broccoli stems with brown ends, for instance.

If you can, buy vegetables and salad greens that are loose rather than prepackaged. That way you can see and feel the entire item to be sure it's fresh. Not only can you then select items based on freshness, but you also can choose your own quantities and your own "mix"—more arugula, for example, or no chicory. However, if you're too tired, too rushed, or too whatever to bother preparing fresh salad and you don't mind overpaying, those packaged salads sure come in handy. Take advantage; just be sure the greens look fresh, crisp, and moist.

Many people choose organically grown vegetables to avoid what they consider to be health risks posed by products grown in commercially fertilized soil or sprayed with chemical pesticides. This is a personal choice. There is no readily apparent difference in flavor between many regular and organically grown produce; however, organically grown potatoes and other root vegetables seem to have a more intense and sumptuous flavor.

Kitchen Clue

Most experts will tell you that potatoes, onions, and garlic should be kept in a cool, dark place—not the refrigerator. However, if you lack space, you can keep them in the basket (not moisture drawers) in your fridge. Do not store them in plastic bags (you may use paper bags or towels) because they may perish more quickly.

You have to use common sense about storing vegetables. You also have to use your eyes and nose. Refrigeration guidelines are given for each vegetable discussed below, but don't feel married to the numbers. Go by appearance and smell, not by the actual time the vegetable has been in the refrigerator, and discard or keep the vegetables accordingly.

For optimum storage, keep fresh vegetables and greens in the refrigerator in special vented plastic vegetable bags. The tiny holes help maintain the perfect balance of air and moisture needed to keep the produce at its peak.

Speaking of storing vegetables, if you're one of those lucky people with a garden and a green thumb, you might find yourself with a bounty of produce at the end of a season. You can only store your harvest for so long in the fridge—then what should you do with the leftovers? There are lots of options, depending on the vegetable.

Tomatoes, particularly plum tomatoes, make terrific sauce (you can make a big batch and freeze it in small containers). You can prepare chutney, chow-chow, or other relishes with bell peppers, corn, zucchini, carrots, and beans. Cabbage can become sauerkraut or coleslaw. You can make a big pot of vegetable soup or stew.

Some people preserve vegetables in jars using a bain-marie. To do this, follow the jar manufacturer's instructions. Other people freeze vegetables, but frozen veggies can be watery. If you can't think of anything else to do with the bounty, why not give it to neighbors, friends, soup kitchens, and homeless shelters?

A Primer on Fresh Vegetables

The word *vegetable* sometimes makes people grimace. But people who think they hate vegetables probably have eaten them overcooked all their lives. Old-fashioned recipes from days gone by recommended cooking vegetables until they were mush. Today we know better. We have learned to cook vegetables to tenderness but to keep them as crunchy as possible. Although some vegetables, such as spinach and other leafy greens, wilt, even they don't have to suffer from too much time over the heat.

Shorter cooking time benefits vegetables' flavor and texture. It also means healthier eating because fewer nutrients are lost.

With so many varieties of vegetables, it's impossible to give one rule to determine when vegetables are done. But here are two important guidelines to keep in mind: Cut vegetables to a uniform size so that they cook evenly, and cook them for the shortest time possible, so that they become tender but still keep their nutrients and vibrant color. The "Vegetables" recipe section gives approximate cooking times for several vegetables.

The following sections describe the vegetables you're most likely to see in the market. For most vegetables, 1 pound will serve three to four people as a side dish. In cases where this estimate does not hold true, I will indicate the serving quantity under the specific heading. Storage time refers to refrigeration unless otherwise noted.

Artichokes

This unusual-looking vegetable is best in fall and spring. Look for tight, closed leaves and an even-colored surface. If the leaves have sharp points, snip the tops with scissors before you cook the artichokes. Cut surfaces turn color quickly, so rub them with the cut side of a halved lemon to prevent discoloration. Artichokes keep four to five days. One artichoke serves one person. Remember to use a stainless steel or enamel pot with artichokes (and asparagus) because they "react" chemically with other metals (such as aluminum).

Something Simple

People will think you're a genius if you serve artichokes. They look difficult to prepare, but they really aren't. Cut 1 inch from the stems of four large artichokes, put the artichokes in a stainless steel or enamel pot just big enough to hold them, and cover them with water. Add half a lemon. Bring the water to a boil, cover the pan, lower the heat, and cook for about 35 minutes. (When they are done, the stem feels tender when pierced with the tip of a sharp knife.) Remove the artichokes with tongs, holding them with the leaves pointing downward to drain the water. Serve them hot with melted butter or oil and vinegar, or cold with mustard or mayonnaise. That's all there is to it.

Asparagus

These regal-looking spears taste best in the spring. You decide whether you like the fat ones (you must peel these) or skinny ones. You may steam asparagus standing up in a pot that keeps the tips above the water (because the tips cook more quickly) or poach them in a stainless steel or enamel pan. Look for firm, straight spears with tightly closed tips and unwithered stems. Cut off the purple-white section at the bottom. You may see white asparagus, which is grown completely underground to prevent the formation of chlorophyll. White asparagus has a more delicate flavor and texture than green asparagus. Asparagus will last up to five days if you wrap the bottoms in moist paper towels.

Avocados

The avocado is a fruit that we eat as a vegetable. The flavor and texture are rich and buttery. There are two types: large, shiny, and light green-skinned (*Fuerte*) or small, dark, and pebbly skinned (*Haas*). The Haas has a more intense flavor. Store avocados on the countertop until they're ripe. After the surface "gives," or yields, to slight finger pressure, store them in the refrigerator, where they keep about a week.

Beans

Both green and yellow snap beans should be firm, slender, and crisp, and should have no bulging bumps beneath the pod. Snap off the ends before you cook them. Beans keep for as many as four to five days. *Fava* ("broad") beans are thicker and wider. You only use the mature bean inside the pod. Three pounds of favas serve four people as a side dish.

Beets

This dark-red root vegetable is the sweetest one in the larder, with about 10 percent sugar, which is the reason most people like it. Small beets are the sweetest. Look for those with smooth skins. Because beet flesh is claret red, this vegetable makes a stunning side dish. In addition, the leaves are tasty and nutritious. You cook them the same way you would spinach. Beets keep up to four weeks, but the leaves perish after three to four days.

What Is It?

Crudité means "raw thing" and refers to raw (or briefly cooked) cut-up vegetables that people serve as hors d'oeuvres.

Belgian Endive

Endive are small, oval-shaped heads that are best in late fall and winter. Look for pale, compact leaves. Endive is related to chicory; both have a bitter flavor. It is used both raw, in salads, or as a side dish (you need one or two endive per person). You also can use endive raw in salad or as crudités. They last approximately three to four days.

Belgian endive.

Broccoli

Broccoli is more versatile than most people think. Too many people don't use the stem and only buy florets; if you peel the stem, however, it is the tastiest and crunchiest part of the vegetable. Two large spears serve four people as a side dish. Look for tight, dark-green florets and moist-looking stems. Broccoli will last five to seven days.

Broccoli Rabe

This vegetable looks a little like broccoli but the stems are thinner and the rabe contains more leaves. It has an intriguing, bitter taste and keeps four to five days. Be sure the stems look moist, as if they will snap.

Brussels Sprouts

Brussels sprouts are miniature cabbages that are best in the fall, winter, and early spring. Look for compact heads. The tiny ones are the sweetest. Some stores sell Brussels sprouts in cartons; some sell them loose or on the stem. Brussels sprouts keep four to five days.

Cabbage

All varieties of cabbage are available year-round, except for Savoy, which is available in the fall and spring. Look for compact heads that feel heavy for their size. Remove the core before cooking cabbage. Cabbages keep two to three weeks.

Carrots

This yellow root vegetable has almost as much sugar as beets. The slender ones are sweeter than fat ones, and those with the leaves still on top have a more intense taste than packaged ones. Carrots should be firm and stiff. Avoid those that are split or limp. Carrots keep for several weeks.

Cauliflower

Cauliflower usually is sold as a whole white head (there are also green and purple varieties), though some stores sell florets only. Look for heads that are evenly white and, if possible, those that still have green leaves clinging at the bottom. These leaves are edible and quite tasty. Cauliflower keeps five to six days. One head serves four to six people as a side dish.

Celery

Celery is hardy enough to last two to three weeks in the fridge. Look for stiff, crisp stalks. Color is irrelevant; one variety, called Pascal, is darker green than most. Use celery leaves to flavor soups or as a garnish. Consider peeling the celery; peeled celery is less stringy and easier to digest. Use a vegetable peeler and start at the smaller end of the stalk.

Celeriac

This vegetable, the celery root, is fat, squat, and brown and has a lovely, delicate celery fragrance. It must be peeled. It is often shredded for salad, but also wonderful when pureed and combined with equal amounts of mashed potato or cooked apple. Look for firm knobs; they keep for weeks in the fridge.

Chard

There are red and green varieties of chard, which is related to the beet. Only the leaves and stems are eaten, not the root, and you can use it as if it were spinach, only it may take slightly longer to cook if the stems are thick. The leaves are large and sometimes curly and usually dark green or green with red veins. The red varieties are a little sweeter and the thin-stemmed ones more tender. Look for crisp stalks. Chard wilts quickly so it's best to use it within two days of purchase.

Chayote

This is a gourd-like fruit that we eat as a vegetable. It has a ribbed, greenish-white skin and a very mild flavor. Look for very firm chayotes that are evenly colored and use it as you would zucchini.

Corn

Corn is America's favorite vegetable. The sooner you cook the ears after you buy them, the better; over time, natural sugars turn to starch. The kernels can be white, yellow, or mixed. Peel the husk back and look for medium-size, even kernels. Overly large kernels will taste woody; teeny ones will not have flavor. The husks should feel moist and be tightly wrapped around the corn, and the silk should be golden brown. Remove the husk just before you cook the corn. For serving, figure one to two ears per person.

Kitchen Clue

Never buy ears of corn whose husks have been removed. Removing the husks accelerates the speed at which the sugar in the corn turns to starch and adversely affects flavor and texture.

Fein on Food

Everyone knows that our third president, Thomas Jefferson, was a genius. Along with some of his other credentials (such as writing the Declaration of Independence and founding the University of Virginia), he also offered some sage advice about corn. He recommended that as soon as you pick an ear of corn, rush it to a pot of boiling water, before the sweet sap that comes from the stem stops flowing. The best cooks still follow this advice.

Eggplants

Western eggplants have either dark purple or creamy white skin. Smaller Asian egg-plants are light purple with white streaks. In either case, look for skin that is shiny and firm. Eggplants last about one week. Although a medium-size Western eggplant will serve four as a side dish, you need one to two Asian eggplants per person. Because Western eggplants can be bitter, some cooks salt the flesh and let it rest for 30 minutes, then dry it with paper towels before cooking the vegetable.

Fein on Food

People once thought eggplants were deadly. Others claimed they caused insanity and called them "mad apples."

Fennel

This bulbous vegetable is called *anise* in some markets. It has feathery leaves in the center and is best in the late fall and winter. Fennel has a faint licorice-like flavor. The crunchy texture makes it ideal when used raw for salad or crudités, but it becomes delightfully tender when cooked. The leaves make a pretty garnish. Look for compact, even-colored bulbs. One bulb serves two people. Remove the core and stalks before cooking fennel. You may use the feathery leaves as a seasoning. Fennel lasts four to five days.

Kohlrabi

Kohlrabi, a member of the cabbage family, is a roundish, light-green, fall-winter vegetable that has a crunchy texture. Look for evenly colored, moist-looking skin. Larger bulbs need peeling. You need two to three small bulbs per person. They keep one week.

Leafy Greens

Leafy greens have large leaves that range from mild (*chard* and *beet greens*) to hearty (*kale* and *collards*) to bitter or spicy (*mustard, dandelion, escarole,* and *turnip greens*) to sour (*sorrel*). All are fragile, lasting only a few days in the fridge, but are excellent additions to your repertoire and add variety to the diet. Leafy greens should look moist and crisp.

Kohlrabi.

Greens are typically overcooked but, as with all vegetables, if you treat them right, they'll treat your palate right. Cook them just until they soften. When cooked, leafy vegetables wilt and lose volume. You need approximately 2 pounds for four people.

Okra

Okra is a summer vegetable in most parts of the country. The long, slender pods should be crisp-looking and bright green. Okra becomes sticky when it is cooked. The pods keep three to four days.

Parsnips

Parsnips look like cream-colored carrots, and they are sweet, too, but you can't eat them raw. They are available in fall and winter and keep one to two weeks. Look for firm, straight parsnips without cracks.

Peas

English (or "common") *peas* are available only in the summer, which is why so many cooks use the frozen kind. Only the seed, found inside the pod, is edible. *Snow peas*, available all year, have flat pods with teeny seeds inside. *Sugar snap peas* are short, plump, and dark green with small seeds. Snow peas and sugar snaps are entirely edible, pods and all. All should look crisp and vibrantly green. Peas keep two to three days; after that, English peas taste too starchy and pod peas wither.

Kitchen Clue

Leafy vegetables can be quite sandy. Wash them thoroughly a few times.

Potatoes

New varieties of potatoes come and go, but the basic types remain consistent: waxy and starchy. You use different potatoes for different purposes. In general, the round, thin-skinned, waxy kind (such as *Red Bliss*) are best for salads; the starchy oval ones (such as *Idaho russets*) are best for baking and French fries; the large round all-purpose, moderately starchy varieties (such as *Maine, Long Island,* or *Yukon Gold*) are best for mashed potatoes. Avoid buying potatoes that have green spots (indicating the presence of toxic solanine, which is bitter).

Fein on Food

Europeans discovered potatoes quite by accident. Driven by a lust for gold, the sixteenth-century Spanish conquistadors set out to find El Dorado, or "land of plenty." What they found were plenty of potatoes among the Inca tribes of Peru. They brought potatoes back to Europe but no one would eat them. Most people thought the vegetable was poisonous. It took centuries for this renowned kitchen staple to gain acceptance.

Spinach

Spinach has much to offer besides good flavor: It's a good source of calcium, iron, and vitamins. Most markets carry the curly-leaf variety, but a more delicately flavored flat-leaf variety is available in late winter/early spring. If the spinach you buy has not been prewashed, be sure to rinse it several times to rid it of sand. Like other leafy vegetables, spinach loses volume when cooked. You'll need 2 pounds for four people. You can eat spinach raw as a salad green.

Squash

Several types of squash are available. *Zucchinis* and *crooknecks* are prevalent in summer; *acorn, hubbard, butternut, pumpkin,* and other hard-shelled varieties are marketed in fall and winter. Thin-skinned summer squashes are entirely edible; however, you only eat the flesh of winter squash. Summer squash last three to four days, but winter squash keeps for several months. One pound of winter squash will serve two people. One interesting variety of fall squash is spaghetti squash, which becomes stringy when cooked. All squash should look firm and unbruised.

Sweet Potatoes and Yams

These two vegetables are the same in the United States. What stores sell as yams are actually dark orange-fleshed sweet potatoes, which are moister, sweeter, and more flavorful than the pale-yellow fleshed ones. Sweet potatoes last only about 10 days. Look for firm, evenly shaped potatoes with tight skin.

Turnips and Rutabagas

These are fall and winter vegetables. Turnips should have tight-looking, thin skin (cream and purple). Rutabagas, which have a waxy coating and must be peeled, sometimes are called sweet turnips or "swedes." Turnips last up to three weeks, but rutabagas are hardier and will keep up to five weeks. You can cook turnips or slice them raw into salad to add a zesty flavor.

Something Simple

Turnips have a bad reputation. One mention of this potent vegetable conjures up images of malodorous meals at a Dickensian orphanage. Turnips aren't easy to love, but once you learn how to temper and take advantage of their unique flavor, you'll wonder what the fuss was all about. Here's Something Simple: Mix cooked, pureed rutabagas with an equal amount of mashed potatoes, carrots, winter squash, or applesauce. Season with salt and freshly grated nutmeg and serve.

Salad Stuff

John Evelyn, a seventeenth-century writer, once said that a good salad should be composed like music, with each ingredient a component part and not one of them overwhelming the other. Good advice. If you want to prepare salad for dinner or as a side dish, make the parts interesting and harmonious: Buy different types of greens and ingredients such as arugula and radicchio.

Experiment with various types of greens. Some are crunchy, some soft, some bland, some hearty. Some salad greens are expensive, but you need only a handful of assertive ones such as arugula, radicchio, or dandelion greens to balance milder Bibb or iceberg lettuces. Although some people like bitter greens alone as a salad, pungent, peppery, and bitter-tasting greens are usually combined with milder greens and lettuces.

Whatever greens you use, do yourself a favor and get a salad spinner. Although prewashed greens and salad mixes are widely available, whole lettuce heads and other salad greens need washing. Wash greens just before you use them and dry them carefully or they won't absorb the dressing properly. If you wash greens before storing them, be sure to dry them thoroughly.

If you go to the bother of buying and preparing salad, don't mess it up with bottled salad dressing; try your hand at making vinaigrette. It's incredibly easy and versatile, and you can make a week's supply and store it in a covered jar in the fridge. See Section 7, "Sauces and Gravies," for some vinaigrette recipes. Always dress a salad just before you serve it, otherwise you'll wind up with a soggy mess. And try not to use too much dressing—use just enough to coat the leaves.

Greens

Always look for fresh, evenly colored, salad greens. Keep the greens in a vented plastic bag in the refrigerator. Fragile varieties such as arugula, mâche, and watercress will last up to three days. Hardier greens and lettuces will keep up to five days.

Arugula

Also called "rocket," this green with dark leaves has a pungent, peppery flavor that adds pizzazz to a salad of milder greens. Use one bunch in a large salad, or half in a small one. (Arugula is also delicious when sautéed and used as a bed for grilled meat or poultry.)

Arugula.

Chicory

This green has curly-edged leaves. The darker outside leaves are pungent; the pale inner leaves are milder.

Dandelion Greens

The long, narrow, tooth-like leaves can be quite bitter. The smaller, paler leaves are less assertive. Older, more fibrous dandelion greens can be cooked as a vegetable.

Escarole

Escarole is a type of endive, but has long, thick, green leaves and a slightly bitter flavor. While escarole is fine for salad, it is also excellent when sautéed with garlic in olive oil.

Frisée

Frisée is a type of mild chicory that has a faintly bitter flavor. Small quantities of its frilly, pale yellow-green leaves add eye appeal and an interesting texture to salad.

Lettuce

There are four basic types of lettuce:

➤ *Iceberg* is a crisp head and, as the name implies, has crisp leaves. Food snobs hate iceberg lettuce because it is so common, but iceberg does have value: It adds a pleasant crunchy texture to salad. Look for heads that are compact and heavy for their size, with no "rust" at the stem.

➤ *Butterhead* lettuces, such as Bibb, Boston, and limestone, have soft, loose leaves that provide a rich, buttery texture and mild flavor.

➤ *Romaine* lettuce has an elongated head and dark leaves that give salads a hearty taste. Always pass up the giant romaines; leaves that are overly large can be bitter and tough.

➤ *Looseleaf* lettuces, such as oakleaf (red or green), are wonderful for the color and delicate flavor they offer.

Kitchen Clue

One way to quickly remove the core from an iceberg lettuce is to hold it with both hands and strike the core straight down on the countertop. The leaves then break apart easily.

Something Simple

Need an easy, snazzy salad to impress company? Wash and dry some Bibb lettuce leaves, put them on a plate, and top them with wedges of goat cheese or Camembert. Let the salad sit out of the fridge for an hour or so to get the cheese to room temperature. Just before serving, drizzle some mildly flavored vinaigrette over it.

Baby lettuces are very popular these days. They are delightfully tender and have a more subtle flavor than their mature counterparts. *Mesclun* is a combination of baby lettuces.

What Is It?

Mesclun is a word that describes a mixture of salad greens. Each mesclun mixture is different. The French include herbs and edible flowers, but you won't find them in most supermarkets here. Store mesclun usually is a combination of baby greens. You can use them as is, but many are very mild and if you add some sharper items, your salad might be a little more distinctive.

Mâche

Mâche is also known as "lamb's lettuce." It has a mild, vaguely nutty flavor and soft leaves. It's expensive, so use it sparingly—just a bit adds color, texture, and variety to the salad bowl.

Radicchio

This salad "green" looks like a small, purplish cabbage. It is slightly bitter, has crisp leaves, and provides super color for salad. Just a few torn leaves invigorate lettuce and other greens. In addition, radicchio goes beyond the salad bowl; you also can grill it.

Watercress

Watercress is sold in bunches. The small, green leaves have a spicy flavor. Use it in salad, inside a sandwich, or sauté it as a side dish.

Mâche.

Beyond Greens—Other Salad Ingredients

The following produce items are kitchen standbys. You can find dozens of uses—in addition to salads—for these items.

Cucumbers

There are three varieties, including the familiar dark-green one. You can peel cucumbers, although it isn't necessary, even if the cucumber has a thin "waxy" coating. Common cucumbers have lots of seeds. The "English," or burpless, type has no seeds. Kirbys are used for pickling but can be used for salad, too. All cucumbers should be firm and evenly colored. They keep six to eight days.

Radishes

The most familiar radishes are red, but Japanese *daikon* is white (and mild), and there is also black radish (which is ultra-spicy). Radishes give salads a crunchy texture and a peppery zing. Red radishes are useful for garnishing dishes, too. Wash radishes and remove the hairy piece at the tip. Daikon and black radish must be peeled. Radishes keep for a week or so.

Scallions

Scallions are sometimes called green onions. Look for straight stalks and a moist-looking white bulb at the bottom. Cut off the roots, but use both the white bulb and the green part of the stalk to add vivid color and a delicate oniony flavor to salad. Scallions last seven to eight days.

Tomatoes

You always can find tomatoes in the market, but nothing beats a vine-ripened summer tomato. (It's worth a trip to a farm stand to find one.) To pick the best one, smell it. If it doesn't smell like a garden, keep sniffing until you find one that does. Summer tomatoes may not be the most beautiful; often the tops are deeply ridged or have small cracks or other blemishes. Good tomatoes should be firm, not mushy, and richly red. Keep partially green tomatoes near a sunny window to ripen.

During seasons other than summer, you may have a problem buying good tomatoes. The hard orange ones that come in a box are so awful it is better to do without. Imported tomatoes are prohibitively expensive and don't always measure up. Here again, go by fragrance and texture. Plum tomatoes are useful for salad, and are the best varieties for homemade tomato sauce because they're fleshy and are drier than other varieties. Cherry tomatoes are ideal for tossed salads. Tomatoes last three to five days.

Something Simple

Need an easy salad? Try one of these. Slice tomatoes, sprinkle with a few tablespoons of chopped purple onion, and drizzle with thyme-seasoned vinaigrette. Or, slice tomatoes and fresh mozzarella cheese, and cover with basil-flavored vinaigrette. Or, slice tomatoes and sweet onions (such as Vidalias), sprinkle with some type of crumbled blue-veined cheese, and cloak with mustard-scented vinaigrette.

All Those Other Little Produce Items

There are still more items in the produce department. Some, such as chili peppers and lemongrass, are used primarily to accent a dish. Others, such as wild mushrooms, can also make a nice side dish. The following are some common produce items you might have occasion to use.

Garlic

Garlic is a bulb covered with a thin papery sheath. Beneath the skin are individual cloves. (These cloves are *not* the same as the spice cloves used for seasoning hams and baked goods.) When buying garlic, choose fat ones. You can buy chopped garlic in oil in a jar, but it lacks the fragrance and flavor of fresh garlic and tastes bitter after a few days. Some stores sell whole, peeled garlic cloves. They're fine, but very perishable and deteriorate in about a week, so buy the smallest package available. Whole garlic lasts a few weeks, even in the fridge.

Garlic *smells*. It gets on your hands and you smell it in your hair, your clothes—everywhere. You can take a few steps to minimize this side effect: First, wear disposable gloves when you work with garlic. Second, peel the garlic by placing a clove on a flat surface and banging it with the side of a large knife. Don't kill it, but use gentle force. The papery peel will come away from the clove, and you can easily remove the paper and use a utensil to lift the clove. You can chop garlic with a utility knife or in a food processor, but a garlic press saves you this step. If you use one, be sure to work over a plate so you don't lose essential juices that could leak out when you squeeze the tool.

Ginger

Ginger is knobby and has thin brown skin that must be peeled. Be sure you choose ginger that has tight skin and no wrinkles. Inside the skin is fragrant, yellowish flesh that might have some hairs, depending on the plant's maturity. Ginger is super as a flavoring for marinades, stir-fries, steamed fish, and vinaigrette dressing. It doesn't taste anything like powdered ginger, and the two are not interchangeable. Ginger lasts two weeks or so.

A ginger root.

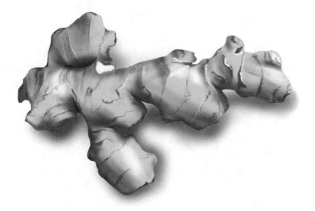

Herbs

Fresh herbs are a must for people learning how to cook. If you know how to use herbs, you'll be a kitchen genius in a flash. Herbs make food interesting and delicious. They also add variety; change an herb and you change the whole dish. Fresh herbs are preferred in salads and all other recipes that you cook quickly (grilled chicken breasts, for example) because dried herbs take too long to soften or impart flavor. Herbs last from 4 to 10 days in a plastic bag, depending on the variety.

Some of the more common herbs are listed below with some suggestions for their use with other foods. But don't let that stop you from trying these herbs with other ingredients.

Herb	Use with ...
Basil	Tomatoes, fish, pasta, chicken, pesto sauce, vinaigrette
Chervil	Fish, shellfish, chicken, tomatoes, peas
Chives	Potatoes, cheese dishes, cream sauces, eggs
Cilantro (also called "Chinese parsley")	Asian, Latin American, and Spanish dishes; shrimp; fish; soup; tomatoes; rice
Dill	Chicken, fish, cucumbers, eggs, tomatoes, beets
Marjoram	Eggplant, tomatoes, beans, potatoes, lamb, pork, chicken, grilled and roasted meats, vinaigrette
Mint	Cucumbers, beverages, yogurt dressings, lamb, marinades
Oregano	Tomatoes, potatoes, mushrooms, zucchini, eggplant, shrimp, lamb, pork, chicken, grilled meats, vinaigrette
Parsley	Almost any savory food you can imagine (the flat type is more pungent than the curly)
Rosemary	Eggplant, beans, beets, shrimp, poultry, lamb, rabbit, veal, pork, swordfish, tuna
Sage	Chicken, duck, pork, sausage, stuffing, dried beans
Savory	Eggs, summer squash, fresh or dried beans and other legumes, veal, pork, chicken, fish, vinaigrette
Tarragon	Chicken, fish, shellfish, eggs, vinaigrette
Thyme	Tomatoes, potatoes, rice, pasta, chicken, duck, pork, fish, shellfish, eggs, vinaigrette

Horseradish

This root is an ugly thing that looks like a tree limb; it has dark-brown, muddy-looking skin. Peel it, and then grate it or chop it in a food processor before you put it to use as a condiment. (The fumes are powerful—don't sniff!) Mixed with ketchup, it becomes cocktail sauce; mixed with sour cream or yogurt, it becomes a sauce for beef and poached fish. Use it to perk up salad, mashed potatoes, or dozens of other recipes. It keeps for more than a week. Store grated leftovers in a container, covered with vinegar. Cover the container and drain the horseradish before you use it.

Leeks

Leeks look like fat scallions. They are less potent than common onions. They can be very sandy, so wash them carefully, especially between the layers. (Cut off the root, slice the leek lengthwise, and separate the leaves with your fingers under running water.) They are useful for stock, soups, and as a flavoring agent, but they also are a delicious side dish when braised. Leeks keep seven to ten days.

Lemongrass

Also called "citronella" or "citronella grass," this looks like a stiff scallion. It has a fibrous outer husk that you have to peel away. The flesh has a delicate lemony taste and is a super flavoring for fish, shellfish, chicken, pasta, and vinaigrette dressing. Stalks keep three weeks.

Lemongrass.

85

Mushrooms

White button mushrooms are familiar enough, but wild mushrooms have an intense flavor that can make a huge difference in a recipe. They can be expensive, though, so use just a few and mix them with white mushrooms to enhance flavors without spending a bundle of money. Here's a list of some of the more common ones:

➤ *Chanterelles* have a small, ivory, trumpet-shaped cap and delicate flavor.

➤ *Cremini* look like common white mushrooms but are toast-colored and have a more intense flavor.

➤ *Enoki* are tiny and cream-colored, and are usually used raw, for salad.

➤ *Morel* mushrooms have a long, spongy-looking cap and an earthy flavor.

➤ *Oyster* mushrooms usually come in clusters. They are mild.

➤ *Porcini* (or *cèpes*) mushrooms have thick stems and an umbrella-shaped cap. They have a woodsy, almost smoky flavor.

➤ *Portabellos* are enormous, dark brown mushrooms that some people eat like steak. They have a hearty, meaty taste. You can brush the caps with olive oil, sprinkle them with herbs, and grill them.

➤ *Shiitakes* have dark brown large, flat caps. The flavor is rich and meaty. Shiitake stems are inedible.

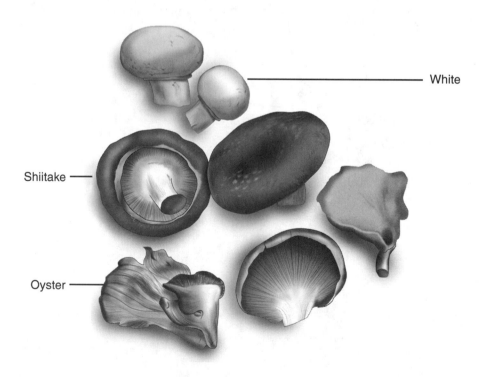

Mushrooms perish quickly and you must use them within three to four days. Most people advise that you clean mushroom caps with a special brush or moist paper towel. If they're really dirty, rinse them quickly in cold running water, cap side up, so no water will get into the gills underneath and make the mushrooms mushy. Trim the bottoms of the stems.

Dried mushrooms have a more intense flavor than fresh ones. When you substitute dried for fresh, soak them in hot water (15 minutes or so) to reconstitute them. Use less than the amount of fresh mushrooms called for.

Onions

Onions are among the more useful ingredients in the kitchen. Use yellow onions unless a recipe tells you otherwise. Yellow onions are strong. You can eat them raw, but they are best for cooking. They should have dry, papery skins and no green sprouts. Onions can last for months, although sweeter ones are more perishable. Other onion varieties include

➤ Sweet onions (Vidalias, WallaWallas, Mauis)—great when raw.

➤ Spanish and Bermuda onions—terrific on burgers and make wonderful onion rings.

➤ Purple (red) onions—suitable for salad and wonderful when grilled.

Fein on Food

No one need shed any tears for onions. They are among the world's worthiest vegetables, revered through the ages. Ancient Egyptians thought the layers symbolized eternity. Ancient Chinese prescribed the vegetable for high blood pressure. In the first known labor strike in history, the slaves who built Pharaoh's pyramids refused to work until they got their daily ration of onions. In addition, onions sustained the armies of Alexander the Great and General Ulysses S. Grant. Not a bad record.

Peppers

This category includes mild *bell peppers* and pale green *Italian frying peppers* as well as hot *chili peppers*. Bell peppers have made a fashion statement in recent times and come in lovely shades of green, yellow, orange, red, and purple. The green ones are the cheapest, red ones the sweetest. Look for peppers with tight, glossy skin and no wrinkles. They last about seven to eight days.

Bell peppers are among the more useful produce. You can cut them into salad or slice them for crudités. You can roast them and serve them as a first course or for an antipasto (see Section 6, "Vegetables"), stuff them for a main course, or sauté them to use as a side dish. Always remove the stem, seeds, and white inside flesh of peppers before you serve them.

Hot peppers are smaller than bells. You use them to give foods a spicy liveliness. Peppers of varying degrees of hotness are available throughout the year. More common varieties include

➤ *Anaheim* (with bright green or red skin) and *Poblano* (cone-shaped with deep green or red skin, called *Anchos* when dried), which are mildly hot.

➤ *Jalapeño* (short and tapered with dark green or red skin, called *Chipotle* when dried), which is medium hot.

➤ *Serrano* (a medium-size pepper with pointy ends used often in Mexican cooking), *Habanero* (stubby, with folds in the skin, which can be green, orange, or red), *Thai* (long, curved, red or green peppers with tapered ends), *Hungarian wax* (also *banana pepper*), and *cayenne* (small, slim and usually red with pointy ends), which are fiery hot.

Always wear rubber or disposable gloves when handling hot peppers, and wash your hands several times when you're finished. Chemicals in the seeds can irritate the skin. Also, be sure not to touch your skin, tongue, or eyes after working with hot peppers—and this is not the time to clean your contact lenses and put them back in your eyes.

Fein on Food

Pepper, as in bell or chili pepper, is a culinary misnomer. The plant's pungency fooled Columbus and his men when they first tasted it on one of their trips to the New World. (Or did it?) The men reasoned that because these fruits of the vine were hot, they must be related to the prized peppercorns (*Piper nigrum*) that the explorers originally set out to find. In those days the word "pepper" guaranteed acceptance and shiploads of money. Maybe Columbus wasn't fooled; maybe he was. In any event, fresh peppers (really *capsicums*) were an immediate success in Europe.

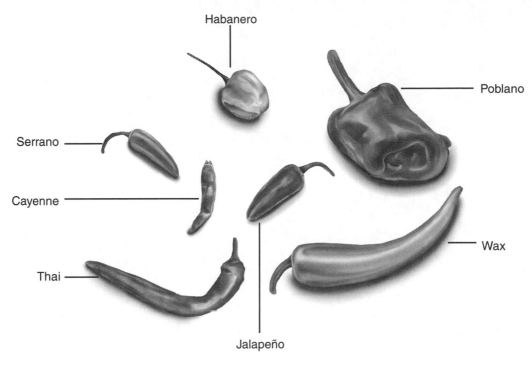

Different kinds of peppers.

Shallots

These look like a cross between onions and garlic. They are mild and are used to season foods in recipes in which onions would be too strong. Look for large shallots that have tight, crispy-looking skin with no sprouts. They can keep for months.

The Least You Need to Know

➤ When appropriate, buy vegetables in season.

➤ Look for firm, fresh-looking vegetables that aren't withered or wrinkled.

➤ You can keep potatoes, onions, and garlic in the refrigerator (but not in the moisture drawers).

Chapter 8

Getting the Skinny on Fruit

In This Chapter

➤ Knowing the common fruits

➤ Learning about the exotic fruits

➤ Using and storing fruit

➤ Trying more nonrecipe recipes to expand your culinary repertoire

After you finish choosing vegetables for dinner, there's more to consider in the produce department—oodles of fresh fruit. You can get almost any kind of fruit anytime these days, thanks to rapid transit: peaches in December, and even exotic items, such as carambolas (star fruit). In this chapter, you'll learn about the fruit you're likely to see, how to make selections, how to tell whether fruit is ripe, and how to store it. And I'll even include a few simple starter recipes.

A General Overview of Fruit

It may seem terrific to have any kind of fruit anytime, but all this availability does have some drawbacks. Out-of-season fruits often have a mealy texture and lack flavor, and the price is typically outrageous because of built-in transportation costs.

Your best bet is to buy fruit in season, when it has the richest, fullest flavor and the proper texture, and also when it's cheapest. Some fruit is available all year, some only for part of the year, as indicated in the upcoming sections. If possible, buy locally grown fruit that hasn't been conditioned for transportation, and loose, rather than prepackaged, varieties.

Depending on the type of fruit, you can use several methods to detect ripeness. In general, soft-fleshed fruit such as peaches should "give," that is, yield slightly, when you press them with your finger. You probably already know not to buy fruit with soft spots and bruises. Unless you want to eat the fruit right away, buy it slightly underripe and let it ripen at home on the counter. You can put fruit in a brown paper bag to make it ripen faster.

Once fruit is ripe, keep it in the refrigerator (except for bananas). You can store fruit loose or in vented plastic bags. The upcoming sections give guidelines for storage, but, as with vegetables, use your eyes, nose, and common sense to decide whether fruit is bad. Keep fruit longer than indicated if it still seems fresh; discard it if it doesn't. Some fruits are useful for cooking when past their prime eating time—overripe bananas make great banana bread, for instance.

Kitchen Clue

Cold fruit doesn't taste good and often hurts your teeth. Take fruit out of the fridge about 15 minutes before you serve it.

Fruit is sweet, juicy, and likable; it's hard to believe it's so *good* for you! Fruit contains no cholesterol and most have no fat. You can use fruit to make simple desserts that replace high-calorie cakes and pies. First, however, you have to understand what different fruits have to offer and how you can use them to your advantage. Try some of the more unusual varieties as well as the old familiar ones.

Apples

The apple is a basic year-round fruit, although the freshest crop is in the fall, when you can buy apples that haven't been in storage. Look for fruit that is unbruised and appears crisp. The best apples for baking are *York Imperial*, *Rome Beauty*, and *Cortland*. Good pie apples include *Granny Smith*, *Rhode Island Greening*, *Golden Delicious*, *Gravenstein*, *Newton Pippin*, *Northern Spy*, *Stayman Winesap*, *Baldwin*, *Jonagold*, *Braeburn*, and *Idared*. For applesauce you can use pie apples plus *McIntosh*, *Macoun*, *Jonathan*, and *Fuji*. Apples keep for weeks. Cut apples darken on exposure to air, so sprinkle or brush the cut flesh with lemon juice.

Apricots

This small, bright-orange fruit is at its peak in summer. The most flavorful ones have a pleasant floral fragrance. Avoid the hard green ones. Store ripe fruit four to five days.

Something Simple

Almost everyone loves applesauce. Here is the simplest recipe you can find: Wash and cut up eight apples and put them—seeds, core, peel, and all—in a deep saucepan with a ½ cup of sugar and ½ tsp. of ground cinnamon. Add a TB. of lemon juice if you wish. Cover the pan and cook the apples over low heat, stirring them occasionally, until they are soft. Then press the ingredients through a strainer.

Bananas

This year-round fruit is best when it's bright yellow with no brown spots. There are red varieties too, which are shorter and sweeter than the yellows. Bananas sweeten and the skin becomes darker with age. Brown spots don't mean the fruit is bad, but if the banana is completely dark, use it for baking breads and cakes. Don't store bananas in the refrigerator; it changes the texture.

Berries

Most berries are spring and summer fruit. Look for plump fruit that glistens but doesn't look wet. If the berries are packed in cartons, lift the carton to see if it contains fruit stains. If so, the fruit on the bottom is crushed; buy another box. Avoid berries with mold. Berries are fragile and perishable. Put them in the refrigerator and eat them within a day or so. Rinse them quickly just before you eat them. Berries freeze well (put them, unrinsed, in a single layer on a jelly roll pan. When they're frozen solid, transfer them to a double plastic bag for long-term storage).

Raspberries may be available through the late fall. Strawberries are available in the early spring and throughout the summer. The tastiest ones are small, even though the big berries may look better. Don't buy strawberries with lots of white near the stem (unless you will be using them for jam). Remove the stem after you rinse the fruit, otherwise the berries may get mushy. Blueberries, available during summer months, are sturdier and can keep for several days. Be sure they are plump looking, not withered.

Fein on Food

Strawberries are one of the most popular fruits in the world and have been for some time. More than 400 years ago, an English physician, William Butler, said, "Doubtless God could have made a better berry, but God never did." King Henry VIII planted strawberries in his garden, and Cardinal Wolsey (who, when played by Orson Welles in the movie *A Man for All Seasons,* looked like he knew how to eat) was the first to serve strawberries with cream. Strawberries were so highly regarded that the leaves were used to symbolize the rank of duke.

Cranberries are usually sold in bags, and available only from September through December. Be sure they look firm and are evenly colored. You can keep them in the bag for a month in the refrigerator or for a year in the freezer. You needn't thaw them for recipes. Buy a couple bags and put them in your freezer so that you can have homemade cranberry sauce in the spring or summer. You'd be surprised how this can lift your spirits and make meals less boring. (For a cranberry sauce recipe, see Section 7, "Sauces and Gravies.")

Carambolas

This unusual, golden-yellow exotic fruit has deep brown-edged ridges. When you slice it, the pieces look like stars—it's sometimes called "star fruit." It is available from August through late winter and is completely edible. You can slice it and eat it raw (don't peel it), and it also makes a terrific salad ingredient and a great-looking garnish. Carambolas have a tart, plum-like flavor and are crispy. Buy ones that look shiny and moist. They last up to two weeks in the fridge.

Cherries

Cherries are at their best in late spring and summer. Look for firm, plump, evenly colored fruit. Sweet cherries (for eating) are darker than sour, bright red ones (for cooking). Keep cherries about four days.

Citrus Fruits

Most citrus fruits are available for most of the year, but grapefruit and tangerines are best in the winter. Citrus fruits are hardy and keep several weeks. You can store them loose or in plastic bags.

Lemons and limes are not eaten as fruit, but are extremely useful for cooking. The best ones have thin, smooth skins. Thicker-skinned lemons with bumpy ends have less juice than the others. In addition to the juice, the skins of the lemon and lime (also called the peel, rind, or zest) are used in recipes.

Look for well-rounded grapefruit with tight, smooth skin. Pink grapefruit are sweeter than yellow varieties. Pomelos and ugli fruit are similar to grapefruit.

There are two basic types of oranges: those for eating and those for juicing. Navel oranges, without seeds, and blood oranges, with dark, reddish flesh, are good to eat. Juice oranges are thin skinned and have lots of seeds. An orange's skin should be smooth, and a spot of green here and there on the surface is okay.

Tangerines have loose, dark orange skin. They are more fragile than oranges but last up to two weeks. Tangelos are a cross of tangerines and grapefruit. They are juicy and tart.

Figs

Figs are fragile fruit that come to market in late summer and fall. There are green and purple varieties, all of which are tender with abundant seeds inside. You eat the entire fruit—skin, seeds and all, fresh or cooked. Figs deteriorate quickly, so you must eat them within a day or so of purchase.

Something Simple

If you're looking for a quick, glamorous first course for dinner, buy some prosciutto ham and wrap a piece around a fresh fig (or, if it's big, half a fig). That's all there is to it. Want a glamorous brunch dish? Boil 2 cups of water with ½ cup of sugar and a slice of lemon. Add some fresh figs, remove the pan from the heat, add ½ tsp. of vanilla extract if you'd like additional flavor, and let the fruit cool. Serve the figs plain or with cream.

Grapes

Green, red, purple, and black grapes are available all year. Look for thick, firm stems that are moist looking. The fruit should be plump and firm. Grapes keep several days.

Kiwi Fruit

You would never guess that inside this small, unassuming oval fruit with the fuzzy brown skin there is flesh that is bright green, like a gemstone emerald. Its taste is a treasure, too, like a cross between a melon and a raspberry. Kiwi fruit are available year-round. You can keep them approximately 10 days. You can't eat the skin, so peel the fruit or slice it in half and scoop the flesh out.

Fein on Food

Kiwis became popular in the 1980s, though they were first imported from New Zealand in the 1950s. They were called "Chinese gooseberries" then, but didn't catch on because of the name. At that time, anything that smacked of communist leanings was bound to be a loser.

Mangoes

This tropical fruit is best in late spring and summer. There are two types, oval and kidney-shaped, in a variety of colors: red, orange, and yellow. Green, hard mangoes don't ripen well; they are used for cooked dishes. Ripe mangoes are good for eating raw or for making dips or salsa; they are juicy and have a spicy flavor. They are difficult to peel, but the taste is worth the effort.

To peel a mango, score the skin with a sharp paring knife into wide, long strips. Pierce the skin near the top and pull back each strip between the knife and your finger. Then cut the flesh into slices down to the pit and scrape each slice from the pit with your knife.

Melons

Melons are summer fruit. Their flesh contains a high percentage of water so, with few exceptions, you cannot cook them. Melons do not sweeten as they soften, they just get juicier. One way to tell ripe melons is to knock on the surface. If you hear a hollow sound, the fruit is fine. Melons keep 4 to 5 days. Cut melons last about 3 days.

Cantaloupes are small and round with a netted surface and smooth orange flesh. The best ones have a fragrance you can smell when you lift the fruit. *Honeydews* are large, green-fleshed, and juicy. *Watermelons* are large, either oval or round, and have dark green skin or green-and-white striped skin. The flesh usually is red, though there are some yellow varieties. Unless you are feeding an army, buy cut watermelon. Look for rich, uniformly colored, moist-looking flesh and dark black seeds (if not seedless).

Less familiar but sweet and tasty are *Casaba* melons, which are round with ridged yellow skin and creamy flesh, and *Cranshaw* melons, which are large and quite aromatic, with mottled skin and spicy-flavored, pale-orange flesh.

Papayas

This tropical fruit looks like a tall, fat pear that starts out green and turns yellow when ripe. It tastes similar to melon but is hardier and lasts 7 to 10 days.

Peaches and Nectarines

These summer fruits are similar, and for culinary purposes are interchangeable. There is only one way to tell which ones are really good: Smell them. Only the ones with the flowery fragrance will ever taste like they should. Color is irrelevant to ripeness or flavor. Smooth-skinned nectarines are sturdier than fuzzy peaches and last a few days longer (about seven to eight days) in the refrigerator. Peaches will keep five to six days. You must peel peaches, but not nectarines, for cooking.

Pears

Everyone asks why pears in the store are always hard as rocks. The reason is that growers have found that pears (unlike most fruits that benefit from tree ripening) ripen better, taste better, and have a better texture when they're harvested before ripening and kept at room temperature. Keep pears out on the counter for several days and they will become buttery-tender. Be careful, though—they bruise easily. The place where you accidentally hit them will be a soft spot, like a black and blue mark. You'll know when they're ripe because they "give" when touched and have a sweet floral scent.

There are several varieties of pears, most of which are available during the fall and winter. You have to taste each to see which you like. All pears are fine for eating out of hand, except the *Seckel*, which is hard and grainy and is usually used for preserves. The best pears for baking and pies are *Comice, Bosc,* and *Anjou.* Ripe pears will keep four to five days.

Something Simple

Here's a special dessert that takes almost no time at all to prepare. Peel some pears, cut them in half lengthwise, and remove their cores. Brush the cut surfaces with lemon juice. Fill the hollows with sweetened cream cheese or, better yet, Mascarpone cheese. Sprinkle the cheese with chopped toasted nuts (especially hazelnuts or almonds) and serve.

Pineapples

This tropical fruit comes from Hawaii or Central America. Although all pineapples are high in sugar, the Hawaiian ones are sweeter. They should have a floral smell, but if the scent is overwhelmingly fragrant it can mean overripe fruit. The center leaves of the stalk should come out easily, and the bottom should be tender but not overly soft. Pineapples keep four to five days.

Plums

Plums are summer and fall fruit, depending on the variety. They should be firm and plump with tight-looking skins. Green and yellow varieties are harder than the red varieties. You can keep them about a week. Although most people eat them out of hand, plums are perfect for poaching, baking, and in pies.

Warnings

Rhubarb leaves are poisonous. Most rhubarb is sold without the leaves but if the stalks you buy have any or if you grow your own rhubarb, remove the leaves. Do *not* eat them.

Rhubarb

This is a spring and summer vegetable that we eat as a fruit. Because it is so acidic, rhubarb requires bountiful amounts of sugar. The stalks resemble celery and are either slim and light pinkish-green (hothouse rhubarb) or thick and dark red (field rhubarb). You can't eat rhubarb raw.

Because of its acidic nature, rhubarb is a terrific side dish for rich meats and poultry such as duck, turkey, and pork. It used to be called "pieplant" because it is such a tasty pie ingredient, especially when combined with strawberries.

Something Simple

Another easier-than-you-can-believe recipe: Cut 1½ pounds of rhubarb into ½ inch-thick slices and put it in a stainless steel or enamel pan with ¾ cup sugar. Add some grated orange peel or a few drops of lemon or orange juice if you'd like some extra flavor. Cover the pan and cook the mixture over moderate heat for 10 minutes. Remove the cover and cook another 15 minutes, or until the mixture has thickened, stirring the ingredients frequently. Chill well before serving.

The Least You Need to Know

➤ Buy fruit in season because you will save money and get the best flavor.

➤ Soft-fleshed fruits should "give" to indicate ripeness, although certain varieties (such as nectarines, peaches, apricots, melons, and pineapple) also should smell fragrant when ripe.

➤ Keep underripe fruit on the countertop until it ripens (or in a paper bag for faster ripening). Then store it in the refrigerator—except for bananas.

Chapter 9

A Trip to the Dairy Barn and Down the Grocery Aisles

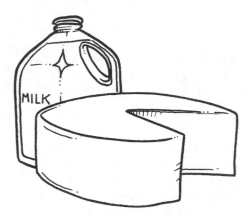

In This Chapter

➤ Using essential dairy products and eggs

➤ Learning about dried beans, pasta, and rice

➤ Selecting and storing canned goods and packages

➤ Buying coffee and tea

Everyone knows how to buy a quart of milk. And you probably also know how to buy peanut butter and ice cream. You don't need lessons on this stuff. But some details are worth repeating. Besides, there's always some little tidbit of information, even about everyday groceries, that can help you be a better and more confident cook. Sometimes the small, seemingly insignificant detail makes a world of difference; for example, most good cooks recommend sweet, unsalted butter for recipes.

This chapter goes over these everyday items, offering buying and storing suggestions. You'll also uncover some crumbs of information here and there that might come in handy when you start to cook and serve meals.

Discussing Dairy Products

Dairy products include milk—usually cow's milk (although some food stores sell goat milk as well as cheeses and yogurt made from sheep, goat, and buffalo milks)—and all foods based on milk: butter, cheese, cream, ice cream, and yogurt.

While margarine, tofu, and eggs are technically not dairy products, I discuss them here for purposes of organization.

Butter

In the United States, butter comes in either 1-pound blocks or ¼-pound sticks. Each stick contains 8 tablespoons and equals ½ cup. That means a pound of butter is 32 tablespoons, or 2 cups. *Whipped butter* has air whipped into it, giving it terrific spreadability. Use it for toast or to fry an egg, but it won't work as a substitute for stick butter in recipes. The two don't measure up the same way.

There are two types of butter: *sweet* and *lightly salted*. The word "sweet" is a misnomer: There's no sugar or any other sweetener in it. Instead, this butter is made from sweet cream and is simply plain butter without salt. Sweet butter has a more delicate flavor than salted butter, and for that reason it is the butter of choice for recipes. Most recipes assume you're using sweet butter. If you use salted butter, cut down the amount of salt in the recipe. Sweet butter usually costs a few cents more per pound than salted. Butter lasts for up to two weeks in the refrigerator and up to a year in the freezer.

Margarine

In many cases, margarine serves as a substitute for butter. You can use the firmer stick margarine to sauté or to bake cakes and pies, for example. In addition, margarine is softer than butter, so it spreads more easily. However, it isn't as rich as butter and is unsuitable for butter-based sauces such as Hollandaise or *beurre blanc*.

Some people use margarine because they think it's healthier than butter. It may not be. Margarine is derived from various vegetable oils and is high in total fat. Recent studies have shown that margarine's transfatty acids may raise blood cholesterol. Stick margarine's calorie count is about the same as butter's. Softer, tub margarines may contain air or water, so they are less caloric. As with whipped butter, however, you cannot substitute whipped margarine for firmer margarine or butter in recipes.

What Are All Those Cheeses?

Cheese is a cook's good friend. You can serve certain varieties for hors d'oeuvres and others for dessert, so when you first learn to cook, you can count on cheese for those parts of the meal you don't want to fuss with while you concentrate on the entrée. Come to think of it, experienced cooks rely on cheese for the same reasons.

Something Simple

Cheese and fruit make a classy dessert. Classic duos include Stilton cheese and Comice pears, cheddar cheese and crisp apples, and Brie cheese and grapes. Soft ripened cheeses, semisoft cheeses, and blue-veined cheeses are the smartest choices for dessert, paired with grapes, peaches, pears, apples, apricots, or oranges. You may accompany the cheese and fruit with nuts and a dessert wine such as port, sauterne, or zinfandel.

There are so many kinds of cheese—with new ones coming to market every day—you might have difficulty deciding what to buy. Some cheeses are mild, some assertive. Some are made from sheep's milk, goat's milk, cow's milk, and so on. Some smell so intense you should make sure you're with good friends before you open the package. No cheese should have a rancid odor, though; even the most robust one should smell fresh, not stale. Don't buy rank-smelling cheese, and if any of your stored cheese starts to smell foul, throw it out.

The assertive, even, shall we say, *odoriferous* cheeses, are among the tastiest and most interesting, and if you haven't given them a chance, consider doing so as you expand your culinary repertoire. In the following lists, I group some of the more commonly available cheeses by type. If you want to serve a cheese board with cocktails, pick from among different categories, not two in the same category. For example, you might serve these cheeses together: Brie, Port Salut, and Cheddar; or Pont-l'Évêque, Gouda, and Fourme D'Ambert; or Chèvre, Jarlsberg, and Saga. Most importantly, try a number of cheeses, and experiment to find your favorites.

➤ Moist white cheeses such as *cottage cheese, cream cheese, Mascarpone,* and *Ricotta* are mild. They perish quickly, so check the dates on the packages. Keep these cheeses in covered containers and use them within seven to eight days. Use them to eat on crackers, make spreads, or cook recipes such as cheesecake and lasagna.

➤ Soft cheeses such as *Brie, Camembert, Boursin, Boursault,* and *Pont-l'Évêque* are useful for both hors d'oeuvres and dessert. Keep them in plastic wrap, changing the wrap every other day, for about two weeks.

➤ Semisoft cheeses such as *Muenster, Gouda, Monterey Jack, Havarti,* and *Port Salut* are suitable with cocktails. They also melt well, so they are terrific for grilled cheese and macaroni and cheese. If you change the wrap every few days, these cheeses will last for two to three weeks.

➤ Firm cheeses such as *Cheddar*, *Edam*, *Fontina*, *Jarlsberg*, and *Emmanthaler* are perfect at either end of the meal, and you can cook with them because they melt beautifully. If you change the plastic wrap every few days, these will last more than a month. If you see any mold, cut it away, but don't throw away the cheese. You can still use it for cooking—even those portions that have cracked or hardened.

➤ Hard cheeses such as *Parmesan* and *Romano* should be firm, but not dry and cracked. They store beautifully for months if you wrap them in plastic wrap and change the wrap every few days. Most accomplished cooks regard these cheeses as staples and would never use the pre-grated canned varieties. The best Parmesan cheese is called *Parmesan-Reggiano*. You can use young, still-pliable Parmesan and Romano cheeses for dessert, but their primary purpose is for cooking. Keep a chunk of fresh Parmesan or Romano cheese in the fridge and grate it just before you use it. Ungrated cheese lasts longer than pre-grated.

➤ Blue-veined cheeses such as *Stilton*, *Blue*, *Roquefort*, *Gorgonzola*, *Saga*, and *Fourme D'Ambert* have varying textures that range from creamy to hard. You can serve any of them for hors d'oeuvres or dessert. They also are super when you crumble them into salad. Wrap them well and change the plastic wrap every few days. These cheeses last more than a month.

➤ *Goat* (Chèvre) *cheese* is tangy and aromatic and comes in an assortment of shapes and sizes. Some are creamy, some firm, some plain, others covered with ash or herbs. Goat cheese is useful for an hors d'oeuvre or dessert, and it is outstanding as a first course at dinner or crumbled into a green salad and even tastes terrific on top of pasta. Change the plastic wrap every other day and it will last up to two weeks.

Something Simple

Here's an easy almost-recipe for a first course at dinner: Cut some goat cheese into small rounds about ½-inch thick, put them on a plate, and sprinkle each one with a teaspoon of olive oil. Grind some fresh black pepper over them, and sprinkle with a small amount of freshly minced rosemary, thyme, savory, or chives.

➤ Sheep's milk cheeses such as *Feta* are tangy, sharp, and sometimes salty. You can use them in casseroles or salads. Change the plastic wrap every few days, and sheep's milk cheese will last up to three weeks.

➤ *Fresh mozzarella* has become a fashionable table and salad cheese. There also is *buffalo mozzarella*, which is tangier than the cow's milk kind. Fresh mozzarella is delicate and spongy, tasting somewhat like solidified milk. It deteriorates quickly, lasting only a few days in the fridge. Keep it immersed in a bowl of cold water and covered with plastic wrap, or in an air-tight covered container. Change the water every day.

Kitchen Clue

Don't serve cheese cold (except for cottage cheese, cream cheese, and ricotta). Let it stand at room temperature for at least an hour before you plan to serve it.

➤ *Packaged mozzarella* just doesn't cut it for out-of-hand eating because it is too rubbery. It is, however, absolutely fine for cooking. It lasts much longer than fresh mozzarella, and you can freeze it for up to six months. For refrigerator storage, change the plastic wrap every few days. It lasts about two weeks.

Understanding Categories of Cream

Cream spoils quickly, though there's less chance of spoilage with *ultra-pasteurized* cream. Check the sell-by date carefully. Heavy cream (36 percent milk fat) is especially perishable. Before you beat it to make whipped cream, pour a drop on your finger and taste it. If it's spoiled, you'll know.

Cream is useful for several purposes, one of which is to enrich sauces and soups. Just a generation ago, people used more cream than they do today; cream is definitely a casualty of dietary fat cutbacks. But you don't have to throw out all your old favorite recipes; most of them can be adapted by using lighter creams such as half and half. The dish won't be as rich, but it still can be delicious.

You can't use light cream (18–30 percent milk fat) or half and half (10–18 percent) to make whipped cream, but you needn't use heavy cream. Medium (whipping) cream (30–36 percent) whips well, too, although heavy cream holds its shape better. Cream lasts from 7 to 10 days. Make sure the container is closed as tightly as possible.

Sour cream also has gone on a diet. There's the standard kind (18 percent fat), as well as low-fat and nonfat varieties. The various types of sour cream differ in taste and texture, but for most purposes they can be used interchangeably in recipes. Sour cream lasts more than two weeks.

Crème fraîche is a tangy cultured cream similar to sour cream or yogurt. You can use it as a dessert topping or to enrich soups and sauces. You can buy crème fraîche in some supermarkets and specialty stores, or make your own (see Section 7, "Sauces and Gravies").

What Is It?

When cream is marked **ultra-pasteurized,** it has been heated briefly to extremely high temperatures that destroy bacteria. This greatly increases shelf life (though it inhibits the cream's whipping qualities).

America's Favorite Dessert—Ice Cream

Ice cream and other frozen desserts, such as sherbet, frozen yogurt, and so on, should be the last items you buy when you shop. They defrost quickly and become crystallized more easily the longer they are out of the freezer. These items lose a lot in taste and texture after three to four weeks, when they become gummy. Eat them in a hurry (as if you have to be told).

Making the Most of Milk

Milk is available as whole milk (which has about 3.5 percent fat), lower fat (2 percent, 1 percent, and .5 percent), and skim (less than .5 percent). You can use these varieties interchangeably in most recipes with a less rich result for lower-fat varieties. Acidophilus milk has added bacterial cultures that help people maintain bacterial balance in their digestive tracts. It frequently is recommended for those who are taking antibiotics and for those who are lactose-intolerant.

Buttermilk also has added bacterial cultures, but while acidophilus milk tastes like regular milk, buttermilk has a tart flavor. It is available in low-fat or 1 percent skim varieties. Buttermilk is underutilized in American kitchens, yet it is one of the handiest items to have—especially if you like to bake. It helps ensure that pie crusts, biscuits, and scones will be flaky, quick breads will be tender and crumbly, and pancakes will be rich and fluffy. You can use buttermilk to replace cream in many soups and sauces. The dish will taste tangier. Buttermilk also is a terrific thirst quencher on torrid days. You can drink it straight or process it with some fresh fruit. It lasts more than two weeks in the refrigerator.

You may also buy packages of dry milk and vacuum-packed boxes of liquid, sterilized milk. These are cupboard items (though you must refrigerate liquid milk once you open the box). They come in handy if you run out of fresh milk.

Yogurt

Yogurt is considered a snack food, but you also can cook with the most common varieties (plain, coffee, lemon, and vanilla, for example). It is a perfect substitute for more fatty sour cream in many traditional recipes for dips and sauces. It also is an outstanding ingredient for thirst-quenching beverages and is ideal for baking, giving baked goods much the same qualities as buttermilk. Yogurt lasts about two weeks.

Tofu

Tofu is made from soybeans and sometimes is called bean curd. Tofu looks and feels like cheese. It has a smooth, moist, satiny texture. There are firm and soft varieties, and fresh and packaged varieties. You have to keep the fresh kind in water (change the water every day) and eat it within four to five days. The packaged kind lasts longer until you open it, but you have to finish it within two to three days (with a fresh change of water every day). Tofu is bland and absorbs other flavors well, so it is especially good for soups, stews, stir-fries, or other sauced dishes. It is also very nourishing because it is high in protein; many vegetarians use tofu in place of meat.

Eggs

Eggs have had some hard times lately. Because they contain cholesterol, people are trying not to use them. On the other hand, eggs are one of nature's perfect foods, with plenty of high-quality protein and vitamin A. They also are one of the kitchen's most useful staples—not just for eating, but in all sorts of recipes: custards and quiches, cakes and breads, cookies and meringue, and more. Most recipes assume that you are using "large" eggs. Egg size depends on the weight of a dozen eggs. Large eggs are a minimum of 24 ounces per dozen; jumbo eggs are 30 ounces per dozen. Therefore, you can't substitute one for the other without doing some arithmetic.

The color of an egg's shell (white or brown) makes no difference in taste or cooking. People in certain parts of the country simply prefer one color to the other. When purchasing eggs, buy grade A or AA from refrigerated cases and refrigerate them as soon after purchase as possible. While many refrigerators have special egg-holding compartments, eggs stay fresher (about four weeks) in the carton. If you separate eggs for cooking, you can store the yolks for two days in a covered container; the whites will keep for four days. You can freeze the whites (one white fits neatly into a typical ice cube freezer tray). Store hard-cooked eggs in the refrigerator, in their shells; they last about one week.

There are two ways to judge an egg's freshness: Place a whole egg, in its shell, into a bowl of salted, cool water. If it stays on its side, it's fresh. If it stands up, it isn't. If it floats to the top,

Warnings

Because eggs can be a source of salmonella, a type of food poisoning, be sure to cook eggs thoroughly. You may choose not to use *any* recipe that features raw eggs (such as classic Caesar salad dressing). Wash your hands carefully before and after handling eggs.

throw it out! Second, crack open the egg. If the white is thick and gloppy, that's good (ropey, white pieces are also an indication of freshness). If it runs out in a thin stream like a leaky faucet, it isn't. Eggs become runny as they age. You can use a runny raw egg for cooking, but it won't taste terrific. By the way, "older" hard-cooked eggs are easier to peel than very fresh ones.

Kitchen Clue

When using eggs in a recipe, crack them one at a time into a cup, and add them individually to the other ingredients. That way, if one egg is spoiled, you can throw it away.

Don't be concerned about blood spots on an egg. They are not harmful. The blood is not an indication of bacteria or of fertilization. Remove the spot if you wish, with a tiny spoon or the tip of a sharp knife.

Never use an egg that is cracked (the cracks can be paths for bacteria) or that smells foul. To avoid possible food poisoning, many people avoid foods that contain raw or undercooked eggs. Cooking eggs to 160°F will kill any bacteria that might have been present.

Lots of people use egg substitutes these days. These products are designed to offer the benefits of eggs without the disadvantages of cholesterol and possible danger from food poisoning. Substitutes are made from a combination of egg whites and a range of ingredients that might include coloring, vegetable oil, gums, and other emulsifiers; some also contain small quantities of egg yolk. They don't taste like real, fresh eggs. They fare better in baking, although cakes and puddings made with egg substitutes lack the richness and moisture of the same recipes made with fresh eggs. If you like eggs but wish to cut down on the amount you use, substitute some egg whites for whole eggs; an omelet of four eggs, for example, can be made with two eggs plus three or four whites.

A Primer on Dried Beans, Pasta, and Rice

People are now eating more dried beans, pasta, and rice. You may use these items as part of a meat meal or plan your entire dinner around them. In either event, you probably want to know much more about how to use them to their advantage.

Dried Beans and Legumes

In the famous fairy tale, Jack's mother scolds her simple son for swapping the family cow for a bunch of dried beans. But Jack was smarter than Mom thought. They are one of nature's best sources of protein. They are cheap. And, when cooked properly, they make for memorable eating.

You can buy dried beans loose or in plastic packages. In either case, be sure to look them over and discard any debris or pebbles. Most dried beans must be soaked before you cook them (to cut down on cooking time). There are two ways to do this: Place the beans in a bowl, cover them with water and let them rest at least eight hours, or, put them in a pot, cover them with water by at least 1 inch and bring the water to a boil. Boil the beans for 2 minutes, remove the pan from the heat, cover the pan and let the beans rest for one hour. In both cases, discard the soaking water before adding fresh water for cooking. Cooking times depend on the particular bean and vary from 15 minutes (for lentils) to two and a half hours for garbanzos.

Several kinds of beans and legumes are available, including the most popular ones described here:

➤ *Black beans* are small and kidney-shaped with a cream-colored interior and black skin. They are mealy, with an earthy flavor, and used extensively in Latin American cooking, frequently partnered with rice.

➤ *Black-eyed peas*, though native to China, were introduced to Africa by Arab traders during the Middle Ages and became an integral part of African and African-American cuisines. They are small and ivory-colored with a black "eye" in one spot. They absorb flavors well and do nicely in stews and braised dishes.

➤ *Chick peas (garbanzo beans)* are used in Middle Eastern, Indian, and Italian cuisines. These cream-colored beans are rounded, with an uneven shape. They have a crunchy texture and nut-like flavor. You can use them whole in numerous preparations or puree them to make the dip called *hummus*. (For a great, spicy hummus recipe, see Section 1, "Hors d'oeuvres and First Courses.")

➤ *Kidney beans* come in white, brown, black, or red varieties. All are rich and meaty. Kidney beans are ideal for soups, stews, and other long-simmering dishes such as chili and minestrone soup, because they absorb flavor well.

➤ *Lentils* are bland and tender when cooked. There are several varieties in several colors, all shaped like curved little circles. Lentils need no presoaking.

Fein on Food

The Latin word for lentil is "lens." When scientists invented the curvy piece of glass that helps people to see better, they named it after the legume.

Kitchen Clue

Canned beans are fine, although their texture *is* somewhat mushier than home-cooked dried beans. If you use canned beans in recipes, rinse and drain them first.

➤ *Lima beans* are named for the capital of Peru, where archaeologists believe this bean originated. Cooked limas have a faintly sweet flavor and soft, velvety texture. They are the classic partner of corn (in succotash) and are fabulous for baked beans.

➤ *Pinto beans* are kidney-shaped, beige beans with pink-brown flecks. (The flecks disappear after cooking.) Their earthy flavor makes them suitable for Tex-Mex cookery; they are familiar components of chili and refried beans.

➤ *Split peas* come in green and yellow varieties. They are used mainly for soup. No presoaking is required.

➤ *White beans* are really several varieties, but all have a mild, delicate flavor and are interchangeable for culinary purposes (in recipes such as baked beans and white bean salad). Common varieties include *Navy bean* (the smallest), *Great Northern* (the mature seeds of the common string beans), and *cannellini*.

All About Pasta

Pasta came of age in the 1980s. Suddenly everyone was eating fusilli and tagliatelle, papardelle and penne, among others. You can choose from numerous shapes and sizes and seemingly never run out of varieties. When buying and cooking pasta, consider the following: Fresh or dried? Imported or domestic? Topped with what kind of sauce?

Fresh and dried pasta have different tastes, textures, and cooking times, but both are delicious. It's your choice. Fresh pasta usually contains eggs. There are several good brands of both imported and domestic dried pasta. Try several so that you can make educated choices. Before you buy a box of pasta, however, check the label to be sure it is made with durum wheat semolina flour.

As a general rule, dried pasta can take a more robust sauce than fresh pasta, but much depends on the pasta's shape. Here are some basic rules of thumb:

➤ *Strands* (spaghetti, capellini, fusilli, angel hair) are best with thin, smooth sauces (pureed tomato sauce, cream sauce, plain olive oil, or butter).

➤ *Flat ribbons* (linguine, fettucine, papardelle, tagliatelle) work with rich butter and cheese and cream sauces, smooth meat sauces, and thick tomato sauces.

➤ *Tubular* (macaroni, penne, bucatini, rigatoni, ziti) taste terrific with hearty, chunky vegetable sauce; with meat or cheese sauces that coat the surface and cling to the pasta's hollows and grooves; and in baked casseroles (such as macaroni and cheese).

➤ *Odd-shapes* (farfalle, orecchietto, rotelle) are perfect with chunky vegetable or meat sauces and cheese sauces.

➤ *Stuffed* (manicotti, shells, ravioli, tortellini) may be filled with meat, cheese, or vegetables and topped with butter or olive oil, or with tomato or cream sauces. Small tortellini and ravioli also make a fine hors d'oeuvre when you dress them with vinaigrette and serve them at room temperature.

➤ *Tiny* (ditalini, orzo, pastina) are best for soups and salads.

Always cook pasta in plenty of lightly salted water (to provide flavor and prevent sticking), and drain it when it is *al dente* (see Chapter 14, "A Compendium of Catchwords Used in Recipes," and recipes in Section 5, "Pastas, Grains, and Rice"). Sauce it as soon as it's drained to prevent the pieces from sticking together. If the pieces do stick, toss them with a small amount of the pasta cooking water to separate them.

Rice Is Nice

Years ago, shopping for rice was simple: You bought either white or brown. A few upscale markets sold wild rice (which really isn't rice at all). But interest in rice has soared and the market has expanded to meet consumer demand. Today there are thousands of varieties. Basically though, there are two types, long-grain (the grains remain separate when cooked) and short-grain (which is stickier when cooked). There are medium-grain rices, too, but they have more of the characteristics of short-grain rice and are included in that category below:

➤ *Long-grain* white kernels are at least four times longer than they are wide. This rice can be lightly fragrant or intensely aromatic, but always cooks to fluffy, separate grains. It's the all-purpose white rice for cooking and the rice of choice for salads and pilafs. Varieties include regular, long-grain white rices, as well as *Basmati, Texmati, Jasmine, Wehani,* and *Louisiana Pecan.* For rice recipes, see Section 5.

➤ *Short-grain* white rice has plump, rounded kernels. This rice contains a large amount of the starch *amylopectin,* which causes the grains to become sticky when cooked. It is best for sushi and paella; *Arborio* rice, a variety of short-grain white is perfect for risotto. Chinese *glutinous* rice (used for desserts) is a type of short-grain white.

➤ *Colored* rice (usually brown, although there are red and black varieties) reflects a particular variety's natural pigment and the mineral content of the soil. It usually is not "milled," that is, only the outer, inedible protective husk has been removed from the grain. The germ and bran remain intact so that this type contains more fiber and vitamins than white rice. Some colored rices are partially milled. Colored rice typically has a robust flavor and slightly firm texture. Varieties include familiar brown rice (unmilled white rice) as well as less well-known *Bhutan Red, Japonica,* and *Wehani.*

111

➤ *Converted* rice is white rice that has been parboiled and dried before milling. The conversion process helps retain nutrients but also removes some starch. The grains are very smooth and don't become as fluffy as regular white rice. While some people like the taste and texture of converted rice when served plain, it is not suitable for many cooked dishes such as pilaf.

➤ *Instant* rice has been precooked and dried before packaging. It doesn't taste at all like real rice.

➤ *Wild* rice is a type of grass, not a grain, but it *looks* like rice; hence, the name. For a recipe, see the "Pastas, Grains, and Rice" recipe section.

About Canned, Jarred, and Packaged Goods

Choosing canned foods is simple. Other than deciding whether you prefer brand name or generic products, the only guidelines have to do with what you shouldn't do. Don't buy cans that bulge, that are dented or rusted, that don't have labels, or that leak. Don't buy cans whose labels have been taped back on. Discard cans in your cabinet that bulge, that make a loud hissing sound when you open them, or whose contents smell bad. All of these are indications of spoilage and poor maintenance. Don't store leftovers in their cans, either. Food deteriorates more rapidly in the can and takes on a metallic taste.

Jellies and preserves in jars keep indefinitely on the shelf and, when opened, in the refrigerator. Sometimes preserves become crystallized in the fridge, but they're still useful; just cut away the sugary stuff. Mayonnaise, Worcestershire sauce, ketchup, mustard, and similar jarred ingredients also keep indefinitely on the shelf; once you open them, store them in the refrigerator. Jarred vegetables last a couple of days in the refrigerator once they're opened. Salsas and pasta sauces last awhile longer. You can store these items in the jars with their covers tightly closed.

Many packaged goods such as crackers have "sell by" dates. These foods taste better before those dates but aren't spoiled after that time. Packaged items such as cookies, crackers, and cereals will keep fresher and crisper if you transfer them to air-tight plastic containers. Keep chips in their bags, but close the bags tightly.

Unless the container says otherwise, you can keep all unopened canned, jarred, and packaged items in cabinets. That includes peanut butter, instant coffee, chocolate chips, rice, sugar, flour, dried beans, oil, vinegar, and the like. Most last indefinitely, although flour can taste stale after nine to ten months.

How About Coffee?

The best coffee begins with whole coffee beans, freshly ground. However, if you pre-fer canned coffee, be sure to buy the right grind for your coffeemaker—automatic-drip coffeemakers use drip grind, percolators use perk grind, and so on. Store unused coffee in the can with the plastic cover on. For a fresher taste, keep the can in the refrigerator—or freezer, if you use less than a pound per week. Keep extra coffee beans in tightly covered containers in the refrigerator or, even better, in the freezer. There are several types of whole-bean coffee, from every part of the world and with a multitude of flavors. You can grind your own beans or buy them preground. There's more on coffee in Chapter 18, "So You Thought You Were Done? What About Beverages?"

Tea

Tea comes in several forms and flavors. Buy it in individual, single bags or as loose tea leaves that you steep and strain. There are commercial blends, herbal teas, and classic, selected teas such as Darjeeling, oolong, Keemun, and Ceylon. There are also blends of different teas, including English Breakfast, Irish Breakfast, and Earl Grey. Store tea in an air-tight container in a dark place for maximum freshness and flavor. There's more on brewing tea in Chapter 18.

The Least You Need to Know

➤ Fresh eggs have thick whites and rounded yolks. Older eggs are thin and runny, but may be used in recipes. Discard any eggs whose shells are cracked or that smell foul when you crack them.

➤ Don't buy or use food in cans that bulge, are rusted, dented, or leaky, or don't have labels attached.

➤ Keep coffee or coffee beans in the refrigerator or freezer.

➤ Check the labels on jars and store open jars of perishable food in the refrigerator.

Part 4

Getting Ready to Cook

You must be shopped out by now. Your drawers and cabinets are filled with gadgets and goodies. Now the fun begins—you're ready to cook.

Or are you? You can't just cook; you've got to know how to do it. Do you know how to choose a good recipe? To carry out recipe instructions? To measure ingredients?

If a recipe tells you to "fold in" whipped cream, will you know what to do? Is folding whipped cream anything like folding laundry? If the recipe tells you to sauté chicken, will you know what that means and what to sauté the chicken in?

If you're not sure about cooking how-to's, keep reading. In the next few chapters, I will show you how to read and follow a recipe so that it works for you. I will explain how to measure ingredients and how to substitute one ingredient for another. And I will explain the various cooking terms and cooking methods you'll need to know to be a confident and competent cook.

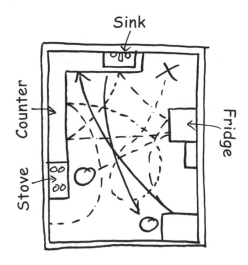

Sink

Counter

Stove

Fridge

Chapter 10

Making a Game Plan

In This Chapter

➤ Reading a recipe

➤ Choosing and using a good recipe

➤ Planning your cooking strategy

➤ Planning how to serve the meal

Now that you know how to sniff out a ripe peach, tell the difference between a frying chicken and a roaster, and recognize lemongrass when you see it, you're on the way to becoming a virtuoso cook. All you have to do is learn some fundamental cooking techniques. Of course, you can read cookbooks and gain bits of culinary wisdom from good cooks, but the best way to master the techniques is to get in the kitchen and start cooking. You will learn from practice and, yes, from your mistakes. Because it's almost time for you to actually cook a meal, this chapter tells you how to choose a recipe, organize the preparations, and serve the meal.

A Good Meal Begins with a Good Recipe

Some people, even beginners, are instinctive cooks. They know without reading a recipe that if they add some chopped parsley and a few squirts of lemon juice to steamed white rice, it will taste pretty good. But most people, especially people who feel unsure in the kitchen, need recipes. As you practice cooking, you'll see how and why good recipes work—and bad ones don't.

If you really want to know how to cook, follow this one basic rule once you have a recipe in front of you: Read it, read it, read it!

Read *carefully*. Misreading is one of the biggest pitfalls of cooking, and often the reason people consider themselves bad cooks when they really aren't.

How to Read a Recipe

A well-written recipe lists the ingredients in the order they're used. It usually states the quantity to the left and the ingredient to the right, as shown here:

> 8 apples

Sometimes the ingredient is more specifically described. For example, because apple pie is made with a different kind of apple than is applesauce, an apple pie recipe may say:

> 8 Granny Smith apples *or* 8 pie apples

In addition, sometimes an instruction appears directly before or after the named ingredient:

> 8 Granny Smith apples, peeled, cored, and sliced

or

> 8 peeled, cored, and sliced Granny Smith apples

This extra description provides precise directions without going into lengthy detail in the instruction section. After you know how to peel, core, and slice an apple, you'll be grateful for this shortcut.

A very helpful recipe gives alternative amounts, like this:

> 8 Granny Smith apples, peeled, cored and sliced (about 3 lbs., or 8–9 cups)

Or like this:

> 8 cups of peeled, sliced apples; about 8 apples, or 3 lbs.

Then you know precisely how many apples to buy. After you make this recipe a few times, if you see another apple recipe, you'll know that a certain number of apples of that size weighs an approximate amount and equals a certain number of cups of sliced fruit.

Judgment Calls

Some recipes call for a cook's judgment. A "pinch of salt" or "season to taste" are ones that seem to annoy many people. Recipe writers do this for two reasons. First, to let you know that when they say "pinch," they mean for you to use a teeny amount but that exactness isn't critical. If you have small fingers, your pinch will be a bit different than that of a person who has large hands. The point is, it doesn't matter, and you shouldn't feel imprisoned by minutiae.

The second reason is that people's tastes are different, especially regarding seasoning. When a recipe says "season to taste," you should taste the dish, add the seasoning, and taste the dish again. These steps help you focus on how much of the ingredient you like, and encourage you to trust your taste buds, not someone else's.

Recipes include other kinds of judgment calls; some recipes give "options." A recipe for blueberry muffins, for example, may say:

> 1 tsp. freshly grated orange peel, optional

That lets you know that you can vary the taste and texture of the dish by using the optional ingredient, but that the recipe doesn't depend on it.

Other recipes give "choices." For example, a recipe for sautéed chicken may call for the following:

> ½ cup white wine or chicken stock

or

> 1 tsp. fresh thyme or rosemary leaves

That means the recipe works whether you use wine or stock, or thyme instead of rosemary, and you can decide which you like better, or use the one you have on hand. If you have both ingredients, try it one way one time, and the other way the next time. You'll soon realize that you can improvise in other recipes, too—even ones that don't offer alternatives. Next time you see a recipe for sautéed chicken that calls for stock, you'll know that you can probably use white wine.

Fein on Food

Old-time recipes require lots of judgment calls. In fact, the person who gave the recipe usually assumed that anyone preparing it would know how to cook. Look in antique cookbooks, especially community cookbooks and those from charitable organizations. Look at your grandmother's spiral recipe notebook. Some recipes say things like "Bake as usual," or "Cook in a hot oven until done." Hmmmm. Still, these recipes can be treasures. To salvage such a recipe, find a similar recipe to see how the dish is prepared. Then you'll know what "bake as usual" means. A "hot oven" means 400°F or above, a "moderate oven" 350°F, and a "slow oven" 300°F or less. Knowing when it's "done" depends on the recipe and is discussed in Chapter 16, "Timing Is Everything: Creating Your First Masterpiece."

What Else You See in a Recipe

Recipe instructions usually follow the list of ingredients. The instructions will tell you at what temperature to cook the dish and how long it will take until the dish is done. The instructions may also tell you how many people the recipe will serve. (Sometimes serving information comes at the beginning of the recipe, right after the title.) Informative recipes specify any special pans or utensils you might need. Some recipes tell you how long preparation and/or cooking take, and some provide nutritional information.

How Can You Tell If a Recipe Is a Good One?

A good recipe is like a map to buried treasure. Both give logical and concise clues, and when you figure them out, you get something really valuable in the end. So, in the first place, look for the logic—that is, be sure the ingredients are listed in the order they're used. Why would a writer list 2 TB. chopped chives first when the chives are added as a garnish at the end? Ingredients listed out of sequence are distracting; you can't follow the recipe because you're too busy looking through a confusing list. The recipe may, in fact, work; but if it's confusing, you're more apt to forget a step or an ingredient, and it won't come out right.

To find out if the ingredients are listed in order, you have to read the instructions. When you do, you will notice if an ingredient has been omitted from the recipe by mistake (for example, if the recipe says, "mix the sugar and the egg yolks together," but no eggs are listed). Sometimes these omissions happen on purpose if you ask for a recipe from someone who really doesn't want to give it to you. If it does happen, by mistake or on purpose, the recipe is useless. A good recipe tells all.

Speaking of telling all, a good recipe should also be descriptive. When it says "cook until thick," it should tell you *how* thick. Thick enough to coat the back of a spoon? As thick as ketchup?

Good recipes should describe time elements in two ways when appropriate, so they give you both actual time and visual cues. Consider this instruction: "Cook for about 10 minutes or until the sauce thickens enough to coat the back of a spoon." Suppose you cooked the sauce for "about" 10 minutes, and it was still as thin as consommé? Or as thick as jellied cranberry sauce? Your stovetop may cook more quickly, or the ingredients you used may be colder or warmer than the writer's. Cooking times are approximate; it's important to know what the dish should look like.

Descriptions also should cover pan size where applicable. If you bake a cake that is designed for two 8-inch cake pans and you use one 8-inch square pan—well, you can guess what happens. And if you use two 10-inch cake pans for the same amount of batter, you're going to have flapjacks instead of layer cake.

Sometimes giving sizes isn't necessary. For example, if you have to beat eggs and sugar, and the recipe doesn't say "beat eggs and sugar in a medium bowl," the recipe will be fine no matter what size bowl you use. Common sense is important here. You know you can use a small bowl to beat one egg but will need a large pot to fit apples for applesauce.

A good recipe should also tell how many servings it yields. Those quantities are averages. Some people eat more, some less. After awhile, you'll know if one broiler-fryer chicken is enough for your family, or if you always have a piece of chicken left over for lunch.

Good recipes don't contain obvious errors, so use some common sense. You know a recipe can't possibly work if it calls for ¼ cup of baking soda when every other recipe for the dish calls for ¼ teaspoon. A recipe that calls for teeny amounts of certain ingredients can't possibly be right, either. A pinch of salt or ⅛ teaspoon nutmeg is okay, but ¼ teaspoon ketchup? How can ¼ teaspoon ketchup possibly make a difference? If you aren't sure about something, look at a similar recipe in another cookbook. You'll soon know if the recipe is off base.

Also look for reasonable combinations. Innovative recipes are fine, but they have to make sense; something about Jalapeño Pepper Chocolate Cake and Dijon Mustard Vanilla Ice Cream doesn't jive.

Finally, good recipes should encourage you to use fresh foods. Recipes that tell you to take a can of this and a jar of that and mix it all up with some frozen stuff are just ways to put together food to fill your stomach. They don't teach you how to cook or eat well.

What You Get from Reading a Recipe

Before you begin cooking from a recipe, read it several times. Your first reading tells you whether the recipe is good. The second reading is for familiarity. If you're more familiar with what to do, you'll be less intimidated and less likely to make mistakes. As you read, picture what you will be doing. If you feel like a fool, then feel like a fool and laugh at yourself. It's better than feeling frustrated if the recipe doesn't come out right.

Reading the recipe first also lets you know what ingredients to buy (make a written list) and what pans and utensils you will need (make note of them and get them out before you begin to cook). You will get some idea of the amount of preparation time.

Visions of Math Monsters: Doubling and Dividing Recipes

Many recipes can be doubled or divided, but there are a few things you should bear in mind. First, you'll have to do some math. If a recipe for pancakes calls for 2 cups of flour and you want to make ⅓ of a recipe, you have to take ⅓ of 2, which equals ⅔ cup. That one's easy.

But suppose your recipe calls for ⅓ cup of shortening and you were making half a recipe. Then you would have to figure out half of ⅓. You would have to go to an equivalency chart (there's one in Chapter 11, "Do I Really Need to Measure?") to find out that ⅓ cup is the same as 5⅓ tablespoons and that there are 3 teaspoons in each tablespoon. Then calculate that half of 5⅓ tablespoons (5 tablespoons plus 1 tea-spoon) would be 2½ tablespoons plus ½ teaspoon or 2 tablespoons plus 2 teaspoons.

Although ingredients for baked goods require mathematical accuracy, not every recipe that you double or divide has to be so precise. Take soups, for example. Suppose you wish to make a double quantity of chicken soup but you only have six carrots instead of the requisite eight. It's okay; use what you have. You also will find that when you double a recipe that calls for onions, garlic, or other similar items to be sautéed in oil first (as in tomato sauce, for example), you won't need as much oil. So if you're doubling a recipe that calls for 2 tablespoons of oil, 1 garlic clove, and 1 onion, you can use 3 tablespoons of oil, 2 garlic cloves, and 2 onions.

First Timer? Follow the Recipe!

It's always a good idea for a cook who isn't confident to follow a recipe precisely the first time. That way you know what the goal is, although it still may taste different than you expected. Suppose you get a recipe from a friend because you liked the way a particular dish tasted. Even if your friend gave you the exact recipe and wrote it well, it may not taste the same. Flavor and texture depend on the brands you use, the freshness of the ingredients, how you measure your ingredients, your oven's heat, the weather, and many other factors. As you gain experience and learn more about ingre-dients, you can substitute ingredients in recipes to suit yourself.

You Need a Cooking Strategy

After you read and familiarize yourself with the recipe, it's time to plan the meal. If you feel tremendously insecure about your ability, stick to one recipe and fill in for the time being with takeout for the other parts of the meal.

Pick recipes that are easy, or use only one that's difficult. If you've made an entire dinner previously, prepare familiar items and try one new recipe. Pick recipes that suit your kitchen; if you have only one oven, you can't make two items that must be baked at the same time at different temperatures (roast chicken at 350°F and baked potatoes at 400°F, for example). Select one oven recipe and one for the stovetop or vegetable steamer (roast chicken and sautéed rosemary potatoes, for example).

Setting the Table

Planning the meal involves more than just cooking. You have to eat somewhere. Sure, you can eat with your dishes on your lap (or on the coffee table) while you watch TV. Lots of people do it. But if you are having dinner with family and want to have some conversation, or if you are serving dinner to company, you'll be eating at the table. That means you have to set the table. Your table setting doesn't have to be formal, but you may want to indulge in some niceties.

If you're preparing a family dinner, you may or may not want to use place mats or a tablecloth, depending on the type of tabletop you have. If you're having company for dinner, however, place mats or a tablecloth look more gracious. Set the plate in front of each diner with the napkin to the left of the plate. In general, the forks go on the left, on top of or to the right of the napkin. The folded part of the napkin should be closest to the plate. Knives and spoons generally go to the right of the plate with the sharp side of the knife pointing toward the plate and the spoon to the right of the knife.

A simple family-dinner table setting.

What Are All These Forks and Knives For, and Where Do I Put Them?

If your dinner calls for more than one of the same kind of utensil (a salad fork and a dinner fork, for example), place them next to each other in the order in which they will be used, from outside in. (The salad fork goes to the left of the dinner fork if you serve the salad first; a cake fork goes to the right of the dinner fork.) This rule has one exception: A coffee or teaspoon goes to the right of the knife.

Dinner fork

Cake fork

Teaspoon

Dinner knife

Here's how to set the table if you're serving a main course, dessert, and coffee.

If you get really fancy someday and have a more formal dinner with several courses, you'll need additional flatware pieces. In this case, items such as dessert spoons and forks go above the dinner plate. You lay these pieces horizontally. The spoon goes right above the plate with its handle facing right, and the fork goes above the spoon with its handle facing left.

123

Sterling silver and silver plate tend to tarnish even in their cloth bags. If you plan to use silverware, look at it the week before your dinner. You may need to give it a polish.

Dessert Forks? Fruit Plates? Are You Kidding?

Just because you serve a multi-course meal doesn't mean you have to own a utensil of every size and shape. If you don't have dessert forks and spoons, you can reuse the ones you do have. After you clear the table of salad forks, quickly wash them to use later for dessert, or use your dinner forks. Likewise, a soup spoon can double as a dessert spoon.

If you don't have all the different sized plates you think you need, you can double up on the ones you have. Serve fruit or cake on a salad plate or even a dinner plate, if that's all you have; just garnish the plate with some berries so your dessert won't look lost.

You Only Have Odd, Assorted Plates? Not to Worry

When plates match and you have all sorts of lovely silverware to go with them, the table looks elegant. But dinner is a total experience, not just a matter of whether or not you have the "right" dishes. Feel free to mix and match plates, with this caveat: Use dinnerware that is similar in feeling and texture. If you have odds and ends, for example, group and use the ones that look rustic or use only the pieces that have a delicate look or feel to them, and so on.

What to Do with Those Extra Plates

Suppose you do have a variety of plates of varying sizes. If you want to use them for a multicourse meal, the general rule is this: Eat to the left, drink to the right. The extra plates (salad, bread, and butter) or salad bowls go to the left of the dinner plate above the fork. If the salad plate is too large to fit there, put it next to the fork with its top in line with the fork's top.

Glassware goes to the right above the knife. If you are serving both wine and water, the water glass goes above the knife, and the wine glass goes to the right of it.

Dinner table set for salad course, main course, one kind of wine, dessert, and coffee.

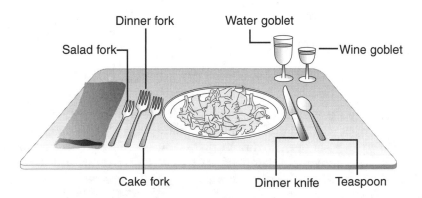

The Big Bonus: Flowers and Candles and Stuff Like That

Even a casual dinner is more appealing if you decorate the table. For company dinner, flowers are always appropriate, but buy them a day ahead so they are in full bloom at your dinner. Try to buy flowers that go with your dinnerware, tablecloth, or place mats. You can save money by taking your own vase to the florist instead of paying for the one he or she provides.

Regardless of whether you bring your own vase, flowers can be expensive, and you can do very well without them. Specialty items such as dried corn, Christmas ornaments, or tiny American flags all make attractive centerpieces or place setting decorations for seasonal dinners, and you can use them over and over again. Fresh herbs in tiny pots with ribbons around them will do for a spring dinner. You can also arrange fruit attractively, make puffs out of ribbons, or use knickknacks, tree branches, and the like.

Don't forget candles. They add a decorative touch, and candlelight gives a meal more charisma.

Napkin Folds and Nightmares

If you know how to make fancy napkin folds for cloth napkins, you can make your dinner more stylish. But folding napkins can give some people nightmares. If you think you're all thumbs and can't make your dinner napkins look like some gorgeous origami creation, here are a few simple tricks you can do with cloth napkins:

➤ Buy napkin rings. Ringed napkins go in the center of the dinner plate.

➤ Make simple "napkin rings" by tying satin ribbons into bows around each napkin.

➤ Pick up an unfolded napkin in the center and stuff it into a wine glass.

➤ Place a tiny flower within the folded napkin, so that the flower sticks out on top of the napkin.

➤ Use fancy cloth or paper napkins with borders or patterns. These are attractive enough to use flat.

Help! I Can't Make a Tomato Rose!

Meals are much more enjoyable when the food is presented attractively. But no one expects you to be a food designer who can "paint plates" the way they do in restaurants, or make roses out of tomato skins or swans out of daikon radishes. Besides, if the garnish is too fancy, it can be intimidating. Here are a few tips to keep in mind when garnishing food:

➤ Use fresh herbs. The old standby, a sprig of rich green parsley, is never wrong—and it's cheap. But also consider a sprig of rosemary, some dark, fuzzy sage leaves, or a cluster of shiny basil leaves. Just be sure your garnish complements the meal. Garnishing with a whole sprig of any herb used in the recipe is always appropriate.

➤ Use any small, fresh-looking, colorful food, such as berries, grapes, cherry tomatoes, or green olives placed here and there on the plate. Other good garnishes include bell peppers cut into strips or crosswise into "circles," lemon wedges, chopped chives, carrot or orange slices, scallions, radishes, and small greens such as watercress or mâche.

➤ Try adding prepared foods—they make terrific garnishes: cranberry sauce or mango chutney inside a mushroom cap, for example.

➤ Experiment with unusual-looking foods such as slices of *carambola*. Arrange the star-shaped slices on the side of the plate.

What Is It?

A **carambola** is an exotic ridged fruit. When you cut the fruit crosswise, the slices look like stars.

➤ Make sure the garnishes are edible. You don't want guests putting plastic, paper, or other nondigestible items in their mouths.

➤ Garnish with edible flowers such as nasturtiums. They're expensive, but you only need a few to make a good impression.

➤ Put sauce on the plate first, then place the food on top; or use the sauce to separate halves of the plate.

➤ Keep the garnishes simple.

Yes! You Can Make a Tomato Rose!

If you want to get a little fancier, you can learn to make some easily sculpted garnishes, including tomato roses, strawberry fans, scored and sliced zucchini, or cucumber and lemon rounds.

To make strawberry fans, hold each berry in the fingers of one hand with the hull (stem) side down and the point side up. With a sharp paring knife, slice thin, parallel slices down from the point to the stem, but do not cut through the stem. Gently fan the slices to show some of the cut side of each slice.

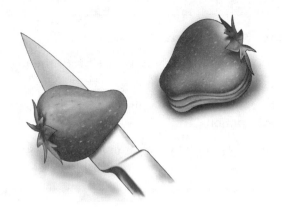

Turn strawberries into fans.

To create scored and sliced vegetables (for zucchini, cucumber, and lemons), use a zester, small paring knife, or vegetable peeler to remove narrow strips of the peel down the entire length of the vegetable or fruit. Then cut the vegetable or fruit cross-wise into slices.

Even the simplest scored and sliced vegetable rounds make gorgeous garnishes.

To make tomato roses, with a sharp paring knife, cut the tomato's thin skin in a con-tinuous, long strip, starting from the top of the tomato. The width of the strip should be between a half-inch and an inch. Loosely roll the strip with the skin surface out and shape it into a flower. You can use the rest of the tomato, of course, so don't throw it away.

You *can* make a tomato rose!

127

The Least You Need to Know

➤ Read a recipe *before you start cooking* to familiarize yourself with the ingredients and the techniques.

➤ Use your own judgment in recipes that say "use a pinch," "season to taste," "use *this* or *that*," or "*ingredient,* optional."

➤ Garnishes add appeal to the meal, but avoid over-garnishing and be sure all garnishes are edible.

Chapter 11

Do I Really Need to Measure?

In This Chapter

➤ Measuring for success

➤ Measuring dry and liquid ingredients

➤ Interpreting a "pinch" and a "dash"

➤ Using measurement equivalents for foods

➤ Measuring for comparison and substitution

After you choose the recipes and plan your cooking strategy, it's time to don your apron, get out the ingredients and pots and pans, and start cooking. The recipes you will be using most likely instruct you to measure certain ingredients, which means you must get out some measuring tools as well.

Is it really necessary to go to the bother of measuring? If so, how do you measure and with what? Keep reading. There are some foods you can't measure when you buy them. For example, your recipe may call for 1 teaspoon of freshly grated lemon peel or 1 tablespoon of chopped shallots. How many lemons and shallots do you buy? You'll find some tips about that in this chapter, too.

Why Bother with Measuring?

Experienced cooks seem pretty blasé about measuring ingredients. To see what I mean, watch a cooking show on TV. One famous chef or another tells you to pour in a table-spoon or two of wine and then proceeds to add half a bottle. The audience laughs.

You laugh. Then you wonder whether you should use a tablespoon or two—or a half-bottle.

Cooking experts don't have to measure precisely for several reasons. First, they're on TV to entertain you, not merely to teach you about cooking; the antics make the show more fun. Second, because you never get to taste what they are preparing, you don't know whether they have overwhelmed the recipe with wine. Most important, experienced cooks have developed a "feel" for precise measurements. They can pour salt into their hands and know what a half teaspoon looks like, or chop an onion and know it equals about a half-cup. And they know something else, too. They know when it isn't necessary to measure precisely—even when the recipe says to.

Warnings

Don't skip the measuring steps when you bake, even as you become more experienced. Recipes for most baked goods are precise formulas that will not work if you don't measure the ingredients properly.

As you become more expert, you, too, will develop a feel for measurement. You will understand when it is important to measure and when it is not. Until then, however, measure ingredients carefully to ensure that the recipe will work with consistent results.

What You Use to Measure

Several types of measuring devices for the kitchen are available. Dry and solid ingredients such as flour and shortening are measured in cups with handles. They come in plastic or metal in sets of ¼-, ⅓-, ½-, and 1-cup measures. (Some sets include ⅔- or ⅛-cup cups.) There also are larger 2-cup size cups.

These cups with handles are for measuring dry ingredients.

Liquid ingredients are measured in a pitcher-like container with a spout. These containers have measurement marks on the side.

Containers for measuring liquids are like pitchers—they have spouts for pouring.

To measure ingredients in quantities smaller than ¼ cup, use measuring spoons. These are also either plastic or metal and most come in sets of ¼-, ½-, and 1-teaspoon sizes, plus a 1-tablespoon size. Some sets include a 1½-tablespoon spoon.

Use these special measuring spoons—not your tableware—to measure small quantities of ingredients.

Something Simple

Need some fabulously easy recipes for terrific things you can do to add flavor to food? Here are some easy and easy-to-measure suggestions:

➤ To make cinnamon sugar, mix 1 cup sugar with 1 TB. cinnamon.

➤ For vanilla sugar, split open a 4-inch piece of vanilla bean and press it into 1 cup sugar (let the sugar stand three to four days before you use it). You can rinse the vanilla bean and reuse it.

➤ To make Java Sugar for use on toast or in cakes and pies, mix 1 cup sugar with 2 teaspoon cinnamon, ½ teaspoon nutmeg, ½ teaspoon powdered ginger, ⅛ teaspoon allspice, and ⅛ teaspoon ground cloves.

➤ For vanilla brandy, split open a 4-inch piece of vanilla bean and put it into 1 cup brandy (let it steep two weeks before you use the brandy). You can use the vanilla bean again to poach fruit or make custard.

131

Kitchen scales measure ingredients by weight instead of by volume. In the United States, most recipes list ingredients by volume, but kitchen scales come in handy for those times when they do not—for example, when a recipe calls for 6 ounces of chopped meat.

How to Measure Ingredients

One reason recipes don't come out right is that the person who prepared the dish didn't measure ingredients properly. Not measuring properly and wondering why your cake fell is like not reading the instructions for your VCR and wondering why it didn't record the movie. You have to follow the rules if you want the cake (or the movie). Follow these guidelines for measuring, and never again ruin a recipe because of measurement mistakes (but good luck learning how to program your VCR):

➤ Measure dry ingredients over a plate or bowl so you can catch the excess and put it back in the container.

➤ Spoon flour and similar ingredients into the measuring cup. Do not scoop the ingredient using the cup itself because this "packs" the cup too much and the measurement won't be precise.

➤ Add enough of the ingredient to come above the rim of the cup, then level it off with the straight edge of a knife.

➤ Never shake, pat, or pack down dry ingredients. This gives an imprecise measurement. There is one exception: Always pack brown sugar.

➤ To measure salt and other dry ingredients used in small quantities, use measuring spoons, scoop the ingredient, and level off the top as you would for flour.

➤ Measure fats such as shortening at room temperature, when they are easier to pack into the cup.

Kitchen Clue

Don't use your tableware to measure ingredients. The teaspoons and cups you use to drink tea or coffee are not equivalent to measuring cups and spoons.

➤ To measure fats accurately, pack them down in the cup to get rid of air pockets. Add enough to come above the rim, and then level it off with the straight edge of a knife.

➤ When you measure liquid ingredients, don't raise the cup to eye level to see if the measurement is accurate. Leave the cup on the counter where you know it will be level, and bend down to see the cup at eye level.

➤ Measure small quantities of liquids (1 teaspoon, for example) over a bowl so that excess amounts will not go into your recipe.

➤ To save washing and drying in the middle of a recipe, have two sets of measuring spoons handy: one for wet ingredients and one for dry ones.

Do I Measure or Sift Flour First?

One of the most confusing questions in cooking is when to measure flour for a recipe that calls for sifted flour. Do you measure before you sift or after? Here's a simple rule to follow: See whether the word *sifted* or *flour* comes first. If a recipe calls for 2 cups of flour, sifted, you measure the flour first, and then sift it. However, if the recipe calls for 2 cups of sifted flour, the recipe writer has qualified the kind of flour to be used: sifted flour. That means you sift the flour before you measure it. To use the recipes in this cookbook, measure the flour before you sift it.

Kitchen Clue

Butter, margarine, and certain brands of shortening are available in sticks that are marked with tablespoon- and cup-measuring guidelines on the wrapper. If you buy these, use those guidelines instead of packing the ingredient into a measuring cup.

Those Annoying Pinches and Dashes

Why would a recipe ask for a "pinch" or "dash" of something? The answer is that even a tiny amount of that ingredient makes a difference to taste or texture. "Pinch" usually refers to measurements of solid ingredients such as salt or cinnamon and means less than ⅛ teaspoon. "Dash" usually is a measurement for liquids and means about two to three drops. You also may see a measurement of "handful." Old cookbooks used this so-called measurement for lots of ingredients, including flour for bread. Today you only see that term occasionally, and it's usually in reference to fresh herbs. It means use several loose leaves (for example, 12 to 15 basil leaves) that you can cluster in your hand easily.

Equivalent Measurements

Sometimes a recipe asks for measurements by weight but you want to measure by volume. For example, although the recipe calls for 8 ounces of milk, you'll probably want to measure it in cups. How many cups is that?

Likewise, sometimes a recipe lists an ingredient, but you want to cut the recipe in half and the math is not so simple. If the original recipe calls for ¾ cup of milk, you need ⅜ cup. How do you measure that with standard measuring cups and spoons?

Recipes that use liquor may ask you to add a "jigger" of some alcoholic beverage. What's a jigger? The following tables will help you convert these kinds of measurements to make measuring easier and more convenient.

Common Measurement Equivalents by Volume (for Dry Ingredients)

½ TB.	=	1½ tsp.
1 TB.	=	3 tsp.
1½ TB.	=	1 TB. plus 1½ tsp.
1½ TB.	=	4½ tsp.
2 TB.	=	⅛ cup
4 TB.	=	¼ cup
5⅓ TB.	=	⅓ cup
5⅓ TB.	=	5 TB. plus 1 tsp.
⅓ cup	=	5 TB. plus 1 tsp.
6 TB.	=	⅜ cup
⅜ cup	=	¼ cup plus 2 TB.
8 TB.	=	½cup
⅝ cup	=	½ cup plus 2 TB.
⅔ cup	=	10 TB. plus 2 tsp.
12 TB.	=	¾ cup
⅞ cup	=	1 cup less 2 TB.
16 TB.	=	1 cup
2 cups	=	1 pint
2 pints	=	1 quart
4 cups	=	1 quart
4 quarts	=	1 gallon

Common Measurement Equivalents for Liquid (Metric Measurements Are Approximate)

1 TB.	=	½ oz. (15 mL)
2 TB.	=	1 oz. (⅛ cup; 30 mL)
¼ cup	=	2 oz. (4 TB.)
⅓ cup	=	2⅔ oz. (5⅓ TB.; 75 mL)

½ cup	=	4 oz. (8 TB.)
1 cup	=	8 oz. (16 TB.)
2 cups	=	16 oz. (1 pint)
4 cups	=	32 oz. (1 quart; 1 L.)

Liquor Measurement Equivalents

1 pony	=	1 oz. (2 TB.)
1 jigger	=	1½ oz. (3 TB.; 45 mL.)
1 fifth	=	⅕ gallon (750 mL; ⅘ quart; approx. 3 cups plus 3 TB.)

How Many Lemons Make 1 Teaspoon of Grated Peel (and Things of That Nature)

When you start to cook, you will not know how many ounces of cheese to buy to get the 2 cups of grated cheese you need for your recipe. After a while, you will get a "feel" for these ingredients. In the meantime, use the following tables, which provide approximate equivalents for some of the more common ingredients you may use in your recipes. Bear in mind, however, that these are approximations only. For example, although a shallot usually provides 1 tablespoon of chopped shallot, a larger shallot gives you more and a smaller one gives you less. There is no way to measure these items precisely, but there is no need to. Use your common sense here. If a recipe tells you to add 1 tablespoon of chopped shallot, you can chop one average-size shallot and not measure it precisely.

Approximate Food Measurement Equivalents: Dry Ingredients

Breadcrumbs, fresh	1 cup	=	2 oz.; 2 slices white bread
Chocolate	1 oz. baking	=	1 square; 4 TB. grated
	6 oz. chocolate chips	=	1 cup
Cocoa	1 lb.	=	4 cups
Coconut, flaked	3½ oz.	=	1⅓ cups

continues

135

Approximate Food Measurement Equivalents: Dry Ingredients (continued)

Flour	unsifted, white all-purpose 1 lb.	=	3½–4 cups (bleached or unbleached)
	cake flour, 1 lb.	=	4½ cups
	whole wheat, 1 lb. (coarse grain)	=	4½ cups
Nuts	almonds, 4 oz. slivered	=	1 cup
	almonds, 1 lb. shelled	=	3 cups
	almonds, ground, 8 oz.	=	1⅓ cups
	peanuts, 1 lb. shelled	=	3 cups
	pecans, 1 lb. shelled	=	4 cups
	pistachios, 1 lb. shelled	=	3⅔ cups
	walnuts, 1 lb. shelled, broken	=	3 cups
Oatmeal	1 lb.	=	5⅓ cups, uncooked
Rice	8 oz.	=	1 cup raw, white
Shortening	8 oz.	=	1 cup
	1 lb., 4 oz.	=	3 sticks
Sugar	confectioner's, 1 lb.	=	4½ cups sifted
	white, 1 lb.	=	2 cups
	brown, packed, 1 lb.	=	2¼ cups
Unflavored gelatin		=	1 TB., ¼ oz. package
White navy beans	1 lb.	=	2 cups

Equivalents: Fruits and Vegetables

Apples, 1 lb.	=	3 medium, 3 cups sliced
Bananas, 1 lb.	=	3 medium, 1¾ cups mashed
Bell pepper, 1 large	=	1 cup coarsely chopped
Cabbage, 1 medium	=	4½ cups shredded
Carrots, 1 lb.	=	3 cups shredded
Celery, 2 large stalks	=	1 cup chopped

Garlic, 1 medium clove	=	½ tsp. minced
Lemon, 1 medium	=	3–4 TB. juice, 2–3 tsp. grated peel
Lime, 1 medium	=	2 TB. juice, 1–2 tsp. grated peel
Mushrooms, white, ½ lb. sliced	=	2½–3 cups
Onion, 1 lb.	=	3 cups chopped
1 medium	=	½ cup chopped
Oranges, 1 medium	=	6–8 TB. juice; 2 TB. grated peel
Peaches, 1 lb.	=	4 medium
Potatoes, 1 lb.	=	3 medium; 3½ cups sliced; 2 cups cooked, mashed
Raisins, seedless, 1 lb.	=	2¾ cups
Strawberries, 1 pint box	=	2 cups sliced
Tomatoes, 1 lb.	=	3–4 medium; 1½ cups peeled, seeded, chopped

Food Measurement Equivalents: Dairy, Eggs, Meat

Butter	1 lb.	=	4 sticks
	1 stick	=	½ cup; 8 TB.
	1 oz.	=	2 TB.
	1 lb. whipped	=	3 cups
Cheese	8 oz.	=	2 cups grated (firm and hard cheeses)
	4 oz.	=	1 cup crumbled (blue-veined)
	8 oz.	=	1 cup cottage cheese
	1 oz. cream cheese	=	2 TB.
Cream	½ pint heavy or whipping	=	1 cup; 2 cups whipped
	1 cup heavy or whipping	=	2 cups whipped
Eggs	large, 1 cup	=	4–6 whole eggs
	large, 1 cup	=	8–10 whites
	large, 1 cup	=	12–14 yolks
	1 large white	=	2 TB.
	1 large yolk	=	1¼ TB.
Ground meat	1 lb.	=	2 cups

Food Measurement Equivalents: Liquids

Sweetened condensed milk, 14 or 15 oz.	=	1¼–1⅓ cups
Evaporated milk, 12 oz.	=	1½ cups
Corn syrup, 16 oz.	=	2 cups
Honey, 16 oz.	=	1⅓ cups
Maple syrup, 16 oz.	=	2 cups
Vegetable oil, 16 oz.	=	2 cups
Water, 16 oz.	=	2 cups

The Least You Need to Know

➤ Measuring is important to ensure accuracy and consistency.

➤ Do not use your flatware spoons and coffee cups as measuring tools; use the ones specifically designed for measuring ingredients.

➤ To measure flour and similar dry ingredients, spoon the ingredient into a measuring cup to a point above the rim. Do not shake, pat, or pack down the ingredient. Level off the ingredient with the flat edge of a knife.

Chapter 12

Can I Use Something Else Instead?

In This Chapter

➤ Substituting: When it's okay and when it's not

➤ Swapping ingredients in baked goods

➤ Substituting dairy, produce, and miscellaneous ingredients

➤ Using alternate pans

In the last chapter, you learned that it's important to measure ingredients accurately. It is equally important that you use the ingredients called for in the recipe so that you know the recipe will come out as expected, and it will taste about the same each time you make it.

Suppose, however, that you run out of an ingredient and don't have time to shop, or you are cooking at 1:00 A.M. and the stores aren't open. Can you substitute ingredients? What do you do if someone is allergic to a particular ingredient—do you have to disregard an entire recipe just because you can't use one ingredient? This chapter tells you how to use alternate ingredients and explains when it is and isn't okay to substitute.

The Whys and Wherefores of Substituting

Substitutions have to make sense. Obviously, no one would substitute sugar for flour, or orange juice for mustard, but not all substitution issues are that clear-cut. The most important factor you need to consider before you substitute one ingredient for another is the function of the ingredient in the recipe.

The First Time, Follow the Recipe

When you are at the stove ready to cook, you face a moment of truth. Either you are the kind of person who likes detailed instructions that you can follow with precision, or you are one of those people who never reads instructions. Because cooking should be enjoyable, you should never feel bound to arbitrary rules, no matter what type of person you are. On the other hand, you need some discipline to help you succeed in the kitchen. It's good to follow recipes until you understand the nature of the ingredients and some basic cooking methods. Following a recipe means using the ingredients called for as well as proceeding in the order given.

As you gain confidence, you can start to substitute in small ways: Substitute olive oil for butter in a sauté, for example. Use basil instead of oregano in the potato salad, or add wild mushrooms to the chowder. Improvisation unlocks the mystery of cooking. Use your head, and use your senses. Taste the food. Smell it. Watch it. Begin to rely on your own palate and your own judgment.

When It Is Okay to Substitute

Some recipes invite innovation and creativity because so many alternative ingredients perform the same function. In these recipes, follow this guideline: You can substitute one ingredient for another if it does not change the intrinsic nature of the dish. Some examples are soups, rice pilafs, and vinaigrette dressing. If you are making vegetable soup and have no broccoli, for example, you can use green beans or some other vegetable instead. You could add peas and corn if you prefer chunkier soup. Regardless, it's still vegetable soup. You could add meats or vegetables to rice pilaf; it's still pilaf. Lots of changes are possible when you're making vinaigrette dressing. You can use almost any vegetable oil you like, season it with any herb, and switch from vinegar to lemon juice, and the dressing is still a vinaigrette.

If someone is allergic to or otherwise intolerant of an ingredient, you must make substitutions. The guideline here is the same: If the new ingredient performs the same function as the original one, go ahead and substitute. If a person is allergic to legumes, for example, use corn oil instead of soybean oil to sauté fish or prepare salad dressing. Use chopped almonds (or even raisins or chopped dried fruit) in quick bread if a guest cannot eat walnuts.

Kitchen Clue

You don't need to use allergies as an excuse to spark creativity. When any number of ingredients will work in a recipe, try to substitute the original item now and then. For example, change the Chocolate Macadamia Nut Bread recipe in Section 8, "Quick Breads, Brunches, and Breakfasts," by using chopped pecans, chocolate chips, or dried cranberries instead of the macadamia nuts.

When It Is Not Okay to Substitute

When an ingredient performs a unique function in a dish and the recipe would not work without it, there is no substitute. For example, a soufflé will not rise without beaten egg whites. Likewise, you cannot prepare yeast bread without yeast or pie crust without some sort of fat.

What Happens When You Substitute

When you substitute ingredients that are more or less interchangeable, you may end up "inventing" a fabulous new recipe. On the other hand, when you substitute ingredients that are less similar, the recipe may change significantly in any number of ways, including the food's texture, density, taste, or intensity of flavor. Suppose you were making muffins and the recipe called for applesauce. Because the applesauce provides moisture, you couldn't use peanut butter instead; it doesn't have the same moisturizing quality. However, you could substitute canned pumpkin or any other fruit puree without changing anything except the flavor.

A change of flavor is just one type of change. Consider the more significant changes possible when you substitute sweeteners. They all serve the same sweetening function, but some have more powerful sweetening capabilities than others. They also have different weights and textures. If you want to substitute a liquid sweetener such as honey for some sugar in a cake recipe, for example, you will have to adjust the amount of dry ingredients to account for the added moisture. The cake made with honey will also have a heavier, denser texture than one made with sugar.

Kitchen Clue

Never substitute artificial sweeteners for the sugar in a recipe; the measurements are not the same. Use artificial sweeteners in accordance with the manufacturer's directions.

Kitchen Clue

When you substitute honey for 1 cup of sugar in a recipe, use only ¾ cup of honey, add a pinch of baking soda (unless the recipe also calls for an acidic ingredient such as buttermilk, yogurt, or sour cream), and reduce the liquid in the recipe by ¼ cup. Never substitute more than half a recipe's solid sugar with a liquid one.

How to Substitute Ingredients

Most recipes for cakes and pastries are precise formulas and will not come out unless you follow them to the letter. Even with these precise recipes, however, you can substitute if you know how. Consider baking powder and baking soda. Both are agents of chemical leavening (they produce bubbles of gas in dough or batter, for example, which results in baked goods that rise). Baking soda is used in recipes that contain acids (such as chocolate or sour cream). Together, the soda and acid form the needed gas. Baking powder contains baking soda plus an acid (and cornstarch, to keep the ingredients dry) and can produce the needed gas by itself. If you need to substitute soda for powder, you may do so as long as you add an acidic ingredient. (Conversely, if you substitute powder for soda, you will have to change the acidic ingredient in the recipe—buttermilk for regular milk, for example.)

When you want to make specific substitutions in recipes, refer to the following tables.

Substitutions in Baked Goods

1 tsp. double-acting baking powder	=	¼ tsp. baking soda plus ½ tsp. cream of tartar
	=	¼ tsp. baking soda plus ½ cup buttermilk or plain yogurt (reduce liquid by ½ cup)
	=	¼ tsp. baking soda plus ¼ cup molasses
	=	1½ tsp. phosphate or tartrate baking powder
4 extra large eggs	=	5 large eggs or 3 large eggs and 3 egg whites
	=	6 medium eggs
1 cup sifted cake flour	=	⅞ cup (1 cup minus 2 TB.) sifted all-purpose flour
1 cup all-purpose flour	=	1 cup plus 2 TB. cake flour
	=	1 cup fine whole wheat flour
	=	1 cup plus 2 TB. coarse whole wheat flour
1 cup white sugar	=	1 cup brown sugar, packed
	=	1 cup superfine sugar
	=	1¾ cup confectioner's sugar
	=	¾ cup honey, reduce liquid by ¼ cup
	=	¾ cup maple syrup, reduce liquid by ¼ cup
	=	1¼ cups molasses, reduce liquid by 5 TB.
1 cup brown sugar	=	1 cup white sugar plus 1½ TB. molasses
½ cup honey	=	½ cup maple syrup
	=	½ cup molasses
1 pkg. dry yeast	=	1 cake compressed yeast
	=	2¼ tsp. dry yeast

1 2" piece vanilla bean	=	1 tsp. pure vanilla extract
1 square (1 oz.) unsweetened chocolate	=	3 TB. unsweetened cocoa plus 1 TB. solid fat unsweetened chocolate (butter, margarine, or shortening)
1 square (1 oz.) semisweet chocolate	=	3 TB. unsweetened cocoa plus 1 TB. solid fat semi sweet chocolate (butter, margarine, or shortening) plus 3 TB. sugar
¼–oz. envelope gelatin	=	1 TB. gelatin (enough to gel 2 cups of unflavored gelatin liquid)

Dairy Substitutions

1 cup butter	=	1 cup margarine
	=	⅞ cup solid fat (such as lard or shortening)
1 cup buttermilk	=	1 cup plain yogurt or sour milk
	=	1 cup minus 1 TB. warm milk plus 1 TB. vinegar or lemon juice (let mixture stand 5 minutes)
3 TB. clarified butter	=	3 TB. vegetable oil
	=	2 TB. vegetable oil plus 1 TB.butter
1 cup heavy cream	=	¾ cup whole milk plus ⅓ cup melted butter (it will not whip into whipped cream)
1 cup half-and-half	=	½ cup light cream or medium cream plus ½ cup whole milk
	=	1 cup whole milk plus 5 tsp. melted butter
1 cup sour cream	=	1 cup plain yogurt
1 cup whole milk	=	½ cup unsweetened evaporated milk plus ½ cup water
	=	1 cup reconstituted nonfat dry milk plus 1 TB. melted butter
	=	1 cup minus 1 TB. skim milk plus 1 TB. heavy cream
1 cup skim milk	=	½ cup evaporated skim milk plus ½ cup water

Fruit and Vegetable Substitutions

1 TB. fresh herbs	=	1 tsp. dried (approximately)
1 tsp. fresh lemon juice	=	½ tsp. bottled lemon extract
1 tsp. freshly grated orange or lemon peel	=	1 tsp. dried (bottled) orange or lemon peel

Miscellaneous Substitutions

1 TB. prepared mustard	=	1 tsp. dry, powdered mustard plus enough water to make a paste
1 TB. flour to thicken	=	1½ tsp. cornstarch sauce
	=	1½ tsp. potato starch
	=	1½ tsp. arrowroot
	=	2½ tsp. quick tapioca
1 cup tomato juice for cooking	=	½ cup tomato sauce plus ½ cup water
1 cup ketchup	=	½ cup tomato sauce, 1½ TB. sugar, 2 tsp. vinegar
1 cup seasoned bread crumbs	=	1 cup plain bread crumbs plus 1 TB. freshly grated Parmesan cheese, 2 tsp. mixed dried herbs, ¼ tsp. salt, ¼ tsp. black pepper, and ⅛ tsp. garlic powder

How to Substitute Pans

If you don't have the right-sized pan, should you just chuck the recipe, or can you substitute? The answer: It depends. As with ingredients, you should always use the pan size that is specified in a recipe. On the other hand, you don't have to go out and buy an endless assortment of pans. When you haven't the exact pan you need, try to use a pan with similar capacity, size, and depth. To measure capacity or volume, count the number of cups of water needed to fill the pan. Use a ruler to measure size and depth.

What Is It?

Clarified butter is melted butter with the milk solids and sediment removed so that only the butter fat remains.

When you substitute pans, bear in mind that you may have to alter cooking times and temperatures. For example, although you can bake the same cake in an 8-inch square cake pan or a 9 × 5 × 3-inch loaf pan, because the loaf pan is deeper, you must bake the cake longer. Likewise, the same amount of batter that fits into the 8-inch square pan also will make 12 muffins. But because each muffin is so much smaller, baking time will be much shorter. If the pan you use is much deeper than the one the recipe calls for, lower the oven temperature by 25°F. The following table gives approximate substitution possibilities for pans.

Pan Equivalents

Muffin pans	=	½ cup (approx.)
8½" × 4½" × 2½" loaf pan	=	6 cups
7" × 11" × 2" brownie pan	=	6 cups
8" square cake pan, 1½" deep	=	6 cups
8" square cake pan, 2" deep	=	8 cups
9" round cake pan, 2" deep	=	8 cups
9" × 5" × 3" loaf pan	=	8 cups
9" × 13" × 2" rectangular cake pan	=	12 cups
10" springform or bundt pan	=	12 cups

The Least You Need to Know

➤ To obtain consistent results, use the ingredients called for in a recipe.

➤ You can substitute ingredients that do not serve a unique function in a dish.

➤ Ingredient substitutions will change the taste and/or texture of a dish.

➤ If you must substitute a pan, try to use one of similar capacity, size, and depth.

A Compendium of the Top 100+ Cooking Terms

Chapter 13

> **In This Chapter**
>
> ➤ A super-glossary that defines and describes the things you do to foods as you cook

Now that you know how to shop for ingredients, choose a recipe, and measure properly, and you understand when and how to substitute ingredients, you are nearly ready to cook. As you look through a recipe, you may notice an unfamiliar direction or cooking term. Often a recipe will ask you to do something to the food before you cook it or as you are cooking it. Before you roast a chicken, for example, the recipe may tell you to "truss" the bird. How do you truss anything? A recipe for cake may ask you to "beat" or "whisk" the batter. What's the difference? Sometimes the recipe directs you to do something after you cook the food, such as "adjust" the seasonings. Do you know what that means? In this chapter, you will not only find definitions for more than 100 of the most common terms for cooking directions, you will also learn some basic techniques, why a particular technique is important, and how you can master it.

Cooking Terms You Need to Know

adjust   To change the seasonings in a cooked dish by adding salt, pepper, herbs, lemon juice, and so on, after you have tasted the dish and determined that it needs more flavoring.

bake blind   To bake an unfilled pie shell partially or completely. For example, to make a custard tart that requires further baking, you use a partially cooked shell to prevent the crust from becoming soggy after you add the custard. You use a fully cooked shell to make mousse, pudding, and fully cooked custard pies. To bake blind, follow these steps so the crust won't shrink:

1. Place the dough into the pie pan, flute the edge, and prick the surface with the tines of a fork.

2. Place aluminum foil or parchment paper over the dough.

3. Put pie weights (special bean-shaped aluminum or ceramic pellets available in cookware stores) or about 2 cups of dried beans on top.

4. Bake the shell in a preheated 400°F oven for 10–12 minutes.

5. Remove the weights or beans and foil and return the shell to the oven to complete baking.

bard   To cover meat with a thin layer of fat before roasting it. Cooks bard lean meats such as veal to keep the flesh moist. The fat gradually renders into the meat as the meat cooks, so there is no need to moisten manually at regular intervals (as you do when you baste). Bacon is a handy barding fat, but you must blanch it for a couple minutes to get rid of excess salt.

baste   To brush or pour a liquid on top of food at regular intervals as it cooks. The basting fluids keep the food moist and add flavor and color. You might baste with pan-roasting fluids, water, stock, wine, beer, juice, or melted fat, depending on the recipe. A special tool called a bulb baster makes basting easy, but you also can baste with a spoon or a pastry brush. Most recipes for roasted meats and poultry will tell you to stop basting for the last half hour of cooking so that the surface will be crispy.

beat   To mix ingredients quickly and vigorously in order to make them smooth, light, creamy, and well aerated. You can beat with any number of tools, including forks, spoons, rotary egg beaters, handheld mixers, electric mixers, and whisks. The most effective way to beat foods by hand is to firmly grip the beating tool and move your wrist and forearm in a circular motion.

Kitchen Clue

If you use dried beans to bake blind, do not cook and eat them. They will be too hard. However, you could save them and use them over and over for pie crusts.

Sometimes you will see more specific beating instructions that tell you to "beat until stiff but not dry." This is used in reference to egg whites to describe the point at which they have the most volume and are the most stable. If you beat egg whites beyond this point, you might have difficulty incorporating them into the recipe. Here are a few pointers to help you use and separate eggs and beat the whites properly:

➤ Separate yolks from whites when the eggs are cold. To crack the egg most effectively, tap the center lightly on the edge of the bowl.

➤ Open the egg shell by prying it apart at the crack. After the egg is halved, look at and smell it. If it is discolored or has an odor, discard it.

➤ Pour the egg into an egg separator. If you don't have an egg separator, wash your hands immediately before cracking the egg. Pour the egg into your hands, hold the yolk in your palm, and let the whites flow through your fingers into a bowl. Store the yolks in a container for future use. Wash your hands again before proceeding with the recipe. (Separating the yolks using the egg shells, rather than a separator or your hands, increases the possibility, however remote, of salmonella poisoning.)

➤ Use a spoon or a paper towel to remove any tiny specks of yolk from the whites. This step is important because yolk contains fat, and even the tiniest particle of fat prevents whites from reaching their greatest volume.

➤ Beat egg whites just before you use them, or they will deflate.

➤ If possible, beat egg whites in a copper, stainless steel, glass, or ceramic bowl. Do not use aluminum because it discolors the whites. Do not use plastic, if you can avoid it, because it retains fats (even if you wash it thoroughly), and you won't get maximum volume.

➤ The best tool for beating egg whites is a whisk or an electric mixer with a whisk attachment. Handheld mixers that have wiry-looking rather than flat beaters, and which do not have posts in the center of the beaters, are suitable as well.

➤ For best results (the most volume), beat egg whites when they are at room temperature. (For optimum results, separate eggs 45 minutes before you beat them.)

➤ Don't add cream of tartar, salt, or sugar until the whites look "foamy."

➤ Start beating egg whites at a slow speed, and then increase speed gradually.

Your goal is one of the following:

➤ *Soft peaks* means the whites tip over softly when you lift the beater from the beaten egg whites.

➤ *Stiff peaks* means the whites tip over only a tiny bit on top when you lift the beater from the beaten egg whites. Do not beat stiff egg whites past the point where they look moist.

There also are special tricks to achieve the most tender and voluminous "whipped cream." Here are some easy guidelines:

➤ Thoroughly chill the cream, bowl, and beaters.

➤ Do not use your copper egg white bowl for whipped cream (or any other ingredient that contains fat). If possible, use a metal bowl because it stays cold longer.

149

Kitchen Clue

Use a copper bowl to get the greatest volume and most stable foam from beaten egg whites. If you use a copper bowl, however, don't add cream of tartar. Use cream of tartar for stability when beating egg whites in stainless steel, glass, or ceramic bowls. If you don't have cream of tartar, use a small amount of salt or sugar to help stabilize the foam.

Egg whites tip over only a tiny bit on top when you beat them to stiff peaks.

➤ The best tool for beating cream is a whisk or an electric mixer with a whisk attachment. Handheld mixers that have wiry-looking rather than flat beaters, and which do not have posts in the center of the beaters, are suitable as well.

➤ Both heavy cream and whipping cream are suitable for whipped cream. Whipped cream made with heavy cream keeps its shape better.

➤ Start beating cream at a slow speed, and then increase speed gradually.

➤ Add sugar gradually after the cream has thickened slightly.

➤ Beat the cream only until the mixture stands in soft peaks. If you beat too long, the mixture will curdle.

➤ If you want to make whipped cream (with whipping cream, not heavy cream) early in the day, stabilize the cream by dissolving 2 TB. non-fat dry milk to each cup of cream.

bind To add an ingredient that holds other ingredients together. For example, in classic tuna salad, you use mayonnaise to bind the tuna fish, celery, and hard-cooked eggs.

blanch To plunge food briefly into boiling water (usually followed by a plunge into or rinse under cold water; see *refresh*). You might do this to set a vegetable's color, to remove the strong flavor of an ingredient such as bacon or onion, to help remove an ingredient's skin or peel (tomatoes and nuts, for example), or to prepare foods for freezing.

blend To mix foods thoroughly until they are smooth, but in a less vigorous way than beating. Blending also refers to processing foods in a blender.

bone To remove the bones, sinew, and gristle from meat, poultry, game, and fish.

bread To coat foods with a dry ingredient such as bread crumbs, cracker crumbs, cornmeal, or flour. You do this to add flavor and a crunchy texture, and to protect a food's surface from intense heat. Fried foods are breaded so that they don't scorch in the hot fat. To assure that the breading will stay in place, follow these simple tips:

➤ Coat the food in milk, beaten egg, or egg white to help the breading ingredient adhere better.

➤ For thicker breading, you can dredge the food in flour, coat it with egg, and then coat it with the breading ingredient.

➤ Let breaded foods rest for 15–20 minutes before you cook them. Resting helps the breading ingredient adhere better.

brown To cook foods quickly over moderately high heat so that they turn a rich golden brown color. Browning foods does more than provide color, though. It also helps seal in natural juices. You can brown foods by frying them in hot fat, cooking them on a grill or broiler, or roasting them in a hot oven. To brown foods properly, be sure the surface is dry. Also be sure not to crowd the ingredients in the cooking vessel, which decreases heat; foods will not brown if the temperature is too low.

bruise To crush an aromatic ingredient slightly to release its flavor and aroma. You generally bruise foods such as garlic, ginger, peppercorns, and cardamom pods.

brush with To use a pastry brush to apply an ingredient (such as melted jelly) to another ingredient (such as a fully baked tart shell).

butterfly To halve food (usually meat, poultry, or shellfish) horizontally without cutting all the way through, so that the food opens like a book or a butterfly's wings.

caramelize To heat sugar or sugar water slowly so that the mixture turns a rich caramel brown. Or to sprinkle food with sugar and brown it quickly under the broiler. Or to cook vegetables until they are soft and their natural sugars have turned them brown.

carve To slice meat or poultry into serving-size pieces. Before you carve a roast of any kind, let it stand for 15 minutes to ensure juiciness and give the meat or bird time to finish cooking.

To make carving a chicken or turkey easier, begin by cutting off the legs and wings; then slice the breast.

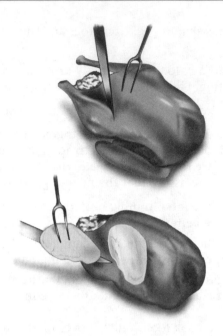

chill   To refrigerate foods. You may also chill foods by placing them in a bowl and putting the bowl in a large vessel filled with ice.

chop   To cut food into pieces, either small (finely chopped, minced) or large (coarsely chopped). When you chop foods, be sure to keep your fingers away from the blade. Put the food on a cutting board and hold it down with one hand, with your knuckles out and fingertips curved in; your knuckles then serve as a guide for the knife blade. You won't cut yourself as long as you keep the blade edge lower than your knuckles. Hold the knife in your other hand with a firm grip around the handle, and cut the food straight down or with a forward motion, depending on the type of cut you want.

When you chop ingredients, use your knuckles as a knife guide so that you don't cut yourself.

clarify   To clear a liquid of solid particles. You clarify stock by adding egg whites and/or shells and heating the liquid gently. The sediment adheres to the solidified egg whites and can be removed easily. You clarify butter by melting it and reserving the liquid yellow oil and discarding the milky white solids.

coat   To cover food completely with an ingredient or food such as flour or sauce. When a recipe tells you to cook a sauce until it is thick enough to "coat a spoon," the sauce will leave a film on the back of the spoon. When you wipe the spoon with a finger, it leaves a streaky finger mark.

coddle   To cook food in simmering water for a very short time. This technique is used primarily to warm foods.

cool   To remove food from a heat source and let it stand until it comes to room temperature (or at least until it is no longer hot).

cream   To mix two or more ingredients until they are smooth, soft, and well blended. It is a good idea to remove butter from the refrigerator shortly before you cream it so that it softens a bit.

Kitchen Clue

To prevent bacteria from growing when you cool foods at room temperature, cool them as quickly as possible. For example, put a saucepan of hot food into a bowl of ice.

crimp   To seal and decorate the edges of a pie crust by pinching the top and bottom crusts together with your fingers or a special tool.

cube   To cut food into squares that are larger than dice.

cut in   To incorporate solid fats such as shortening or butter into flour or another dry ingredient so that the fat turns into tiny flour-coated particles that resemble coarse crumbs. You can use your fingers, two knives, or a pastry blender to cut in. It is easier to cut in fats that are cold.

deglaze   To loosen the natural juices and particles of coagulated foods that have accumulated at the bottom of the pan during cooking and which have formed a "glaze." To remove the glaze, you must add liquid to dissolve the particles. When you add the liquid (it can be wine, water, stock, or juice), you stir and scrape up the bits at the bottom of the pan, often by using a whisk or a wooden spoon. You can use the deglazing liquid alone as a sauce (for a finer sauce, strain the liquid first), or you can boil the liquid until it is reduced to a syrupy texture, and then use the syrup in a more elaborate sauce.

degrease   To remove the fat from food. Fat rises to the top of food, making it easier to scoop off. To remove the fat from hot stock, soup, or sauce, you can use a special fat separator, but a spoon will do the job just as well. Alternatively, you can drop a paper towel gently onto the food, and the fat will cling to the paper towel when you lift it off.

If you have time, the best way to degrease is to chill the liquid. The fat hardens at the top, and you can scoop it off easily. To remove fat from a casserole or roasting pan that contains bulky solid food, tilt the pan so that the juices are in one corner. The fat comes to the top as with stock, and you can scoop it up using the same methods. Always degrease foods before you "deglaze" the pan.

de-seed   To remove the seeds of fruits and vegetables (sometimes called *seeding*). This can be done in several ways:

➤ Crush soft berries such as raspberries and strain them through a sieve.

➤ Slice the cap off bell peppers and pull out the seed cluster.

➤ Cut a cucumber in half lengthwise and use a spoon to scoop out the seeds.

➤ Cut open apples, pears, and similar fruit and use a knife, spoon, or melon-baller to carve out the core and seeds together.

devein   To remove the vein from shrimp. To do this, hold the shrimp curved side out with one hand, and slit the curve open with a small paring knife using the other hand. You will see a gritty-looking black vein that you can pull out with the paring knife or with your fingers.

Here's how you devein a shrimp.

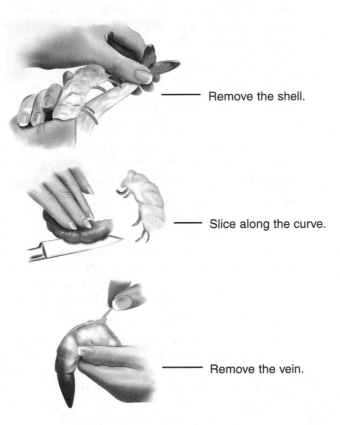

Remove the shell.

Slice along the curve.

Remove the vein.

dice   To cut food into tiny cubes approximately ⅛ inch to ½ inch in size. To dice, first you slice the food, and then you cut those slices into julienne strips (see *julienne*). Turn the strips a quarter turn and cut into cubes.

Dicing food into tiny cubes.

dilute   To make a food weaker by adding water or another liquid.

dot   To scatter the top of a dish with tiny bits of food, typically butter.

drain   To strain food through a colander or strainer to remove liquid. You drain spaghetti, for example. It also means to pour out the fat from a cooking pan.

dredge   To coat food lightly with a dry ingredient such as flour, bread crumbs, or sugar. This is similar to breading foods; however, after you dredge foods, you shake them to get rid of any excess dry ingredients.

dress   To put a sauce or dressing on food. The word usually is used with salad.

drizzle   To sprinkle drops of liquid lightly over food.

dust   To lightly sprinkle a small amount of a dry ingredient over food.

eviscerate   To remove the entrails from an animal in preparation for cooking.

fillet   To remove the bones from fish, meat, or poultry. This procedure is similar to boning. (It is also the word used for the deboned food.)

flambé   A dramatic technique of quickly enveloping a dish in flames by igniting a small amount of heated liquor poured over it. It can create a spectacular effect at the dining room table, but the process is more than visual. When you flambé food you also add flavor. However, to do it properly, you must warm the liquor or it won't catch fire. Never pour the liquor near an open fire; the flames can escape into the bottle and cause it to explode. Move the pan away from the heat source before you set a match to it.

flute   To make a decorative edge on pie, pastry, or vegetables.

fold   To incorporate one ingredient into another using a gentle, lifting motion, preferably with a rubber spatula. To fold, cut down into the middle of the mixture to

155

the bottom of the bowl, scrape the bottom of the bowl, and lift up the spatula, bringing some of the mixture up with it. Repeat this process until the mixture is uniform in color and texture. You may find folding easier if you turn the bowl with one hand as you use the spatula with the other.

You usually fold to incorporate a fragile or delicate ingredient into a heavier one to retain a light, fluffy, aerated texture. If you beat, stir, or mix the ingredient instead of folding it, the mixture will deflate. Folding also is used to incorporate berries, nuts, and other solids into batter for muffins and cakes. This avoids overworking the ingredients, which would activate too much gluten in the batter and cause the pastry to be tough and rubbery.

garnish To decorate food to enhance visual appeal. For tips on garnishing, see Chapter 10, "Making a Game Plan."

glaze To coat food to give it a glossy sheen and enhance the flavor. You can glaze meats, fish, cakes, and candies. Hot meats, fish, and vegetables are usually glazed with a liquid such as stock or juice that has been boiled down to a syrupy consistency. Cold foods are usually glazed with aspic (jellied stock). Cakes are usually glazed with icing.

grate To cut ingredients into small particles using a food processor or a hand grater, which has tiny, sharp holes for cutting.

grease To coat a pan with fat to keep foods from sticking.

grind To make food into tiny particles using a food processor, food grinder, blender, or mortar and pestle.

hull To remove the stem of strawberries using your fingers, a knife, or a special implement called a *huller*.

husk To remove the outside leaves from ears of corn.

julienne To slice food into thin strips. To do this, first slice the food, then place the slices on a cutting board, overlapping each other. Cut through the overlapping slices to make small, matchlike pieces about ⅛ inch wide.

Julienne strips are thin matchlike shreds.

knead   To manipulate food either mechanically or by hand in a pressing-stretching-folding routine. You do this to develop flour gluten when you are preparing bread or to make fondant tender and shiny when you are making candy. When you knead bread by hand, do it on a lightly floured board until the dough is smooth and elastic.

line   To cover a pan or cookie sheet with paper or foil to prevent foods from sticking.

macerate   To place fruits or vegetables in a liquid so that they can absorb flavor and soften in texture. You macerate fruits in liqueur, fruit juice, or sugar syrup. This process is similar to marinating.

marinate   To place food (usually meats but sometimes vegetables) in a liquid so that it will become more flavorful and sometimes more tender. Marinades typically are composed of an acidic ingredient such as wine vinegar, yogurt, or lemon juice plus seasonings and vegetable oil. The acidic ingredients break down tissue and muscle fiber, so these marinades also tenderize foods slightly. Sometimes, however, marinades are simple blends of spices that add flavor but do not tenderize. To prevent food poisoning, be sure to marinate foods either in the refrigerator or for only a short time out of the refrigerator. Do not reuse marinades that you have used for meat, poultry, or fish, and do not use them as sauce for the cooked food. Marinate protein foods (such as meat and poultry) for a short time only, otherwise the flesh becomes either mushy or, ironically, tough.

mash   To mix, press, or otherwise make food into a soft, pulpy mass. Mashed potatoes is the most well-known "mashed" dish.

mince   To chop food into very small pieces; means the same thing as *finely chopped*. The best way to mince foods is to chop them (see *chop*), and then hold the tip of a large knife down with one hand and bring the blade and wider end of the knife up and down quickly on the ingredients using the other hand. Gather the ingredients and repeat the process until you achieve the desired texture.

This is what minced food looks like.

mix   To blend ingredients with a stirring motion using a spoon or fork.

mull   To steep hot tea, wine, or cider with spices or other flavor enhancers.

157

parboil   To partially cook food in boiling water before completely cooking it by some other process. Parboiling is a lengthier process than is blanching.

pare   To remove the skin from fruits and vegetables (the same as *peeling*). Use a paring knife or vegetable peeler.

patch   To repair tiny cracks in dough by pressing two pieces of dough together or using a strip of leftover dough and inserting it between the two cracked pieces. Patching is preferable to rerolling dough because rerolling toughens the pastry.

pipe   To force a smooth, stiff, soft mixture through a pastry tube in order to decorate other foods or a plate.

pit   To remove the seeds, stone, or pit from fruits such as cherries or olives.

plump   To soak foods (such as raisins or dried fruit) to make them soft and tender.

pound   To flatten food, especially meat, to make it thinner, more even, and more tender. To flatten chicken breasts or other meat, place the meat between two layers of waxed or parchment paper. Pound the meat with a meat mallet, cleaver, or wide-bottomed pot until the meat is as thin as you want it.

preheat   To set the oven to a desired temperature so that it is hot enough to receive food. It isn't usually necessary to preheat the oven when you are cooking casseroles and other moisture-laden foods. You should always preheat an oven when you are making roasts and baked goods, however, so that you get a crispy or properly browned surface. Always preheat the oven when reheating fried foods so that they won't be greasy.

prick   To pierce food so that it won't explode, rise, expand, or shrink unnecessarily as it cooks. Use the tines of a fork to prick pie dough; use the tip of a sharp knife to prick a potato for baking.

proof   To test yeast to see whether it is still potent. To do this, dissolve the yeast in a small amount of warm water and add a pinch of sugar. Mix and wait five to ten minutes. If bubbles appear around the edges of the bowl and the top of the mixture becomes foamy, the yeast is okay.

punch down   To hit dough with your hand to deflate it so it becomes more tender and evenly grained.

purée   To blend food until it becomes completely smooth and uniform. You can purée food through a strainer or in a food mill, blender, or food processor.

ream   To remove the juice of a lemon, orange, or other citrus fruit.

reconstitute   To rehydrate dried food (such as dried mushrooms or sun-dried tomatoes) by soaking it in water or another liquid.

reduce   To boil a liquid down to reduce its volume and intensify its flavor. The resulting thicker liquid is called a "reduction" and is the basis of many sauces.

refresh   To place hot vegetables under cold running water or plunge them into a pan of ice cold water in order to stop the vegetables from cooking further, to set the color, and to retain the crisp texture. (See also *blanch.*)

render   To melt fat in order to reduce the solid fat to liquid. Always render fat over low heat to avoid sputtering.

rice   To force food through a strainer or special "ricer" to mash it. This is similar to puréeing, but a riced mixture may not be as smooth as a purée.

scald   To heat liquids to just below the boiling point, when small bubbles appear around the edges of the pan; or to plunge food into boiling water for a short time (as for blanching) or pour boiling water over food.

scallop   To make a decorative edge around a pie crust (see *flute*). Also, to cook foods in a creamy sauce.

score   To cut narrow gashes into the surface of meat or fish to help tenderize the flesh. Scoring also helps the meat or fish retain its shape as it cooks.

scramble   To mix eggs with a fork or spoon while they cook so that curd shapes form.

sear   To brown foods over high heat to seal in juices and create a rich color. You can sear foods in a hot pan, broiler, grill, or oven.

season   To add flavor to food by adding salt, pepper, herbs, or spices.

shell   To remove edible seeds from their fibrous, inedible pods, as with peas and lima beans, or to remove the hard outer covering of shrimp.

shred   To cut food into long, slender pieces using a knife or special shredding blade in a food processor. Shreds are similar to julienne strips.

shuck   To remove the flesh of mollusks such as clams and oysters from their shells.

sift   To remove the lumps and lighten the texture of certain ingredients, especially flour, by forcing it through a sieve or strainer. Special tools are available that are made specifically for sifting flour, but any old strainer will do and is cheaper and easier to use and clean.

simmer   To cook food at temperatures just below boiling. When food is simmering, bubbles appear around the edges of the pan. Most often you will boil foods first, and then lower the heat so that the food stays at a steady temperature just below a boil.

skewer   To place chunks of food to be grilled or broiled onto metal or wooden rods.

skim   To remove the scum (fat and other debris) that rises to the surface of a liquid such as soup or stock.

slice   To cut food into evenly shaped pieces. To slice ingredients, hold the knife the same way you do to chop, but cut across with a forward motion as you push down on the food.

snip　To cut food, typically fresh herbs, into small pieces with scissors.

steep　To pour boiling water or another liquid over dry ingredients, typically tea leaves, and let the mixture stand in order to infuse flavor and color into the liquid.

stir　To combine ingredients in a circular motion using a spoon.

strain　To separate solids from liquids through a strainer or fine sieve.

stud　To insert spices, herbs, or other flavorings into the surface of food. The most common example of this is clove-studded baked Virginia ham.

stuff　To fill a cavity with food or a mixture of ingredients. You can stuff the inside cavity of a chicken, turkey, or other fowl, the circle of a crown roast or acorn squash, the center of a bundt cake, and so on. Never stuff poultry until just before you put it in the oven to roast.

temper　To prepare a cool ingredient before adding it to a hot one in order to prevent curdling. Sometimes, for example, a recipe tells you to add eggs to a hot sauce. If you add the eggs without tempering them, the mixture will curdle. To temper the eggs, you add a small amount of the hot sauce to them, beating constantly. When you have added enough for the egg to feel warm, you can add the egg/sauce mixture to the rest of the hot sauce and continue cooking. Never let the egg mixture come to a boil or it will curdle.

toast　To brown food by the indirect heat of an oven (as you do when you toast nuts) or by the direct heat of a broiler (as when you toast bread or brown foods under the broiler).

toss　To mix ingredients quickly and gently with a lifting motion using two utensils such as a salad fork and spoon. Salad and pasta are typically tossed.

truss　To tie the wings and legs of poultry close to the body so that it will keep its shape during roasting. Sometimes people truss stuffed poultry to help keep the stuffing inside the bird's cavity.

Trussing poultry helps a bird keep its shape during roasting.

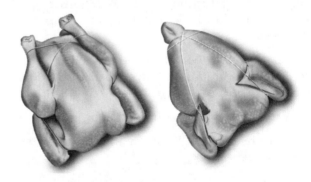

unmold   To turn food out from a container or mold onto a serving plate. Foods that are unmolded include gelatin salads, custards, and cakes. Lots of people have a fear of unmolding. Here are some tips to help you do it successfully:

➤ Grease the pan or mold lightly with vegetable oil or spray before adding the food.

➤ When you are ready to unmold the food, dip the mold to its rim in hot water for 5 to 8 seconds or until you see the edges loosen slightly from the sides.

➤ Place a serving plate upside down over the top of the mold, turn the mold and plate over and gently shake the mold; the filling should slide out.

➤ If your dish doesn't slide out, try the dipping process again for 3 to 4 seconds, or run the tip of a small knife around the edge where the food meets the side of the mold.

whip   The same as beating, except that when you whip you always use a beater or whisk (when it may be called *whisking*)—not a fork. When you whip, you mix ingredients quickly and vigorously to incorporate air, increase volume, and lighten the mixture.

whisk   The same as *whipping,* but using a whisk.

work in   To use your hands or other tools to incorporate one ingredient into another. When making pie dough, for example, you work the fat into the flour.

Al Dente???

Chapter 14

A Compendium of Catchwords Used in Recipes

In This Chapter

➤ A super-glossary that describes food terms

➤ A super-glossary that describes cooking equipment

Even though you understand recipe directions and are acquainted with cooking procedures, as you read a recipe you may come across terms that are unfamiliar to you. The recipe may tell you to cook the pasta *al dente,* or list an ingredient or type of food you don't know, such as "duxelles" or "sole meunière." The recipe may refer to equipment you've never heard of or don't know very much about, such as a "bain-marie" or "nonreactive pan." This chapter describes some important food terms and equipment you are likely to find as you begin your adventure in good cooking.

Al Dente and Other Terms You Need to Know

Is it important to understand every food term? Even though you may never make an aspic or use a liaison to thicken a sauce, a good cook ought to know about them anyway. It makes you more knowledgeable, and that knowledge helps you understand what you are doing as you cook. At the very least, knowing food terms makes you sound smart at parties.

acidulated water Because certain fruits and vegetables—such as artichokes and apples—turn brown when they are cut open and exposed to air, a recipe may tell you to place the food in acidulated water. This is simply a mixture of water and some acidic ingredient such as lemon juice or vinegar, usually in the proportion of 1–2 tablespoons acid to 3–4 cups water.

al dente   An Italian term that translates as "in the tooth" and refers to the way the texture of cooked pasta and vegetables feels in your mouth. Foods prepared *al dente* should offer resistance: tender yet still-crunchy vegetables, pasta that is vaguely chewy.

apéritif   A before-dinner drink (such as vermouth, dry white wine, or champagne) that stimulates the appetite.

aspic   A savory jelly made from meat, fish, poultry, or vegetable stock. This can be a plain aspic that you cut into shapes and serve as a garnish for food, a molded salad containing meat and vegetables, or a glossy coating for cold food.

au gratin   A dish topped with cheese, bread crumbs, and butter that is baked in a shallow dish known as an *au gratin pan* and browned briefly under the broiler. Also known as *gratin*.

au jus   Meat served with natural cooking juices.

au lait   Any food made with milk, although the term usually refers to coffee with milk: *cafe au lait*.

beurre manié   A creamed mixture of flour and butter used to thicken sauces and soups at the end of their cooking time.

bouquet garni   A bundle of fresh and/or dried herbs and spices used to flavor stock, soup, stews, and braised dishes. The herbs and spices are tied in cheesecloth and are removed before you serve the dish. The most common bouquet garni ingredients are bay leaf, thyme, peppercorns, parsley, and sometimes celery tops.

brochette   Skewered meat, poultry, fish, and/or vegetables that are usually grilled. This is the same as a kebab.

canapé   A cracker or small, thin piece of bread or toast topped with savory foods such as smoked salmon or herb-flavored butter and served as an hors d'oeuvre.

chutney   A highly seasoned sweet and spicy relish made of fruits and vegetables (often served as a condiment for meats).

cobbler   A deep-dish fruit pie with a top crust only. The crust can be made of standard pie dough or biscuit dough. When the pie is fully baked, the crust is broken up and pressed gently into the filling so that it looks "cobbled." Sometimes cobbler is made with discs of dough or blobs of biscuit instead of a single crust, in which case it looks cobbled even before it's baked.

condiment   A sauce or relish used to enhance food. The best known condiments are ketchup, mustard, Worcestershire sauce, salsa, and hot pepper sauce.

court bouillon   A liquid mixture of water, wine, vegetables, herbs, and spices used for poaching fish.

crème fraîche   A tart-tasting dairy product that has the texture of sour cream or plain yogurt. It is used plain on top of berries or as a fabulous enrichment for many sauces. You can buy crème fraîche in specialty stores, but it is easy to make at home. See Section 7, "Sauces and Gravies."

crudités   Assorted, cut-up, raw or blanched vegetables, usually accompanied by a dip; one of the most popular hors d'oeuvres in America. You can place the dip in a bowl, but for more dramatic effect, put it inside a hollowed-out crusty, round bread, bell peppers, or a cabbage head.

curdle   The result of heating a mixture too quickly or over too high a temperature, which causes particles to coagulate and separate from each other. Something has gone wrong when a recipe curdles. Egg-based mixtures and dairy products such as milk and sour cream are prone to curdling. Dairy products may curdle when mixed with acidic ingredients. (See Chapter 17, "So You've Made a Mistake?" for ways to remedy curdling problems.)

dash   A tiny amount of any ingredient (less than ⅛ tsp.), although it usually refers to liquid ingredients (2–3 drops).

deviled   Foods that are seasoned with spicy or hot ingredients such as hot pepper sauce or mustard.

duxelles   A classic mixture of minced mushrooms and shallots sautéed with butter. It is used in many sauces and as a stuffing for such diverse foods as stuffed mushrooms and ravioli.

egg wash   A mixture of whole egg, yolk only, or white only, sometimes mixed with a small amount of water to brush onto something. It is used to give a shiny glaze to bread (brushed onto the dough before baking the bread), to patch two pieces of pastry together, to help seeds adhere to dough, or to serve as a "film" that prevents an unbaked pie shell from getting soggy when you pour a moist filling into it.

filo pastry   Also known as phyllo pastry, a tissue-thin dough used primarily in Greek and Middle Eastern cooking, especially to make baklava and spanakopitas.

fines herbes   A mixture of any combination of fresh or dried herbs used to season foods. Unlike a bouquet garni, which is placed inside cheesecloth and is later removed, the fines herbes are scattered into the recipe.

liaison   Any mixture used to thicken sauce, stew, or soup. A beurre manié is a type of *liaison*.

lukewarm   Something that is at room temperature. Recipes often say to heat or cool something to lukewarm.

marinade   A mixture used to enhance the flavor of food. Acidic marinades may also soften and tenderize foods somewhat. Marinades are usually seasoned, acid-based liquids, but they can be dry mixtures, too, in which case they may be called "rubs."

meringue   A mixture of stiffly beaten egg whites and sugar. Some meringues are soft, as in lemon meringue pie. Some are firm and crispy, such as meringue pie shells.

Soft meringues usually contain less sugar than do firm ones. It is difficult to make meringue on a humid day because the whipped mixture tends to soften and "weep."

meunière   A classic sauce made with butter, lemon juice, and parsley.

mirepoix   A mixture of chopped vegetables used to flavor stocks, braised foods, and sauces. They may be removed from the dish (by straining) before the food is finished. However, mirepoix ingredients often are puréed with pan juices and cooking fluids to thicken and enrich a sauce, which means you don't have to use flour or some other starch as a thickener. The most common mirepoix ingredients are carrots, onions, and celery.

mousse   A French word that means "frothy" and refers to a light, ethereal, spongy-textured dish that can be sweet or savory, cold or hot. Mousses are made of puréed food such as meat, fish, fruit, or melted chocolate, which are folded with whipped cream and/or beaten egg whites. Sometimes gelatin is added as a stabilizer.

paillard   A boneless chicken breast that has been pounded thin. Sometimes it is called a *supreme* or *cutlet*. Though the word technically refers to chicken, sometimes it refers to any meat (veal, pork, and so on).

pilaf   A dish containing rice that is sautéed before it is cooked with liquid. Any number of seasonings or textural ingredients, from chopped shrimp to raisins to mushrooms to almonds, may be included in a pilaf. The Spanish dish paella is an elaborate pilaf that may contain seafood, poultry, and meats.

pinch   A tiny amount (less than ⅛ tsp.) of any ingredient, although it usually refers to dry ingredients.

roux   A mixture of fat (usually butter) and flour cooked together before a liquid is added to make a sauce. It is the basis of dozens of sauces from classic white sauce (béchamel) to velouté to Mornay. Old-fashioned macaroni and cheese begins with a roux-based cheddar cheese sauce.

A classic roux contains equal amounts of fat and flour; you vary the texture of the sauce by using different quantities of liquid. For example, a medium-thick white sauce is made with 2 tablespoons fat, 2 tablespoons flour, and 1–1¼ cups of milk. To make a thicker sauce (for a soufflé, for example), you would use 3 tablespoons fat, 3 tablespoons flour, and 1–1¼ cups of milk. If you want to cut down on dietary fat, you can increase the flour by as much as 3 tablespoons without adding more fat. So a thick sauce for croquettes could be made with 2 tablespoons fat, 5 tablespoons flour, and 1–1¼ cups milk.

To make a roux, melt the fat in a small, heavy saucepan over low heat. (Do not use an aluminum pan because it imparts a metallic taste.) Then add the flour and use a whisk to incorporate it into the fat. Continue to cook and whisk the ingredients constantly for about two minutes over low heat. This process assures that your sauce won't have an unpleasantly "starchy" taste. A "white roux" is the most common type and is ready after two minutes of cooking for use in classic white sauce and all its variations. There is also a "blond roux," which is slightly darker (cooked a minute or so longer) and is useful for ivory to light amber-colored sauces. A "brown roux" is just that: Roux cooked over low heat for a few minutes longer so it becomes golden brown. A brown roux goes into brown sauces.

rub   A blend of seasonings that you rub onto the surface of food before you cook it. A rub enhances flavor; it does not tenderize food.

sauce   A blend of ingredients used to enhance, complement, or harmonize with food. Sauces are frequently pourable liquids, but some are very thick (e.g., mayonnaise), and others are chunky and more solid (e.g., cranberry sauce).

Classic French cuisine has given us many of the sauces we use in cooking. These include

➤ Béchamel (white sauce), made by adding milk or cream plus seasonings to a roux (see "roux"). There are several variations on béchamel including Mornay (with cheese), *soubise* (with onion), Nantua (with lobster butter), and Albert (with horseradish). White sauces were once more popular than they are today. Velouté is the same as white sauce but it is made with stock rather than milk or cream.

➤ Espagnole (brown sauce), made from slow, simmering meat stock. In days gone by, cooks simmered the ingredients (including Spanish ham, hence the name), for days. Today you can make brown sauce much more quickly. Variations on Espagnole include *bordelaise* (with red wine) *bigarade* (with orange flavor), *Madeira* (with fortified wine), and Robert (with Dijon mustard). *Demi-glace* is Espagnole that has been reduced to a syrupy consistency.

➤ Emulsified sauces, including *hollandaise* (hot, lemon-flavored butter-and-egg-yolk sauce) and its variations: *béarnaise* (with tarragon), *Maltaise* (with orange flavor), *noisette* (with ground, toasted nuts). Other emulsified sauces are *beurre blanc* (hot, vinegar-shallot-butter sauce) and mayonnaise (cold, thick egg yolks and olive oil).

➤ Vinaigrette, a blend of vegetable oil, vinegar, and seasonings used for salad dressing and marinades.

Today, the term "sauce" goes beyond these French classics to include such items as gravy, pan sauces, and blender sauces, as well as barbecue, tomato, and pesto sauces, salsas and chutneys, and many dessert sauces such as fudge sauce, melba sauce, and puréed fruit sauces. See Section 7.

scallop   A type of seafood (sea scallop, bay scallop), or a thin slice of meat. Also known as a *cutlet.*

smoke point   The point at which fat breaks down, starts to smoke, and gives off an odor. Different fats have different smoke points. To stir-fry or cook by any other method that requires high heat, you need a fat that has a high smoke point: Peanut, canola, corn, soybean, safflower, and sunflower oils are fine. Olive oil has a lower

167

smoke point than these and is not appropriate for high-heat cooking. Butter has a low smoke point and burns easily. Clarified butter has a higher smoke point than regular butter. Sometimes a recipe will tell you to use clarified butter or plain butter plus vegetable oil. This is because the butter provides flavor and a rich color, and the vegetable oil withstands the heat, giving the mixture about the same smoke point as clarified butter.

stock   Sometimes called *broth*; the long-simmering poaching liquid from cooked meat, poultry, fish, or vegetables. The solids are strained from the liquid when cooking is complete. Stock is used to make soup and sauce.

truffles   High-priced types of fungus, these are difficult to find, are hunted down by specially trained pigs or dogs, and are highly prized because they are rare and have an astonishingly rich, earthy flavor and tantalizing aroma. Truffles are used in many dishes, including pâtés and pasta, but also are used to garnish food. (Chocolate and other candy truffles are confections shaped to resemble fungus truffles.)

vegetable cooking spray   This is vegetable oil (plus other ingredients such as alcohol and lecithin) in an aerosol can. You spray it onto pans to prevent food from sticking. A sprayed pan has fewer calories and less fat than one greased with shortening, but also may have a "fake" odor. Use it sparingly or it may also leave an aftertaste.

zest   The outermost layer of the skin of a citrus fruit. It does *not* include the white pith—only the thin, colored part. You can grate zest off the pith with a hand grater or with a special *zester*.

A Bain-Marie and Other Equipment You Ought to Know About

You are probably familiar with the pots, pans, and equipment mentioned in recipes. But sometimes an odd item will pop up or you'll notice something in a store that puzzles you. Do you know what a pastry blender does, for example? A *bain-marie?* The following items are some of the more useful equipment you should know about.

au gratin pan   A shallow, heat-proof pan or casserole dish in which you brown foods by putting them briefly beneath the broiler. You can also serve directly from an au gratin pan or use it as a small roasting pan.

bain-marie   Literally "Marie's bath," a hot-water bath used to provide even heat and a moist environment for foods. You use it to cook foods steadily and slowly or to keep them warm, either in the oven or on the stovetop. A bain-marie comes in handy for delicate items that crack or curdle easily, such as custards, cheesecake, and egg-based dishes.

To make a bain-marie, place a dish containing food inside a larger vessel containing simmering water, or fill the larger vessel with water after you place the dish inside. The water should come about halfway up the sides of the inner pan. The larger vessel may be a roasting pan, cake pan (for the oven), or large saucepan (for the stovetop).

A bain-marie is useful when you cook foods that crack or curdle easily, such as cheesecake or custard.

bulb baster   A two-part device used to baste food. It has a long, tapering tube made of metal or plastic and a rubber bulb at the wider end. To baste, you place the tube in the basting liquid and squeeze the bulb, which sucks the liquid into the tube. Then you aim the tube at the food to be basted and release the bulb. The liquid flows out of the tube onto the food.

This bulb baster has a metal tube; some have a plastic tube.

cake tester   A long, wiry rod with a loop handle on top. You insert it into the center of a cake to see whether a cake is done. If the rod comes out dry—with no batter clinging to it—the cake is done.

chafing dish   A sauté pan that sits inside another pan containing water, similar to a double boiler in concept. The water is heated with canned fuel that sits beneath the pan. Most often, chafing dishes are used to keep foods warm for buffet service at parties, and many are decorative or fancy.

charlotte mold   A container that has gently flared sides and is used to hold charlottes (a type of pudding) and other molded foods.

cheesecloth   A gauzy cotton cloth used to wrap foods such as bouquet garni or whole fish and hold them together during cooking. Food wrapped in cheesecloth is easy to remove from the cooking vessel.

double boiler   A two-part pot in which one pan sits inside another. The lower pan holds water; the upper pan holds food. The water in the lower pan cooks the food, yet protects it from intense, direct heat. Double boilers come in handy for delicate foods and those that would burn too easily over direct heat, such as chocolate, custard, or egg-based dishes. You can buy a double boiler, but it is easy to make your own by placing a bowl over the rim of a saucepan.

Dutch oven   A large, heavy casserole dish or short-handled pan used for braising and other slow, moist-heat cooking methods. You can use it in the oven or on the stovetop.

jelly roll pan   A cookie sheet with a rim around it. Use it to create classic jelly rolls, bake cookies, toast nuts, make bread crumbs, or reheat foods.

nonreactive pan   A pan made of materials that won't react with acidic ingredients such as vinegar, wine, lemon juice, or tomatoes; that is, the molecules of the metal won't combine with the acid to give a bad taste or color to the food. Nonreactive pans include those made of stainless steel, ceramic, glass, enamel, or anodized aluminum. Regular aluminum, cast iron, and copper pans are reactive.

nutmeg grater   A small metal grater with one side curved and fitted with sharp cutting holes and one side flat; it tapers at one end. To grate nutmegs, you rub them against the sharp side and the gratings fall through the middle and out the narrow end. Nutmeg mills, which look exactly like pepper mills, are also available.

pastry blender   A tool used to cut fat into flour. It is made of curved, rigid metal wires that are held together with a thick handle.

pie weights   Ceramic or aluminum bean-shaped pellets used for baking blind so that pie crusts won't shrink.

sifter   A special tool used for sifting flour to make it finer. You can sift without a sifter. A strainer works just as well, is cheaper, and is easier to clean.

skillet   A general name for a frying pan. Skillets come in many sizes and types, including sauté pans, braising pans, and omelet pans. When a recipe does not indicate otherwise, you may use any all-purpose skillet.

skimmer   A utensil used to skim fat, scum, or solids from food. A skimmer has a long handle with a disk-shaped end. The disk is perforated metal with either large holes (for removing solids) or mesh-like holes (for straining scum and fat).

Skimmers help you get rid of fat and scum from stock, soup, and stew.

soufflé dish   A deep, straight-sided casserole dish. The straight sides allow soufflés to rise properly. These dishes are useful for other types of recipes too, including savory casseroles and puddings, as well as cold mousses.

springform pan   A two-part pan with detachable sides that clamp onto a base and can be removed easily by opening the clamp. It is used primarily for cakes that stick, such as cheesecake, or molded cakes and confections, such as chocolate mousse/lady finger cake.

whisk   A wire whip used to beat foods and incorporate air into them. Whisks come in many shapes and sizes for different purposes. A *balloon whisk* is large and wide with flexible wires and is used when you want to incorporate as much air as possible (to beat egg whites and whipped cream, for example). Smaller, more tapered whisks with rigid wires are better for thick batters that don't require much aeration. Those with flexible wires are useful for light batters, marinades, and fragile foods.

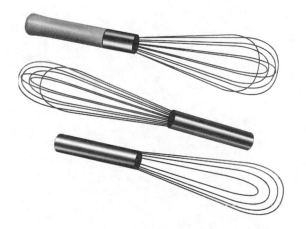

Whisks come in different shapes and sizes to serve different purposes.

171

wok   A round-bottomed pan once used exclusively in Asian cooking, that is useful for stir-fries and other dishes cooked quickly over high heat. The rounded sides ensure quick, even heating, allow you to cook with a minimum of fat, and help keep the food in the pan (instead of falling onto the stovetop).

zester   A small cutting device used to remove the outermost layer of citrus fruit.

This tiny tool can remove the zest of citrus fruit in a flash.

1. Take food.

2. Put food over heat source.

3. Now you're cooking!!!

Chapter 15

Method Acting: How You Cook Food

In This Chapter

➤ Frying: sautéing, stir-frying, and deep-fat frying

➤ Roasting and baking

➤ Stewing and braising

➤ Boiling, simmering, and poaching

➤ Steaming

➤ Grilling and broiling

➤ Microwave cooking

Your apron is on, your recipe is out, and your hands are clean. You are about to cook. You know how to chop the garlic and follow other recipe instructions, and you know what it means to cook an ingredient *al dente*. You know what a springform pan is.

All of these directions and terms lead to the actual cooking of your food. But you don't just cook the food any old way. You roast some foods and stir-fry others. Which ingredients do you poach, and which do you grill? Just as a method actor must understand a role for a film, you must understand the role an ingredient plays in a dish and use the appropriate technique to cook it to advantage. This chapter explains the basic cooking methods and gives tips on how to use those methods successfully.

Frying

Several methods use the technique of frying. All frying methods involve cooking food in hot fat. Most of the differences among these submethods have to do with the kind of food you cook, the amount and temperature of the fat, and the type of pan you use.

Sautéing

When you sauté foods, you cook them quickly in a small amount of fat over moderately high heat for the first couple of minutes to sear the surface, and then finish them over moderate heat. You can use a specially designed shallow pan with straight sides, but any open skillet will do. Because the cooking time is relatively brief, only tender cuts of meat and poultry cut into small pieces and water-rich vegetables such as mushrooms and spinach are suitable. You may sauté firm-textured vegetables if you parboil them first. The best foods for sautéing include skinless and boneless chicken breasts, turkey cutlets, small broiler-fryer chicken parts, beef steaks (such as strip or sirloin), veal, pork and lamb chops and cutlets, fish fillets, shrimp and scallops, and vegetables (such as bell peppers, mushrooms, spinach, onions, and zucchini).

There is no adequate translation of the French term "sauter," which means "to jump." The food doesn't jump, nor do you. The bottom line is that you must keep the food moving in the pan so it won't stick, scorch, or dry out. Shake the pan. Shake the food. Turn the pieces often (except for delicate fish fillets). These quick movements, in which ingredients seem to be jumping in the pan, characterize the technique of sautéing.

Kitchen Clue

Spattering grease is a potential problem when you're frying. Make sure the food to be fried is dry and that the frying pan has some depth so that grease bubbles hit the sides of the pan. If a grease spatter burns your skin, put ice on the burn immediately.

Sautéing requires only a minimal amount of fat to keep the ingredients from sticking to the pan. However, because you have to keep the heat at moderate temperatures, it is important to choose the fat carefully. Olive oil and vegetable oils are good choices. Classic sautés call for butter, which has a luxurious flavor. But butter burns if you heat it too high or for too long. Therefore, if you want to use butter, use clarified butter or mix the butter with some vegetable oil, which doesn't burn as readily. To mix the two, use equal quantities of each: If a recipe calls for 4 tablespoons of butter, use 2 tablespoons of butter and 2 tablespoons of vegetable oil.

While plain sautéed food is delicious as is, you may want to make a sauce to go with it. Before you prepare the sauce, remove the food from the pan and keep it warm (cover it or put it in the oven preheated to 140°F). For the simplest sauce, add some liquid, such as stock or wine, to the pan. The liquid deglazes the pan (loosens the bits and pieces of food that have stuck to the bottom of the pan). To give the sauce a rich, intense flavor and a delicately thickened texture, you must reduce the liquid by boiling it until it reaches about half its original volume. When the sauce is finished, simply pour it (strained if you like) over the food. (You may also rewarm the food by putting it back into the pan and coating it with the hot sauce.)

Follow these tips for successful sautéing:

➤ Bring food to room temperature before cooking, so that it browns quickly and stays juicy.

➤ Make sure the food is dry, or it won't brown properly.

➤ You may sprinkle delicate foods such as chicken, fish, and veal with flour before sautéing them, to add color or thicken the sauce.

➤ Use a pan that conducts heat well (see Chapter 4, "The Bare Essentials Part Deux: Equipment Staples").

➤ Make sure the pan is big enough to allow space between the pieces of food. If the pan is crowded, the food will steam rather than fry, and it won't be browned and crispy.

➤ If you only have a small pan, sauté the food in batches.

➤ Use uniformly sized pieces that cook evenly.

➤ Drain excess fat from the pan before you add liquid.

➤ If you sauté cut-up chicken parts, you may have to cover the pan for a short time to be sure the meat cooks through completely.

Kitchen Clue

Sautés are among the most versatile recipes. You can vary almost any dish by changing the meat (veal cutlets to chicken cutlets, e.g.), changing the liquid (stock to wine), or changing or adding embellishments (changing onions to leeks, or adding shrimp or sausage to a dish of sautéed chicken).

Stir-Frying

As the name implies, this method involves stirring as you fry, moving the food very quickly. It is similar to sautéing, except you use higher heat for a longer time; the food is cut into bite-size pieces and you "toss" rather than turn or shake it. Like sautés, you must use ingredients that cook quickly and can withstand high temperatures. The best foods to stir-fry are tender cuts of meat such as sirloin beef, boneless chicken, firm-fleshed fish and shellfish, water-rich vegetables, parboiled vegetables, or vegetables that you can steam in the pan fluids when you finish stir-frying.

A wok has rounded sides that help radiate heat quickly and evenly.

While you can use any type of skillet to stir-fry, the handiest pan is a wok. A wok is a rounded pan of Asian origin; the rounded shape helps radiate heat quickly and evenly up the sides of the pan so that the food cooks more evenly. In other words, pieces of food on the sides of the pan benefit from the heat as much as those at the bottom of the pan. Therefore, you can use even less fat than you need with a wide-bottomed skillet. An excellent alternative is a stir-fry pan or "chef's pan," which has a flat bottom and rounded sides. These pans radiate heat almost as well as a wok and are more stable.

Kitchen Clue

You can stir-fry fibrous vegetables, but they need special attention. In addition to parboiling or steaming them prior to or at the end of stir-frying, you should peel them. Broccoli is a particular stir-fry favorite. To peel broccoli stems, cut off about a half-inch of flesh at the bottom of the stalk, and then use a paring knife to peel the topmost layer of skin. Peel this skin to the place where the stem meets the florets. Peeled stems are delightfully tender. You can save the peel to make vegetable stock.

Because you stir-fry at high heat, you must use a cooking fat with a high smoke point—that is, one that will not burn and become smoky at high temperatures. Butter is unsuitable. Olive oil works well only when you will stir-fry an ingredient such as spinach that cooks exceptionally quickly. The best choices are bland-flavored vegetable oils such as peanut, soybean, corn, canola, safflower, and sunflower.

As with sautés, stir-fries sometimes include both meats and vegetables. You usually cook the meats first so that the vegetables don't soften too much while you wait for the meat to finish cooking.

Follow these tips for successful stir-frying:

➤ Get out all your ingredients and tools before you cook, including any thickening mixtures such as cornstarch and water.

➤ Organize the ingredients into separate containers so that you can easily and quickly add them to the pan.

➤ Be sure to cut the ingredients into same-sized pieces so that they cook evenly.

➤ Preheat the wok or other pan. It should be very hot before you add any ingredient.

➤ Add a minimal amount of oil to the pan. If you use a wok, swirl the pan to coat the sides with a film of oil.

➤ For better flavor, always stir-fry seasoning ingredients such as garlic and ginger before you add other ingredients.

Deep-Fat Frying

Deep-fat frying is less popular than it used to be because most people now try to avoid excess fat. Amazingly, however, when some deep-fat-fried foods are properly cooked, they contain less fat than foods prepared using other methods. French-fried potatoes, for example, are less fatty than a baked potato that has been topped with butter and sour cream.

There are two different ways to deep-fat fry food, and both involve cooking food in hot fat over moderately high heat until it is cooked through and the inside is juicy while the surface is crunchy and golden brown. In some cases, the food is cooked in about an inch of fat, so you can use a regular, straight-sided sauté pan. In this case, you must turn the food so that it cooks evenly on both sides.

Sometimes, however, the food is cooked by completely immersing it in the fat; in this case, you need a deeper pan or specially designed deep-fryer, and no turning is necessary. Most foods that are suitable for deep-fat frying can be cooked by either method.

Deep-fat-fried foods must be protected from the fat's intense heat. One way to protect the food is by coating it. The most delicate, quick-to-cook foods, such as flat-fish fillets and thinly sliced vegetables, need only a light coating of flour or bread crumbs. Thicker pieces, such as boneless chicken breasts, do better when you coat them with batter or with beaten egg or egg white plus flour or bread crumbs. Soft-centered foods, such as croquettes, need additional protection: Coat them with flour first, then beaten egg, and then bread or cracker crumbs. Starchy foods such as potatoes and doughnuts need no coating.

Another way to protect fried foods is to "double-fry" them. To double-fry, fry the food for a short time to brown the surface, and then remove it from the fat for a minute or so to cool down the outside and let the heat penetrate the inside. When the food has cooled slightly, return it to the fat to finish cooking. This is the ideal way to fry chicken parts and French-fried potatoes.

Kitchen Clue

Grease-free frying has nothing to do with which brand or type of shortening or vegetable oil you use. It has to do with the temperature of the fat. Frying fat must be hot enough to seal the food's surface quickly so the fat will not be absorbed during cooking. Keep the fat at the proper temperature throughout the cooking process, and you will have grease-free, crunchy food.

The temperature at which you deep-fat fry food depends on what you are cooking. The larger the food, the lower the temperature (so the outside won't burn before the inside is fully cooked). For deep-frying, you can use a special thermometer that tells you the temperature of the fat; an electric deep-fryer has a built-in thermostat. Otherwise you can use the bread-cube test. Drop a small piece of bread into hot fat. If it sizzles slowly and bubbles form gently around the edge, the fat is about 350°F. If it bubbles briskly and the bread browns quickly, the fat is about 365–375°F. If the fat is above 375°F, you will see a haze begin to form on the surface of the fat; above 400°F, the fat will start to smoke. Obviously, it is important to choose a fat with a high smoke point. Butter, margarine, and olive oil don't qualify. Use vegetable shortening or peanut, soybean, corn, canola, safflower, or sunflower oils.

Follow these tips for successful deep-fat frying:

➤ Cut foods into uniform pieces so that they cook evenly.

➤ Do not fry extremely large pieces such as a half chicken.

➤ Do not add too many pieces of food to the fat at one time or you'll lower the temperature too much.

➤ Fry food in batches and let the fat return to its proper temperature (from 350°F to 385°F, depending on the ingredient) between batches.

➤ Never add wet ingredients to hot fat.

➤ Coatings stick to fried foods better if you coat the foods 15–20 minutes prior to frying time.

➤ You can reuse frying fats about three times. Strain the fat and store it in the refrigerator in a covered container. Do not add used fat back to the original container of uncooked fat. Before you use the fat again, add about ⅓ of its volume of fresh fat.

➤ Remove fried foods with a skimmer, slotted spoon, basket, or tongs. Drain the food on paper toweling.

Use tongs to remove fried foods from cooking fat.

Roasting and Baking

Roasting and baking are almost exactly the same: You cook the food in an enclosed oven with dry currents of hot air. There is no apparent reason why one is called baking and the other is called roasting. The distinction seems to be that you roast meat and poultry. But what about baked ham? It really makes no difference.

Roasting

Roasting usually involves cooking large pieces of meat, which means you must cook the food in a large pan. However, the pan's sides must be low enough to allow air to circulate freely around the food. It is best to put a roast in the pan fat-side up so that as the fat renders in the heat, it bastes the meat. You may also want to use a rack that raises the roast out of the rendered fat so that the roast won't burn or become soggy. If you are roasting foods that are exceptionally lean, you can bard them (cover them with a thin layer of fat such as bacon) or baste them frequently to keep them moist.

Just because a meat is labeled a roast doesn't mean you should roast it. Only tender cuts of meat such as rib or top round can withstand dry heat. Chuck "roast," shoulder "roast," and other fibrous "roasts" cut from the more exercised parts of the animal need moist heat cooking methods to soften them. All poultry except older stewing hens are suitable for roasting. You also may roast cut-up chunky vegetables.

The best way to roast meat is to cook it first at a high temperature for a brief time, and then cook it to completion at moderate temperatures. This helps give the surface a deep, rich color and keeps juicy fluids inside.

Follow these tips for successful roasting:

➤ Make sure you preheat the oven.

➤ Make sure the pan is slightly larger than the roast. If it is too small, rendered fat will drip onto the oven. If it is too large, rendered fat will burn in the pan and the roast won't cook evenly.

➤ Never cover a roast with a foil "tent." This steams the meat.

➤ Use a meat thermometer to be sure of proper temperature. The thermometer goes into the thickest part of the meat (or the thigh or breast of poultry), but do not let it touch a bone. If it does, the thermometer will give a false reading.

➤ Remove a roast when the temperature is 5 to 10 degrees below the desired temperature. Roasted foods continue to cook even after being removed from the heat.

➤ Let a roast stand for 15 minutes before you carve it. This lets the meat reabsorb fluids and remain moist and juicy.

To carve a boneless roast, place it on a meat board and hold the meat with a large fork. Slice down for a small roast; stand a large roast on its end and slice across.

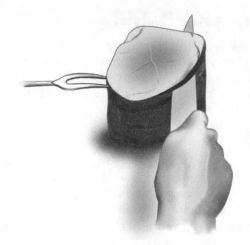

Baking

You bake foods such as cakes, pies, cookies, and other pastries, as well as soufflés, casseroles, small portions of meat, and fish. These foods generally are smaller than roasted foods, so you bake them in smaller pans, such as casserole dishes, muffin or pie pans, or on baking sheets. As in roasting, however, the air must be able to circulate freely in order for food to cook evenly, so you should not crowd the oven with too many pans. If you have to use two oven racks, try to alternate the pans: one to the left, one to the right.

Follow these tips for successful baking:

➤ Make sure you preheat the oven. This is especially important for cakes, pies, pastries, and cookies.

➤ Bake cakes on the center rack, except for angel food cakes, which go on the lower rack.

➤ Don't open the oven door during baking unless basting is necessary.

➤ Keep your oven clean so that foods will cook more evenly.

Stewing and Braising

Stewing and braising are methods for cooking sinewy, fibrous cuts of meat such as chuck, shoulder, bottom round, rump, brisket, and shank; older poultry such as stewing hens; and hardy vegetables such as celery and endive. Both methods use moist heat to cook foods slowly; that is, the ingredients cook in a covered pan over low heat for a long period of time. Tough foods become incredibly tender with these methods; meat sinews melt into rich, glossy gravy, even if you are using a so-called "inferior" cut. In fact, most people like stewed and braised foods because of their satiny sauces.

There are some technical differences between a dish that's stewed and one that's braised. Textbook definitions say that braised foods are large and that you brown them before adding liquid. Braised foods usually call for a minimum amount of liquid (about ½ inch of fluid), and they often contain a *mirepoix*, or mixture of diced vegetables. A stew usually has smaller pieces of food that may or may not be browned first, and calls for a large quantity of liquid (enough to cover the food).

But you may see recipes for braised foods that call for a lot of liquid. Likewise, some stew recipes tell you to brown the meat first. The point is that you cook these foods more or less the same way. Sometimes these methods are called "pot roasting," which isn't roasting at all, and sometimes foods cooked by these methods are called "fricassees."

The best type of pan for stewing or braising is a braising pan, a heat-proof casserole dish, or a Dutch oven.

Stews and braises are the ideal dishes to cook ahead. Their flavors mature as they stand, so they are even better a day or so after you cook them. In addition, when you chill a stew or braised dish, pan fat rises to the top and you can scoop it out easily. You also can freeze stewed and braised foods for future use.

Follow these tips for successful braising and stewing:

➤ Dry the food before you stew or braise it.

➤ If you brown the meat, cook it in batches so that the pan has enough room for the food to brown properly; otherwise, the meat will "steam" and look unpleasantly gray.

➤ If you brown the food, you may cook it in its own fat or add a film of vegetable oil to prevent sticking. Drain excess fat before you add other ingredients.

➤ You may cook a stew or braised dish on a stovetop at low to moderate heat or in the oven at 325–350°F.

➤ Do not let the stewing or braising liquid come to a hard boil. Keep it at a simmer or the food will be tough and rubbery.

➤ Stew and braise food for a long time; that's what it takes for it to become tender.

Boiling, Simmering, and Poaching

Boiling, simmering, and poaching are similar processes: All involve cooking foods by immersing them in hot liquids. To boil is to cook food in water at a temperature of 212°F, when water bubbles rise rapidly to the surface of the liquid. Foods are rarely boiled; even hard-boiled eggs (properly called hard-cooked eggs) aren't really boiled. That's because most foods fall apart if you cook them in rapidly boiling water. The only foods you actually boil are pasta products and vegetables, such as sugar snap peas, that cook quickly. Cooking these vegetables rapidly in boiling water preserves their nutrients and sets their color.

To simmer food is to cook it at temperatures just below a boil. The bubbles form around the edges of the pan and rise slowly to the surface. Most so-called boiled foods (potatoes, eggs, and meat) should be cooked at a simmer. You may or may not cover the pan, depending on the ingredient being cooked.

Poaching is more of an art form than boiling or simmering, but it follows the same principles. When you poach food, you must keep the liquid just below a simmer, so the food cooks more slowly.

Poaching is ideal for delicate fruits and also for fibrous fruits and vegetables that take a long time to cook. You also can poach fish (it is an especially good method for firm-fleshed fish such as salmon and halibut) and shellfish, eggs, meat (such as corned beef and short ribs), chicken breasts, and small whole chickens.

There are two poaching methods. The first is to immerse the food in the near-simmering liquid. This is the best way to poach small foods such as fruits and eggs. You also can poach food by covering the ingredient with cold liquid and bringing the liquid to a near-simmer. This is the best way to poach larger foods such as whole fish and chickens.

You can use any deep pan for boiling, simmering, or poaching. Although there are specialized pans for poaching fish, you can create your own fish poacher using a roasting pan. Many foods are poached in water, but you also may use wine, stock, or *court bouillon*. You may keep the liquid plain or season it with herbs, spices, and vegetables (such as onion and celery tops) for meats and fish, or with orange peel, lemon slices, or vanilla beans for fruits. The poached food absorbs flavor during the slow-cooking process.

Follow these tips for successful poaching:

➤ Don't let the liquid come to a boil or the food will toughen or disintegrate.

➤ Let poached fruit cool in its cooking liquid.

What Is It?

Court bouillon is a blend of water, wine or vinegar, and seasonings. You can use a court bouillon to poach fish and shellfish.

Steaming

Steaming involves cooking food with moist, hot steam. Ingredients are placed in a steamer above simmering liquid; as the steam rises, the moist heat envelops and cooks the food. This method has become extremely popular because it is quick and easy, uses little or no fat, and preserves nutrients. It is an ideal method for cooking fish, chicken, shellfish, and vegetables. Steamed foods have a lovely, delicate flavor and a moist, succulent, and tender texture.

Several utensils are appropriate for steaming. You can place a ready-made stovetop steamer inside a saucepan (these come in many sizes, shapes, metals, and prices), concoct a steamer by setting a colander or strainer above the water in a saucepan, or set Chinese tiered bamboo steamers in a wok. Of recent vintage are electric steamers that make the process of steaming a cinch.

Most often, steamed foods are cooked over water. However, for added flavor, consider using stock, wine, or juice in whole or in part, or add herbs, spices, and vegetables to the water. If you use an electric steamer, be sure to follow the manufacturer's instructions regarding steaming fluids.

Follow these tips for successful steaming:

➤ Don't crowd the steamer. Steam must be able to circulate freely around the food.

➤ Don't let the liquid touch the food.

Keep boiling water nearby when you steam. If you have to replenish your steamer with water, you must use boiling water.

Warnings

Be extremely careful when you use an electric steamer; these handy appliances build up a lot of steam. Lift the cover quickly and keep your hands and face as far away as possible to prevent the steam from scalding your skin.

Grilling and Broiling

Grilling and broiling are substantially the same and refer to food that's cooked one side at a time over (or under) high, intense dry heat. You control the cooking not simply by adjusting the temperature but by raising or lowering the cooking rack from the heat source. When foods are grilled or broiled, the high heat sears and browns the surface and keeps the natural juices in the food. Grill larger pieces of food about 6 inches from the heat; grill thinner foods about 4 inches from the heat. An oven broiler is not as hot as an outdoor grill, so it's better to broil foods about 3–4 inches from the heat.

Only tender meats that can withstand high, intense heat and quick cooking should be grilled. Even so, never grill a piece of meat more than 2 inches thick or the surface will be charred before the inside is cooked. Best bets for grilling or broiling are beef steaks, veal, pork and lamb chops, cutlets, broiler-fryer chickens, and shellfish such as lobster or soft-shelled crabs. You also can grill or broil water-rich or tender vegetables such as onions, eggplant, zucchini, leeks, and bell peppers. Grilling time depends on the type and thickness of the food.

Foods cooked on an outdoor grill have a smokier flavor than those prepared in an oven or other indoor broiler. Outdoor grills may use gas or natural charcoal or charcoal briquettes. Most gas grills also come with stones that resemble briquettes. Gas grills don't require much heating time; charcoal must be hot enough to turn to white ash before you can cook above it, and that takes some time. When you grill large, longer-to-cook foods on an outdoor grill, you may speed the grilling process by closing the lid. This traps heat and "roasts" and grills the food simultaneously, allowing it to cook more quickly. It also imparts a woodsy taste. You can enhance the flavor of grilled food by adding flavor chips (such as hickory or mesquite) to the charcoal. Soak the chips in water for about 30 minutes before you add them to the fire.

Follow these tips for successful grilling and broiling:

➤ Brush grill grids or broiler racks with vegetable oil to prevent sticking.

➤ Preheat the broiler; let the coals on an outdoor grill turn to white ash before you cook.

➤ Remove any excess fat to prevent fire flare-ups.

➤ Use tongs to turn the food so that natural juices won't escape.

➤ When you broil in an electric oven, you may want to place some foods on a rack in a pan to keep fat from dripping down and burning in the oven (this is ideal for meat and chicken but not necessary for vegetables, chicken breasts, or fish fillets). Leave the oven door slightly ajar.

➤ For additional grill flavor, you can add flavor chips, such as mesquite or hickory chips, to the coals.

Fein on Food

Archaeologists have found evidence that prehistoric people cooked their food on a grid over a fire. Europeans lost touch with grilling, but native Americans didn't. Columbus brought news of Carib Indians cooking food on a *barbacoa* (later Anglicized to "barbecue"). The cult of grilled cuisine has been growing ever since, particularly after WWII, when the GI Bill enabled folks to move to the suburbs, and build patios perfect for barbecues.

Microwaving

Judging by the number of microwave ovens sold each year, microwave cooking has millions of advocates in America. It is a clean, fast cooking method that keeps a kitchen cool and is remarkably convenient.

Microwaving is a good method for cooking plain vegetables because the vegetables retain nutrients and keep their crunchiness and color. It also is useful for cooking fish and chicken breasts, both of which stay remarkably tender and juicy. Melting chocolate in a microwave oven is a cinch, and there is much less of a chance than with other methods that the chocolate will scorch. Microwave ovens are handiest for thawing frozen food and reheating foods such as casseroles.

However, microwave cooking will never produce foods with a crispy crust or richly browned surface, and so it has limited usefulness. Don't expect microwaved foods to taste or look like roasted, grilled, or sautéed dishes. Many people are disappointed when they try to use a favorite old recipe and adapt it to microwave cooking. Microwave-cooked foods have a distinct texture that is unlike that of foods cooked by conventional means.

If you use a microwave oven, understand that cooking times vary significantly, depending on the oven. Wattage varies. Some ovens have carousels to rotate the food; others do not. Some are small; some are large. Your best bet is to pay attention to the manufacturer's instructions regarding cooking times until you get used to your oven.

Not all foods cook faster in a microwave oven. Dried grains and rice, for example, which require cooking in large quantities of water, take as long to cook this way as they do on the stovetop.

Follow these tips for successful microwaving:

➤ Always use microwave-safe dishes, usually made of porcelain, certain types of plastic, glass, ceramic, or paper. Never use metal plates, trays, utensils, or aluminum foil in a microwave oven.

➤ Never put food directly on the oven floor; always use a dish or paper towel.

➤ Never turn on the microwave oven unless it contains food.

➤ To ensure even distribution of heat and avoid overcooking in spots, rotate and/or stir foods two or three times—especially if the microwave oven has no carousel.

➤ Place foods with their thickest parts out, facing the oven walls.

➤ Use a pot holder to remove foods. Dishes can be very hot.

➤ Remember that microwave ovens with higher wattage cook foods faster.

➤ Increase cooking time as you increase the amount of food you microwave.

➤ Remove microwaved foods when they are slightly underdone. They continue to cook for a few moments after you remove them from the oven.

➤ If you cover foods to be microwaved with plastic wrap, pierce the wrap with a few holes to allow steam to escape.

➤ Pierce water-rich foods such as potatoes and hot dogs with the tip of a sharp knife or the tines of a fork so that the food won't burst from a build-up of steam.

➤ Do not microwave whole eggs, foods to be deep-fried or reheated after being deep-fried, large turkeys, whole grains, or uncooked rice.

The Least You Need to Know

➤ Successful frying depends on careful control of the heat. Keep the cooking fat hot and foods won't be greasy.

➤ Cut stir-fried foods into like-size pieces so that they cook evenly. Prepare and organize all stir-fry foods and tools before you begin to cook.

➤ Always preheat the oven before you put in a roast or food to be baked; pre-heat the broiler or grill for broiled or grilled foods.

➤ Don't let braised or stewed foods boil, or they will be tough and rubbery. These foods depend on long, slow cooking for tenderness and flavor.

➤ Don't boil eggs in their shells; cook them at a simmer, just below the boiling point.

➤ If you put too much food in a steamer, the steam won't circulate around the ingredients properly.

➤ Always use microwave-safe dishes in a microwave oven; never use metal plates, trays, utensils, or aluminum foil.

Part 5

Now You're Cooking

Can you believe it? You're finally ready to cook! The next few chapters will help you prepare your first dinner. When you serve the food, you'll want all the parts (the entrée and side dishes) to be ready at the same time, so I'll make some suggestions on how to accomplish this feat. I'll also offer advice on when to do everything else (like set the table). If you make a mistake, I'll show you how to correct it, if it's possible.

After you've cooked a few dinners, you might be ready to take the plunge and invite company over so that you can show off your culinary skills. One chapter in this part—complete with menus—considers three types of get-togethers, and another chapter tells you all about beverages.

Let's begin to cook for real.

Chapter 16

Timing Is Everything: Creating Your First Masterpiece

In This Chapter

➤ Making everything come out at the same time

➤ Cooking food in advance

➤ Freezing for the future

➤ Knowing when a dish is done

➤ Everything else besides the cooking

The reason you're cooking is so you can serve a meal. That means you have to consider details other than the food itself. For instance, you must get the entire meal, not just a particular dish, to "come out." This chapter deals with the details and the "whens" of cooking: timing the foods so they all come out simultaneously. It talks about which foods you can cook ahead, knowing when you should do all the other meal-related tasks (such as setting the table), knowing when foods are done, and so on. The more you master the details, the more confident you will be. The best cooks are the confident ones.

Are You Kidding Me? Reread the Recipe?

Before you start to cook, you need to read the recipe again. The first reading helped determine whether the recipe was good. The second reading enabled you to make a shopping list, figure out what equipment you need, and familiarize yourself with the procedure. Reading a third time helps you get noncooking, secondary chores out of the way. Do you have to grease a pan? Do it before you mix the ingredients. Do you have to preheat the oven? Do it *before* you begin to cook.

As you reread your recipe, you can begin to prepare the ingredients: chop the onions, bring a pot of water to boil, wash the meat. You also can take out the proper pots, pans, and utensils. If you're cooking ears of corn, you'll need tongs to lift the ears out of the water, for example. If you reread the recipe, you'll know enough to have tongs ready so you don't have to go searching for them at the last minute and maybe overcook the corn.

When you reread, you should also consider what you'll do with the food when you've finished cooking it. What will you do with the contents of the pan? (Do you need a platter? A bowl?) How will you remove the food from the pan? (With a spatula or a large spoon?) Get these details out of the way before you begin to cook.

One of the most important reasons for rereading the recipe is to help you prepare a timetable of what you have to do and when you have to do it.

Is This a Railroad Station or a Kitchen?

If you were meeting a friend at a train station and both of your trains were scheduled to arrive at 7:03, you'd be upset if either one of them was an hour late. The same holds true for recipes: When you're making several different dishes for dinner, you want them to come out at the same time. So you've got to prepare a schedule of arrival times to make sure they do.

Arrival times take everything into consideration, not just cooking time. Suppose you decide to prepare roast chicken, cooked rice, and stir-fried spinach. A roasted chicken should stand about 15 minutes after you remove it from the oven (to keep it juicy). In addition, it will take you about 5 minutes to carve the bird and put it on a platter. Therefore, if the roasting time is 2 hours, resting time is 15 minutes, and carving time is 5 minutes, the arrival time is 2 hours and 20 minutes after you begin. Because rice takes about 20 minutes to cook and needs 10 minutes of standing time, its arrival time is 30 minutes after you begin it. So you begin to cook the rice about 1 hour and 50 minutes after you put the chicken in the oven. Then factor in the time for the third recipe so that you can have all three dishes ready within minutes of each other.

Kitchen Clue

Timing is everything. Help yourself out and use a kitchen timer ... or two or three, when preparing different foods for one meal. There may be a working timer on your oven, or you might have a separate timer (some of which can be set for up to three different times). If necessary, use both timers if the two different sounds will help you remember what you're timing.

Early in your culinary adventures, you'll want to choose at least one recipe that you can prepare ahead and reheat, or serve cool or at room temperature. Whatever recipes you choose, write the timetable on paper and use it as a cooking guide.

Like train schedules, recipe arrival times aren't always precise. And even when they are, it can be nerve-racking trying to get the dishes to the table on time, present them attractively, and be sure they're hot. A few tricks of the trade can help. Preheat the serving dishes; warm dishes help keep the food warm. You can rinse them with hot water or place them for a brief time in the oven before you put the food in them. You can also pop the filled serving platters and bowls into the turned-off oven while you finish up the last item.

What You Can Cook Ahead

Instead of getting yourself into a frenzy about arrival times and schedules, consider making some foods ahead of time. You can completely cook many dishes in advance (moisture-laden casseroles or chili con carne, for example). Soups, stews, pot roasts, and braised foods taste even better when they're reheated, so these are ideal to prepare ahead. Likewise, you can partially prepare some foods ahead of time, up to the point at which you would place them in an oven (macaroni and cheese, for example).

You can cook many deep-fried foods (such as fried chicken or fritters) ahead of time, too. Although these lose something in texture, for the sake of convenience you can make them ahead and re-heat them by placing them on a rack on a cookie sheet and putting them in a preheated 400°F oven.

Warnings

Certain foods are breeding grounds for bacteria and should never be cooked partially. Chicken, turkey, and other poultry fall into this category. Don't *ever* partially cook poultry.

What You Can't Cook Ahead

There are some foods that you simply can't cook ahead of time. These include dishes in which texture is critical. For example, many steamed and stir-fried vegetables are supposed to be crunchy. If you make them ahead of time they become soggy. Canapés on little rounds of bread are supposed to be firm. If you make them more than 2 hours ahead of time, the bread will be too damp or, on the other hand, it may dry out (depending on the topping). Salad greens are supposed to be crispy. If you dress the salad more than 10 minutes before you serve it, you'll have soggy salad. Foods that rise to the occasion, such as soufflés, also can't be cooked ahead. They fall fast after you take them out of the oven.

What You Can Prepare a Little Ahead

Even if you can't cook a dish ahead of time, you can prepare the separate parts that constitute the whole dish, just up to the point of actually putting it together. For example, you can wash and cut all the vegetables and seasonings for steamed and stir-fried vegetables. You can prepare the pasta and many sauces for sauced pasta dishes, rice for fried rice dishes, and so on.

While it's all right to prepare the separate parts of a dish ahead of time, you've got to use some common sense about how far ahead. For example, you can chop many sturdy vegetables (such as broccoli, cauliflower, carrots, and green beans) the day before you need them. But more delicate vegetables (such as zucchini, snow peas, and mushrooms) will lose freshness more quickly, so it is preferable to chop them the same day you'll be cooking them (early in the day is fine). Garlic also loses its zip if you chop it too early. Wait until just before you cook.

You may wash and store salad greens, provided you dry them thoroughly, a day or so ahead. Vinaigrette dressing keeps well for at least a week, with this caveat: If you use fresh herbs for your vinaigrette, add these to the dressing just before you pour it onto the salad. You can cut bread for canapés the day before you cook (keep the pieces in plastic bags), and you can prepare many toppings for canapés (flavored butters and smoked trout spread, for example) as much as two days ahead.

You surely are not going to want to carve a radish swan or swirl tomato skins into a rose at the last minute. Get your garnishes cut, carved, and cleaned early in the day.

What You Can Freeze

Some foods are fine to cook ahead and freeze. Foods ideal for freezing include tomato sauce, stew, pot roast, many soups, cooked casseroles, meat and poultry pies, quiches, crepes, cookies, fruit pies, cakes, and breads.

You can't store food in the freezer forever, of course. Tomato sauce is good for about six months, as are fruit pies and cookies. Other freezables can lose taste and texture if kept for more than three or four months. Be sure to let foods cool slightly before you wrap them for freezing. Wrap the food in plastic wrap and then freezer paper, or put it in airtight plastic containers. Don't forget to label and date each item.

With the exception of items such as breads, cakes, and cookies, it is not a good idea to defrost food (particularly meats) on the countertop because of the risk of food poisoning. Though it takes a lot of time, use your refrigerator. (Don't forget to put a plate beneath the food to catch the drippings.) Smaller items defrost within 24 hours, but a roast may take up to two days to defrost, and a large turkey may take as many as three to four days.

You can plunge large items into cold water to speed up the defrosting process; change the water occasionally and be sure the food is sealed tightly in plastic wrap. You also can defrost by microwave, but you must cook those foods as soon as you defrost them to prevent possible food poisoning.

What You Can't Freeze

Some foods don't hold up well in the freezer. Sorry, but you can forget freezing such things as cooked pasta (as opposed to pasta casseroles such as lasagna); lettuce and salad greens; cooked potatoes; foods made with cream cheese, mayonnaise, vinaigrette dressing, or gelatin; egg-based dishes; grilled foods; delicate, lightly sautéed foods; meringue; and whipped cream. If you have cake with cream cheese frosting or whipped cream on it, go ahead and freeze it, but don't expect it to be as smashing as it was when it was fresh.

Going Together

You'll find that if you prepare as much of the dish as possible beforehand, you won't be as rushed and stressed when you actually have to cook. Here's another tip: If you are preparing two recipes with the same ingredient (onions, for example), chop it at the same time. Keep all the ingredients for one recipe together, either on one large platter or in small separate bowls or plates. Cover the platter and/or bowls with plastic wrap until you are ready to use the ingredients, and then add them one by one or together as the recipe states. If you are preparing several recipes with some of the same ingredients, it's a good idea to label all the bowls. That way you'll know which bowl of onions is for which recipe.

When Do You Set the Table?

You can set the table for a company dinner early in the day or even the night before. Some people worry that dust will fall on the plates and glasses. If this is a concern for you, turn the plates and glasses over until just before your company arrives.

Take everything out: the candlestick holders and candles, bread basket, serving utensils, and platters. You'll then be sure you have everything you need. If you forgot to buy candles, you'll know early enough to do something about it. If you will be serving cocktails and hors d'oeuvres, don't forget to get out the cocktail napkins, corkscrew, and such. Before you call your guests into the dining room for dinner, fill the pitcher with ice and water.

Kitchen Clue

Cooking a meal gives you a sense of accomplishment and lots of memories. Keep a journal of your important dinners so that you can reminisce about them. Journals have other advantages, too: You know what you served so that you don't duplicate a meal for the same people, and you know which recipes you liked (or didn't) so that you can prepare them for others (or make sure you *don't* prepare them again).

How Do You Know When a Dish Is Done?

Even though a good recipe will tell you how long to cook the dish, that time is only an approximation. The approximation may even be within a time range. For example, a recipe might state, "bake the pie 45–55 minutes." Always check for doneness at the minimum time given (in this case, after 45 minutes).

There are various ways to tell when food is done after the given amount of time. You can tell some things by sight, some by taste, some by feel. For some foods, however, you must use special tools to test for doneness.

As a general rule, a cake or quick bread is done when you can see that the sides are starting to pull away from the pan. If you touch the top gently, the cake will feel spongy and bounce back a bit when you lift your finger. Alternatively, you can use a cake tester, long wooden skewer, or toothpick. Insert one of these into the center of the cake, and if it comes out clean (with no liquid batter on it), the cake is done.

Kitchen Clue

Want to save even more time? As you're preparing food, clean up as you go. That way there isn't a big mess when you finish the recipe. And take advantage of old tricks of the trade: Line a roasting pan with aluminum foil to keep the pan cleaner, or soak crusty pots overnight so you don't have to scrub.

When pasta is done, it will be tender but still somewhat resilient (remove a piece from the water and test by biting into it). Rice will be soft, and all the water in the pan will be gone. All fully cooked vegetables should be vibrantly colored: jewel-green peas, fire-colored carrots. If they're drab, you've overcooked them, so watch out next time. Thick vegetables such as broccoli, Brussels sprouts, and carrots are done when they are still firm and resilient but are tender enough for you to pierce them with the tip of a sharp knife. Vegetables such as sugar snap and snow peas should be crunchy but tender; taste one to know if the batch is done. Soft vegetables such as kale or spinach are done when they have just wilted and are soft but not mushy.

Pork and poultry are done when you prick the thickest part (the center of the roast, the poultry thigh) with the tines of a fork or the tip of a sharp knife and the juices run clear. A meat thermometer can be very helpful here. There are two types of meat thermometers: "instant-read" thermometers, which you insert into the meat briefly (about a minute) to check the temperature, and the more traditional kind that you leave in the meat throughout the cooking process. Either is fine. Insert the thermometer into the thickest part of the roast and make sure it doesn't touch a bone (or it will give a false reading). The thickest part of a turkey or roasting chicken is either the thigh (the area near where it meets the breast) or the breast. Insert the thermometer deep into the flesh at an angle (from the lower part of the thigh upward, or in the breast, from the neck toward the back).

The USDA offers guidelines as to when meat is cooked enough to be free of harmful bacteria. However, many people prefer their meat rare and juicy, at a temperature reading below the numbers listed in the guidelines. Naturally, there is always some risk in consuming protein foods that are cooked rare or medium rare, but because the risk is remote, rare and medium-rare meat is very popular. The choice is yours to make.

The following table indicates internal temperatures to which various cuts of meat and poultry should be heated to achieve proper juiciness. However, for those who prefer to follow the more conservative USDA guidelines, these are also listed. In either case, be sure to follow safe food handling basics (wash your hands and wrap, refrigerate, and defrost the meat properly) to keep pathogens away. You will learn to satisfy your own particular requirements after you have worked with a meat thermometer for a while. Remember that meat continues to cook for a short time after you take it out of the oven. That means you should remove the food 5 to 10 minutes before it reaches the temperature you want.

Temperatures for Roasted Meats and Poultry

Type of Meat	Best Temperature	USDA Suggested Temperature
Beef	120–135	145–170
Veal	140–150	160–170
Pork	155	160–170
Lamb	120–135	145–170
White meat chicken	160	170
Dark meat chicken	165	180

The following table gives approximate roasting times for meats and poultry. Bear in mind, however, that times may vary depending on variations in your oven and on the cut of meat, as well as various circumstances such as how thick it is or how cold it is when you put it in the oven.

Approximate Roasting Times for Meat and Poultry

Type of Meat	Minutes Per Pound
Roast beef, boneless	15–20
Prime rib of beef	15–20
Roast veal, boneless	25
Roast pork, boneless	20
Pork loin, bone in	20
Fresh ham, bone in	20

continues

Approximate Roasting Times for Meat and Poultry (continued)

Type of Meat	Minutes Per Pound
Leg of lamb, whole	12–20
Turkey	20
Roasting chicken	22

Fish is done when the flesh has softened and is opaque; you should be able to put a fork completely through it. A whole fish is cooked when a meat thermometer registers about 145°F. Shrimp are done when they turn pink and are firm; scallops when they become creamy-white; and clams, oysters, and mussels when the shells open. (Discard any that do not open.) Casseroles are done when their tops are golden brown or the top layer of cheese is bubbly, lightly browned, and obviously hot.

Pancakes should be turned when the batter on the top starts to bubble. The pancakes are done shortly thereafter, when the second side has browned. To be sure it's done, lift the pancake slightly with a rigid spatula to see the underside.

Pies are done when the top crust is golden brown. Most cookies are done when the edges are browned and crispy. If you make homemade whipped cream, you know it's done when it stands in soft mounds and there appears to be no liquid left in the bowl. Whipped egg whites are done when they stand in stiff peaks but still look glossy. Here's a trick to tell whether egg whites are completely whipped: Start to turn the bowl over. If the egg whites don't move as you move the bowl (they don't even fall out when you turn the bowl completely over), they are done. If they swish back and forth, you need to beat them some more.

The Least You Need to Know

➤ Plan ahead when cooking a meal (you can even write out a time chart) so that several different dishes will be ready at the same time.

➤ You can cook casseroles, stews, soups, quiches, pot roasts, filled crepes, fried foods, and braised foods ahead of time.

➤ Certain foods such as stir-fries, many cooked vegetables, dressed salad, and other foods that are intended to be crispy cannot be cooked ahead, but you can prepare the component parts in advance.

➤ Set the table, make garnishes, and do other noncooking tasks early in the day or the day before a company dinner.

So You've Made a Mistake?

During the days when Louis XIV ruled France and gastronomy was considered one of the highest art forms, a chef named Vatel committed suicide because the fish he ordered for dinner didn't arrive on time. If a culinary calamity occurs while you're cooking, of course you are not going to kill yourself, but you may want to kick yourself!

Even the best cooks make mistakes. The heat may have been too high. The phone rang and distracted you. You forgot a step. Forgive yourself. Many mistakes can be remedied. This chapter discusses mistakes that you can correct and those you cannot correct. It also deals with the most common mistakes people make in cooking, and tells you how to avoid making them.

Mistakes with Different Types of Foods

Some cooking mistakes are total disasters: You have to throw out the dish or the ingredient. But not every disaster is total. The following sections outline some of the more common mistakes people make and tell whether or not you can salvage the food—and if so, how.

Mistakes with Fruits and Vegetables

If you see vegetables beginning to discolor because you cooked them too long, remove the pan from the heat immediately, place the pan in ice-cold water, and quickly scatter a pinch of baking soda into the cooking water. If the vegetables are already overcooked and dull-looking, purée them (add some butter and seasonings), and serve them as is or use the purée to create soup or to thicken gravy or soup. If a baked potato has burst, salvage the parts that haven't scattered over the oven and make them into mashed potatoes.

If peeled fruit has begun to turn brown, use a vegetable peeler to cut off a film of flesh, then rub the fruit with the cut side of a lemon or put it in acidulated water (water with a small amount of lemon juice—see Chapter 14, "A Compendium of Catchwords Used in Recipes") to prevent further browning. Browned fruit is fine as-is for pies, cobblers, and the like; fruit darkens as it bakes anyway—especially when coupled with richly colored spices such as cinnamon.

Kitchen Clue

You can prevent guacamole from discoloring by storing it with the avocado pit stuck in the center until serving time.

Mistakes with Meat, Poultry, and Fish

Pot-roasted, stewed, and braised meat can be tough for several reasons, but it's often because you haven't cooked the meat long enough or over low enough heat. Give the meat more time. If possible, add an acidic ingredient such as tomatoes or wine to help tenderize the meat. If you don't have a lot more time, slice the meat exceptionally thin and let it sit in the pan juices for 10 to 15 minutes.

If a roast beef, chicken, or turkey is not browning well, your roasting pan is probably too deep. Put the roast in a shallower pan. If you overcook meat, you can no longer serve it rare, but you don't have to throw it out, either. If you don't like to eat well-done meat, make hash, chili, pot pie, or some other type of casserole dish. If the meat is not cooked well enough, give it more time. If dinner guests are waiting, you may need to cut the meat into serving portions and put the portions back in to cook. Fish that's dried out and overcooked can still be okay if you make a rich sauce to cloak it with or if you mash the fish for fish cakes.

Mistakes with Dairy Products

If you have heated butter too long or over too high a heat, it will turn brown. Although you can't use over-browned butter in recipes that call for delicate butter sauces, some of the best-tasting recipes have been created out of over-browned butter (plain old scrambled eggs, for example). If the recipe is for a dish that can stand a creative touch (soup, for example), use the browned butter.

If you cook cheese and it becomes rubbery, your heat was probably too high; try cutting the mass into chunks and processing the pieces in a food processor or blender for 10 to 15 seconds before trying to use it in the recipe.

If you have over-whipped whipping cream, don't throw out the ingredients. Keep whipping the cream until the solids and liquids separate completely. Discard the liquid and knead the solid matter to extract as much liquid as you can. The result is sweet butter.

Mistakes with Soup

If a soup tastes too salty, you have several options for remedying it. If there is time, add more liquid and let the soup cook more. If you have no time or the soup cannot stand to be thinned, add sugar or brown sugar, beginning with ¼ tsp. and adding more until the soup tastes as you want it. Although the sugar will not eliminate the salt, it will cover the salty taste. Or, you could add a peeled, sliced, raw potato and let the soup cook 10 minutes. (The potato will absorb some of the salt.) Remove the potato and discard it before serving the soup. Always add the minimum amount of salt to soup as you cook it, and taste for seasoning after the soup has cooked awhile.

If soup is too thin, cook it longer so that it reduces. Alternatively, add a *liaison*, such as beurre manié or cornstarch and water mixed to a smooth paste, or add raw rice or pasta and simmer the soup, covered, until the rice or pasta is fully cooked. If you don't have time for these options, you could stir in leftover pureed vegetables, mashed potatoes, or cooked rice.

> **What Is It?**
>
> A **liaison** is any kind of mixture that you use to thicken a sauce, soup, or stew. Beurre manié, for example, is a particular type of liaison made from equal parts of butter and flour, which are stirred until the mixture is smooth.

If you made stock and it looks cloudy, add crumbled egg shells or a couple of lightly beaten egg whites, let the stock simmer 2 to 3 minutes, and then lift out the shells or poached egg whites and strain the stock.

Mistakes with Bread, Dough, Pasta, and Pastry Products

Yeast dough doesn't rise for several reasons. Most often it is because the yeast is too old. You need to proof yeast (see Chapter 13, "A Compendium of the Top 100+ Cooking Terms") before you use it for baked goods. Sometimes the dough doesn't rise because the place you have set it to rest is not warm enough. The best place to let yeast dough rise is in a warm oven. To warm the oven before you put yeast dough in to rise, turn the oven to 450°F for 2 minutes; then turn off the oven. Don't open the door while the dough is rising. Another way to make the oven warm is to put a pan of very hot water beneath the bowl of dough.

If a cake doesn't rise, the baking powder you used might be too old. Throw the cake out. However, if the cake rises but then falls, you may be able to salvage it. Cut it into small pieces, cover it with ice cream, whipped cream, and/or fudge sauce, and call it pudding. Although you should never open the oven door while a cake is baking, you can peek through the oven window. If you do so and notice that a cake is rising lopsided in the pan, gently open the oven door and turn the pan halfway around for the remainder of the baking time.

Over-baked cookies can be turned into tasty crumbs for pie crusts. Let them cool, then crumble and process them in a food processor or blender or crush them under a rolling pin.

If cream puffs come out limp, there is too much moisture inside them. Slit a cap off the puff and scoop the soggy insides. Return the puff with its cap to the oven to re-heat for a minute or so at 400°F.

If your pasta sticks to itself, plunge it into near-boiling water for a few seconds and gently separate it with a spaghetti fork, chopsticks, or a wooden spoon. Or set it in a colander and let very hot water run over the pasta as you separate it.

Mistakes with Chocolate

One of the most common cooking mistakes is letting chocolate stiffen to a dull-looking, hard-as-a-rock mass. The main reason chocolate *seizes* is that water or steam droplets fall on it as it cooks. Here's what to do if your chocolate seizes: For each ounce of chocolate, add 1 teaspoon shortening—*not* butter—to the pan and slowly melt the chocolate again over low heat.

To prevent chocolate from seizing the next time, here are some tips for how to melt chocolate:

What Is It?

When you're melting chocolate and it **seizes,** it stiffens into a hard, dull-looking mess—the opposite of melted.

➤ Chop the chocolate into small pieces so that it melts faster.

➤ Melt the chocolate in the top part of a double boiler. Be sure that the top pan fits snugly into the bottom one so steam cannot escape from the lower pan. (If you use a makeshift double boiler, be sure the bowl fits snugly in the lower pan.)

➤ Heat the water in the bottom pan over low heat, but do not let the water boil. The water in the lower pan should be at a near-simmer, about 200°F.

➤ If you prefer, you can melt chocolate in the microwave oven. Follow the manufacturer's instructions.

➤ If you burn chocolate, throw it out. It will have a burnt flavor.

Mistakes with Rice

If rice is undercooked, sprinkle 2 to 3 tablespoons of water over it, cover the pan, and continue to cook it for another few minutes. If rice is overcooked, some of it will stick to the bottom of the pan. You can use the unstuck portions the way you planned, but you will have less of it. Lift out the crusty part at the bottom with a rigid spatula and deep-fry it in hot oil for 2 to 3 minutes or until it is crispy. Serve the crisped rice as a bed for stir-fried vegetables.

If rice is burned at the bottom, the taste often permeates the entire pot of rice. Taste the unburnt portions. If they taste burnt, try adding a chunk of rye bread to the pan, covering it, and letting the rice stand for 5 minutes. Taste the rice again. If it still tastes burnt, you'll have to throw it out. (Sorry.)

Mistakes with Gravy

If you have a knack for making lumpy gravy, here's what to do: Beat the lumpy gravy with a whisk or hand mixer with a vigor that shows you're angry at it. That should straighten out the gravy. Otherwise, put the gravy in a blender or food processor and process it until it is smooth. You also could strain the gravy through a fine sieve.

If your gravy is too salty, slice a potato into it and let it cook 8 to 10 minutes. If the gravy is too thin, let it cook longer, or bind it with one of the following mixtures (per cup of gravy) and cook and stir the gravy another minute or so:

➤ 1 teaspoon cornstarch dissolved in 1 tablespoon water

➤ 1 tablespoon flour dissolved in 2 tablespoon water

➤ 1 tablespoon beurre manié

Mistakes with Meringues

Meringues can weep (become watery), bead (display amber-colored droplets), or be too soft or sticky. Failed meringue often happens in humid weather because sugar absorbs moisture from the air. It also can happen because you didn't dissolve the sugar properly. When you make a meringue, add the sugar gradually so that the egg whites can dissolve the granules properly. When a meringue weeps, beads, or becomes soft, you can't do anything about it. It still tastes okay; it just doesn't have the best texture.

Mistakes with Egg Whites

The most common mistake with egg whites is overbeating. (For instructions on how to beat egg whites properly, see **beat** in Chapter 13.) If you do overbeat egg whites (they are no longer glossy and the fluff looks dry and brittle), add one more raw egg white and beat it in.

When Something Burns

You can save some burned foods, but, as with chocolate, you sometimes have to throw them out. The question to ask yourself is "How does it taste?" For example, if you burn a cake layer, you may be able to slice off the burnt part. Taste a crumb from the unburnt part, and if it tastes okay, use the cake. To make the cake taste even better, heat ¾ cup water with 1 tablespoon brandy for 2 to 3 minutes, and then brush this mixture on the bottom cake layer.

Burnt vegetables usually are gone for good. If you catch the vegetables just before they burn, however, you can try to correct the error by plunging the bottom of the pan quickly into some very cold water. You also can try cutting away the burnt parts, putting the rest over very low heat in a new pan, and covering the pan with a damp kitchen towel for a few minutes; the towel may absorb some of the burnt odor.

When Something Curdles

Foods curdle for several reasons, such as when you cook products that contain eggs at too high a temperature or when you mix an acidic ingredient with milk or cream. To prevent foods that contain eggs from curdling, cook them over low heat or in the top part of a double boiler set over near-simmering (*not* boiling) water. Before you add eggs or egg yolks to a hot sauce, temper them—that is, gradually add about a half-cup of the hot sauce to the eggs before you add the eggs to the sauce. Stir the ingredients in the pan constantly so that all portions of the food reach the heat. If possible, add a small amount of flour to the recipe; recipes containing flour will not curdle.

If you're too late and the mixture has already curdled, try one of these remedies:

➤ Remove the pan from the heat and plunge the bottom into ice water. Obviously, when you cook a sauce that could curdle, it helps to keep a large bowl of ice water on the side, just in case.

➤ Beat the sauce vigorously with a whisk or hand mixer. If that doesn't work, add an ice cube to the sauce and beat it in.

➤ Add 1 tablespoon of sauce to 1 tablespoon cream or milk and mix until creamy. Then gradually add more curdled sauce and beat it into the creamed mixture until all the curdled sauce has been incorporated.

➤ Make a new sauce and gradually whisk or beat in the curdled sauce 1 tablespoon at a time.

In cases where you must mix an acidic ingredient (such as lemon juice or wine) with milk or cream, be sure to cook the ingredients over low heat, add the second ingredient gradually, and whisk or beat the ingredients vigorously.

Miscellaneous Mistakes

There are oodles of other cooking mistakes. Here are some tips to avoid common errors:

➤ If you are making a recipe that contains gelatin (mixed with water) and the mixture becomes too firm, set the mixture over a bowl of very hot water. It will soften.

➤ If your cheesecake cracks, sift some confectioner's sugar on top of the cooled cake.

➤ If the brandy for a flambéed dish won't ignite, warm it separately in a pan. If you've already added the brandy to the other ingredients, raise the heat of the pan in which the mixture is cooking.

The Least You Need to Know

➤ To reduce the salty taste in oversalted dishes, add a small amount of sugar to cover the taste or a sliced raw potato to absorb some of the salt.

➤ Burnt chocolate must be discarded. Many burnt foods also cannot be saved. Taste the food first, and if the entire dish tastes burnt, throw it away.

➤ To salvage "seized" chocolate, melt each ounce of it with 1 teaspoon of shortening.

➤ Always temper eggs before adding them to a sauce by first mixing a small amount of the hot sauce into the eggs.

Chapter 18

So You Thought You Were Done? What About Beverages?

You already know that preparing a meal means more than making the food. You'll probably be serving a beverage, too. Not everyone drinks a cocktail before dinner, wine or beer with dinner, or coffee or tea after dinner. If you wish to serve these, however, this chapter tells you how.

Serving Cocktails

Cocktails are not the popular predinner drinks they once were. These days many people pass up the old-fashioned, heavy, sweet, mixed alcoholic beverages in favor of wine or bottled water before a company dinner, or nothing at all before an everyday dinner. Still, many people enjoy a predinner cocktail. Certain classics, such as martinis, margaritas, and bloody Marys, continue to be favorites. Other people prefer a straight alcoholic beverage such as Scotch or bourbon "on the rocks" or mixed with "soda" (club soda) or ginger ale. If you plan a cocktail time, consider these pointers:

➤ Serve cocktails with a nibble of food that will moderate the effects of the alcohol. Predinner food and drink should stimulate, not satisfy, the appetite, so the rule is to serve a little of each.

➤ Have an ice bucket filled with ice and tongs handy for serving the ice.

➤ Use different size glasses depending on the drinks: short glasses for drinks "on the rocks" and taller or stemmed glasses for mixed drinks.

➤ Be sure to have ginger ale, tonic water, club soda or seltzer, and orange or tomato juices on hand for mixed drinks. You also want to have sliced lemon or lime and olives or cocktail onions as garnishes.

➤ Chill the beverage glasses if you have room in your fridge.

How to Choose and Serve Wine

There's an old adage that says, "The more you learn, the less you know." On one hand, people today are more knowledgeable than ever about wine. On the other hand, they are more intimidated about choosing wine because they may know a little something, but not enough. Some experts will advise you to stick to the classic rule: White wine with fish and chicken, red wine with meat and cheese. Others tell you not to pay any attention to those rules. It can seem very confusing. The following sections give you some guidelines for selecting and serving wine with dinner.

White Wine with Fish, Red Wine with Meat, and All That

While the rules regarding which wines to serve with foods may have relaxed, beginners will still feel more comfortable starting with classic combinations. In general, you serve *dry* white wine with fish, chicken, and veal, and red wine with beef, pork, lamb, and rich poultry such as duck. Rosé wine goes with fish and chicken also, as well as with cold summer foods and baked ham. Sweet white wines are suitable for dessert.

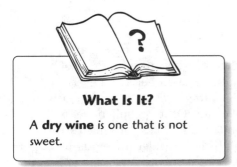

What Is It?

A **dry wine** is one that is not sweet.

When in doubt, you can always serve champagne. While it is a favorite aperitif, champagne is a delightful choice to continue throughout the meal.

Which White Wine? Which Red Wine?

Saying that white or red wines go with particular foods is only the first step. When you go into the wine store, you will see so many different types of wine that you soon will realize exactly how much is involved in your choice. Here's a tip: Befriend a wine merchant. He or she will not laugh at you because you don't know about wine. A smart businessperson will teach you about wine to keep you as a happy customer. Ask questions.

It's smart to visit a wine store for advice even if you usually buy wine in a grocery store or warehouse outlet. Most wine stores carry popular brand name wines at competitive prices. They usually don't carry (or at least don't feature) expensive vintage wines, so you don't have to be intimidated going in. And it may actually be worth an extra dollar, if that turns out to be the case, to buy wine this way because of the education you'll get.

What you communicate to the wine merchant is important. It isn't enough to say you are planning to serve chicken. Describe the recipe, list the seasonings, and describe the sauce. Is the dish heavy? Light? Mild? Rich wines go with rich foods, delicate wines with delicate foods, and so on. The best rule is to speak up so your wine merchant can help you pair the proper wine with the dish. Make a note of which wine you buy and what you serve with it. That's the best way to gain experience.

If you don't want to shop in a wine and liquor store, your next best bet in getting a wine education is to take a wine-appreciation course or buy a book—many good ones are available. Look for one that explains which wines are dry, which fruity, which spicy, and so on, so you can get a better handle on which one to buy for your dinner.

Keep this easy tip in mind: If you cook with wine, serve the same wine (or at least a similar type of wine from the same area) with the dish. For example, if you prepare Coq au Vin with burgundy wine, serve a burgundy wine with it.

When Not to Serve Wine

Wine is sometimes inappropriate. Foods that are highly spiced or acidic overwhelm wine, so don't serve wine with foods such as Cajun-style blackened meats, salad, or antipasto. You usually don't serve wine with soup, either (although sherry or Madeira wines are swell with onion soup). In addition, egg dishes and wine don't couple well.

When You Serve More Than One Wine

If you wish to serve more than one wine at a meal, the general rule to follow is to serve a white wine before a red one, a dry wine before a sweet

Kitchen Clue

Don't serve red wine in the same glass as the white wine you served with a previous course. Likewise, don't serve two different whites or two different reds in the same glass.

one, a light wine before a full-bodied one, and a young wine before a more mature one. It is important to progress to heavier, more complex flavors. If you serve the heavier or more complex wine first, it may overwhelm the one to come.

What Is It?

When you **decant** wine, you pour it from its bottle into another container, such as a special wine decanter. This step hastens the breathing process and makes wine more mellow tasting.

How to Keep and Serve Wine

Once you have made your wine selection, bring the wine home and store it in a cool, dark, dry place. Lay it down horizontally so that the cork will continue to soak. After a bottle of wine is open, you can store leftovers for approximately one week. Put the cork back in the bottle or use a special vacuum-type gadget that removes the air from wine bottles and keeps the contents from spoiling.

Always serve champagne, sparkling wines, white wines, and rosé wines chilled. "Chilled" doesn't mean so ice cold that your teeth hurt; if the wine is too cold, you won't be able to taste it. Most red wines are served at room temperature. (Seasonal Beaujolais Nouveau is sometimes served slightly chilled.) Ask the wine merchant for the proper temperature of the red wine you have chosen, and ask whether the wine must be decanted before serving. If so, *decant* the wine (or at least remove the cork to let the wine breathe) some time before you serve it.

About Beer

When you're quaffing a frosty beer at the ballpark with a hot dog or a plate of nachos, it's all right to go with your favorite lager. But pairing beer and food for dinner can be a bit trickier. The meal may call for a full-bodied ale, stout, or porter, or for a specialty microbrew where nuance or depth can match the simplicity or complexity of the main dish. Several books are available to help you pair the proper beer and entree. As with wine, however, some general guidelines can help you make a wise beer selection. First, beer is a particularly good partner for heavy, robust foods such as sausages or pork. It also stands up well to spicy foods (Thai, Sichuan, and Indian cuisine, for example), to smoked dishes (such as salmon, turkey, and so on), and to foods that contain cheese (Welsh Rabbit) or vinegar (sauerbraten).

If you like beer, it is a good idea to experiment with different kinds to see what tastes you prefer with particular food. As with wine, however, you'll usually want to pair a light-bodied beer with milder food, a more robust beer with heavier and spicier dishes. Some examples: bock beer or ale with ham, pork roast, or pot roast; dry porter with smoked salmon or grilled steak; lager beer with grilled chicken or fish.

Some Info on Bottled Water

Bottled water has become extremely popular in recent years. Varieties include ...

➤ Mineral water, which has a higher mineral content than most tap water.

➤ Spring water, which comes up to the surface from underground sources.

➤ Sparkling water, which is carbonated water. It may be naturally or artificially carbonated.

➤ Seltzer and club soda, which are artificially carbonated waters.

About Coffee

These days, more people are drinking more coffee and they are more particular about its quality. It pays to know how to prepare a good brew.

Fein on Food

According to conventional wisdom, coffee was discovered centuries ago by accident in the Ethiopian village of Kaffa. A herd of goats began to dance around shortly after nibbling on some wild coffee beans. A monk who happened to be passing by witnessed the scene and munched on some of the beans himself. Then he spent time experimenting with the beans until he realized how good the stuff tasted when steeped in hot water. The first canned coffee was produced in 1878 by Chase and Sanborn.

Help! Buying Coffee Is Almost As Confusing As Buying Wine!

Sure, you can go into a supermarket and choose a can of coffee; perhaps it's the same brand you always saw around the house when you were growing up. But these days supermarkets and specialty coffee shops tempt you with fresh beans, which most coffee lovers say makes the best brew, and the fragrance can be tantalizing enough to make you rethink buying the canned stuff.

There are only two types of coffee beans: robusta and arabica. *Coffea robusta* beans are the type used for most canned coffee, although canned coffee may also include some arabica beans. *Arabica* beans are more flavorful; most specialty coffees are arabica beans. Because the best-tasting arabica beans are grown at higher elevations, some packages boast that the product is "mountain grown." Flavor differences have to do with the type of beans and also with the soil and climate where the coffee grows. Decaffeinated coffee can be made from either type of bean.

From arabica and robusta come dozens of varieties. Some familiar names are mocha, which is a light-roasted coffee; Colombian, which has a full-bodied flavor; and French roast, which comes from a dark, hearty-flavored bean. If you use specialty coffees, try several to see which kind you like.

The best way to store coffee is in a tightly covered container in the refrigerator or freezer, depending on how often you use it. Whole beans last up to four weeks in the fridge before they begin to lose flavor and up to six months in the freezer. Freshly ground or opened, canned coffee will stay fresh for up to 10 days in the fridge and 2 months in the freezer. Unopened canned coffee is fine for about a year.

There are several grinds of coffee. "Drip" is a moderately fine grind for manual and electric drip coffeemakers. You also may use "drip" for "pressed" coffee made in a French press or plunger pot. "Perk" is a coarse grind for percolator pots. "Espresso" is a very fine grind used for espresso coffee and cappuccino.

Grinding Coffee Beans

You can have fresh beans ground for you at the store, but for the best flavor and aroma, grind the beans yourself at home just before you make the coffee. Use a special machine meant for coffee beans, not your blender or food processor. Coffee oils can leave an odor on the blades.

Two types of machines are available. The smaller, canister-shape coffee grinders chop the beans; these are inexpensive and easy to use. You add the beans and press the cap or a button until you see that the grinds are the consistency you need. Unfortunately, some guesswork is involved because you have to determine both the quantity of beans and when to stop processing. Also, choppers create heat, which can cause coffee beans to be bitter.

Larger mills grind the beans through special burr grinders. This process doesn't generate heat, so it is better for the coffee beans. Some models let you preset the quantity of beans needed for the amount of coffee you want (four cups, six cups, etc.). All have settings for the type of grind needed. There's no guesswork here. The downside is that coffee mills are more expensive than canister-shape choppers.

Buying an ADC Coffeemaker

Most Americans make coffee in an electric automatic drip coffeemaker (ADC). So many brands and models are available that you could go nuts in the housewares department picking the coffeemaker of your dreams. Most of the differences among machines from the same manufacturer have to do with extra features—that is, the basic coffeemaking unit is the same, but one has a timer that lets you program wake-up coffee, another has a permanent gold-mesh filter, and so on. You have to decide whether those extra features are important to you and whether they are worth more money.

ADCs come in several sizes, though most make either 10 or 12 cups. It is almost impossible to brew a small quantity of full-bodied coffee in the large machines. If you usually prepare only two to four cups of coffee, buy a small machine that makes up to four cups, or buy a larger unit that has a special switch for brewing small quantities. This switch slows down the brewing process so that small amounts of coffee will have flavor and body. It is a very valuable feature that gives the large machine terrific versatility.

How to Make Good Coffee

To make good coffee, you must brew ground beans with near-boiling water slowly enough to extract the most flavor from the beans, but quickly enough to prevent the coffee from becoming bitter. There's an art to making a good cup of coffee. Some people like percolator pots; some like plunger pots; some like drip pots. All of these make good coffee. Regardless of which method you use and which type or variety of coffee you use, follow these guidelines for brewing a tasty cup:

➤ Use fresh beans; the freshest beans make the best-tasting coffee.

➤ If you buy preground coffee, be sure to buy the proper grind for your coffeemaker. If you grind your own beans, be sure you grind them to the proper texture.

➤ Use 2 tablespoons coffee for each 6 ounces of water. If you like your coffee stronger, use more.

➤ To brew small quantities of coffee in an automatic drip pot, use a small machine or one with a switch for brewing small quantities; otherwise, the coffee will be weak and lack flavor.

➤ Always begin with cold, fresh water. The best coffees are made with water that brews to 190–200°F.

➤ Remove wet grinds from the coffee maker as soon as the coffee is brewed.

➤ Use brewed coffee quickly (coffee deteriorates after about 45 minutes), or store brewed coffee in a thermal carafe.

➤ Make new coffee instead of reheating old coffee.

➤ Be sure to keep your coffee pot clean. Residual coffee oils become rancid and leave a bitter taste.

➤ To make iced coffee, double the strength of the grinds to water. You can freeze leftover coffee in ice cube trays to use for chilling iced coffee.

Kitchen Clue

Don't reuse coffee grounds or let coffee water boil.

What About Espresso/Cappuccino Machines?

It seems everyone is drinking espresso coffee and cappuccino lately. You can make it at home using a stovetop model, but it is easier to use an electric machine. Two types are available: "steam" machines and higher-powered "pump" models. Steam machines have smaller capacities but are much cheaper and are easy to use. Pump machines usually produce better espresso, with a thick layer of foam (called *crema*) on top. They also are quicker, but can be costly. Many people find espresso machines difficult to operate. It takes practice using standard models, however; these days there are many fully automatic and semi-automatic models that make espresso brewing a cinch. Whatever type you buy, be sure to look for machines made of metal or heavy, durable-looking plastic and that don't have unnecessary knobs and removable parts to make the coffeemaking process even more confusing.

Teatime

Tea also has become more popular in recent years, and as with coffee, there are lots of decisions to make. It's not just a matter of grabbing the most familiar box of tea bags.

Fein on Food

The biggest tea party in American history took place near teatime (actually 6:00 P.M.) on December 16, 1773, when groups of anti-British citizens of Massachusetts dumped 90,000 pounds of tea into Boston Harbor as a protest against newly imposed taxes. After the famous Boston Tea Party, patriotic Americans gave up drinking tea. Now, hundreds of years later, tea finally is gaining popularity in the United States.

How to Choose and Buy Tea

Tea is available as loose leaves or in bags. There are commercial teas, made from tea leaves blended for consistent flavor, and there are specialty teas. Stores also sell the makings for several other beverages that we buy and prepare as tea: dried leaves, herbs, seeds, roots, and bark that are brewed in hot water to make such "teas" as chamomile and rose hips.

True tea comes from the leaves of a plant called *Camellia sinensis*. Flavor differences among the various kinds, such as Darjeeling or Assam (specialty teas) have to do with the soil and climate where the tea plant grows and how the leaves are processed. True tea is processed in three ways:

➤ *Black teas* come from tea leaves that are allowed to ferment (oxidize) and darken in the sun. They produce deeply colored, full-bodied teas such as Darjeeling, Ceylon, Assam, and Keemun. Earl Gray is a blend of several types of black tea plus citrus flavoring. English Breakfast Tea generally consists of blends of Keemun, and Irish Breakfast Tea usually combines Assam and Ceylon teas.

➤ *Oolong tea* (the kind you get in Chinese restaurants) comes from semi-fermented tea leaves. These teas are hearty and flavorful and are medium amber in color.

➤ *Green tea* leaves are not fermented. They are steamed soon after harvesting to prevent oxidation and are always pale in color and delicate in flavor.

Spice teas are any of these varieties to which spices have been added. The words "pekoe" and "orange pekoe" have to do with the size of the tea leaves. Commercial bags of tea labeled with these words are blends of small, cut-up tea leaves.

Teas of all types should be stored at room temperature in airtight containers, preferably dark tins that are kept out of the sunlight. They will stay fresh for up to one year.

How to Make Good Tea in a Teapot

You will enjoy a greater variety of flavors if you use specialty teas, and you can control strength better if you use loose tea instead of bagged tea. However, you can make good tea with tea bags or loose tea, commercial blends or specialty tea. Whatever you decide, follow these tips when brewing a potful of tasty tea:

➤ Prewarm your teapot by filling it halfway with hot water, swirling it, and pouring out the contents. An earthenware, porcelain, or glass pot works well (although the best tea is brewed in a silver teapot). Aluminum pots discolor tea.

➤ Put 1 rounded teaspoon of loose tea in the teapot for each 6 ounces of water (two bags per 3 cups of water). If you like your tea stronger, use more tea, but do not let the brew steep longer than the recommended time.

➤ Always begin tea preparation with cold, fresh water (that you boil in a saucepan or tea kettle). Be sure the water comes to a full boil or the tea's full flavor will not be extracted.

➤ Pour the boiling water over loose tea leaves and let them steep three to five minutes. (Tea bags steep for two to three minutes.) Pour the tea into cups through a small tea strainer. If you desire more tea, refill the pot with boiling water.

➤ To make iced tea, double the strength of tea leaves to water and let the brew cool. To make iced tea immediately from hot tea, triple the strength.

➤ Serve tea plain, with sugar and lemon, or with milk.

The Least You Need to Know

➤ Serve some edibles with cocktails to moderate the effects of alcohol.

➤ The old rule of white wine with fish and chicken, red wine with meat and cheese still applies in a general way, but other considerations include serving light wines with light foods, rich wines with rich foods, and so on.

➤ To help you pair the right food and wine, provide a wine merchant with a detailed description of the dinner you're serving.

➤ Fresh ground beans make the best-tasting coffee. Use the proper coffee grind for your coffee pot.

➤ Loose specialty teas make the best-tasting tea. Make sure to use boiling water, and let the tea steep for a few minutes before you pour it.

Chapter 19

Inviting Company: A Menu and Planning Guide

In This Chapter

➤ Planning a cocktail party, with menus

➤ Planning a small dinner party, with menus

➤ Planning a casual cookout, with menus

By now you can be confident about your cooking skills. You can shop and chop, grill and garnish. Why not show off your newly acquired skills by inviting company? In this chapter, I talk about three simple ways to entertain. Once you get the hang of cooking for company, you'll see how rewarding it can be to serve at home and relax with family or friends or to be a competent host or hostess to business associates.

Your First Cocktail Party

Cocktail parties are a good introduction to entertaining. These parties typically are short (about two hours) and can take place in one room. The food can be easy and simple and, for the most part, prepared ahead of time. A cocktail party can be easier on your wallet, too.

In addition to the food and drinks, you need several other items, including a bottle opener, corkscrew, jigger for measuring, pitcher, stirrers, cocktail strainer, knife and cutting board, ice bucket, ice, and tongs. You'll need glasses (two per person), cocktail napkins (approximately three to four per person), and mixers such as club soda, tonic water, and ginger ale. And don't forget lemons, limes, green olives, cocktail onions, and perhaps some maraschino cherries.

Choosing the Liquor for a Cocktail Party

Most people today do not drink creamy, heavy, or overly sweet cocktails. But it's smart to keep vodka, Scotch, blended whiskey, bourbon, rum, and gin on hand. (A particular type of alcohol may be more popular in one part of the country than another.) You will need dry vermouth for martinis and tequila for margaritas, and you will need white and red wines (approximately two bottles of white for every bottle of red) for those people who do not drink hard liquor. Keep some beer handy, and don't forget soda and juice for people who prefer not to drink alcoholic beverages. As a general rule, each person will drink one alcoholic beverage per hour. One bottle of wine will serve two to three people.

Choosing the Food for a Cocktail Party

For your first cocktail party, the key is this: Keep it simple. Serve pre-prepared finger foods that don't require plates and utensils. Make sure the foods aren't messy so that they are easy to eat. *Don't* make foods that require cutting or need more than two to three bites. Preferably, you also should offer both hot and cold edible tidbits in a variety of colors and textures. If you don't want to make all the hors d'oeuvres, you can supplement homemade morsels with upscale store-bought items. In this case, choose foods that are obviously store-bought (herb-coated French salami and mini-mozzarella cheese rounds, for example), so that everyone will know you cooked the rest.

Your life will be easier if you set out some of the food (crudités and dip or cold canapés, for example) on platters or in bowls here and there in the room and pass around the remaining hors d'oeuvres. In general, each person will eat about eight to twelve hors d'oeuvres during a 2-hour party.

Sometimes you will want special friends or relatives to stay past cocktail party time. If you do, have some more substantial food ready (a casserole or salad, depending on the weather). Party "post-mortems" with good friends can be fun, but you may feel exhausted, so an oven-ready dish or a salad is perfect.

Cocktail Party Etiquette

For a party to be successful, you need more than food and drink. Here are a few tips that can make an evening at your home special to your guests:

➤ Be sure your invitation is clear that yours is a cocktail party, not a dinner party. Setting beginning and ending times and writing "hors d'oeuvres and cocktails" is one way to convey this information.

➤ Arrange trays of food strategically in the room so that guests will spread out.

➤ Don't invite all the people to whom you owe social obligations. It involves too much work. If you invite more than 18 people, consider getting serving help.

216

➤ Decorate the pass-around platters to make them attractive. You don't have to fuss: Use edible flowers, a sprig of basil, or slices of lemon.

➤ Have some music playing in the background.

➤ Have lots of ice on hand.

➤ Provide some nonalcoholic beverages.

➤ Make sure you put out coasters so people don't place wet drinking glasses on your furniture.

Warnings

Never let any guest drink and drive. Everyone knows this but it can't be said enough.

Menu Suggestions for Cocktail Parties

If you're planning your first cocktail party and are unsure what to serve, consider the following menu suggestions for simple hors d'oeuvre combinations. You can find all the suggested recipes in Part 6, Section 1, of this book, "Hors d'oeuvres and First Courses."

Menu I

    Crudités and Pita Bread and Spicy Hummus

    Royal and Not-So-Royal Potatoes

    Wrapped Shrimp

    Stuffed Mushrooms

    Tomato and Basil Bruschetta

Menu II

    Guacamole (with corn chips)

    Ham and Asparagus Roll-Ups

    Roasted Garlic (with crackers or pita bread)

    Herb and Cheese Gougères

    Kielbasa en Croûte

> **Menu III**
>
> Stuffed Mushrooms
>
> Kielbasa en Croûte
>
> Tomato and Basil Bruschetta
>
> Wrapped Shrimp
>
> Sweet and Pungent Tropical Dip (with chips)

If you don't mind using serving plates, you can supplement these menus with Corn and Barley Salad, Roasted Red Peppers, or Shrimp Cocktail. If you are having some friends stay after the party, consider such items as Gillian's Ziti Casserole, Crunchy Crusted Macaroni and Cheese, Chili Con Carne, Easy Tuna and White Bean Salad, or Chicken Salad Provençale.

Your First Dinner Party

You will remember your first dinner party forever. You will remember who you invited and what you served. A first dinner party is an accomplishment, and you deserve applause. Of course, you will be nervous; but if you have mastered some cooking skills and equipped yourself with a few good recipes, you can be confident that it will turn out wonderfully.

The first rule of the road when planning a dinner party is this: Expect the unexpected. Someone may cancel, the roast may take longer than you thought it would, and so on. Leave yourself enough time for possible pitfalls. Even if you are a last-minute person who works well under stress, give yourself extra time before a dinner party— enough time to relax before your guests come.

Small dinner parties of six to eight are large enough to make the evening lively, yet cozy enough to exchange real conversation. You can easily adapt most recipes to serve this number of people.

A few days before the dinner, make a list of what you need to do. Plan your menu, but be flexible and market-sensitive. If the pears you wanted to serve look awful, you might have to switch the dessert. Shop for staples the week before, and pick up everything else (including ice and flowers) the day before. Get out your tablecloth, flatware, serving platters, and utensils, as well as dessert plates, cups and saucers, and a coffeepot. Prepare a cooking schedule as suggested in Chapter 16, "Timing Is Everything: Creating Your First Masterpiece."

In addition to all the cooking-related things you have to do, remember these tips for successful dinner parties:

➤ Make sure you have enough chairs.

➤ Hang clean towels in the bathroom.

➤ Prepare your clothes the day before.

➤ If you are preparing the dinner with some-one else, decide beforehand what each of you is responsible for.

➤ If appropriate, get wood for the fireplace.

Some Menu Suggestions for Dinner Parties

Kitchen Clue

Some of these menus will take more time and effort than oth-ers. Remember, you don't have to make every item suggested. Supplement with store-bought foods until you feel confident you can do it all.

If you're planning your first dinner party and are unsure what to serve, consider the following din-ner party menus. The majority of the menu items can be prepared ahead of time, leaving you stress-free for your guests. You will find most of the recipes in Part 6; however, the first (and easiest) menu contains many "nonrecipes" called "Something Simple" that are scattered throughout Chapters 6 through 9.

Menu I

Hors d'oeuvres: Figs Wrapped with Prosciutto, Crudités and Pita Bread with Spicy Hummus, Roasted Garlic with crackers or pita bread

First Course: Cooked Artichokes

Main Course: Broiled Lamb Chops, Baked Potato, Steamed Carrots, Applesauce *or* Cooked Rhubarb

Dessert: Fruit and Cheese

Menu II

Hors d'oeuvres: Herb and Cheese Gougères, Ham and Asparagus Roll-Ups, Kielbasa en Croûte

First Course: Shrimp Cocktail

Main Course: Lemon-Oregano Roasted Chicken, Mashed Potatoes *or* Cooked Rice; Sautéed Sugar Snap Peas *or* Steamed Broccoli

Dessert: Apple Brown Betty

Menu III

Hors d'oeuvres: Tomato and Basil Bruschetta, Wrapped Shrimp, Royal and Not-So-Royal Potatoes

First Course: Salad Greens with Pignoli Nuts and Shaved Parmesan Cheese

Main Course: Pearl J. Fein's Famous Standing Rib Roast, Baked *or* Baked Stuffed Potatoes, Broccoli with Garlic and Lemon *or* Creamed Spinach

Dessert: New York Cheesecake

Menu IV

Hors d'oeuvres: Sweet and Pungent Tropical Dip (with chips), Stuffed Mushrooms, Wrapped Shrimp

First Course: Thick-as-Fog Pea Soup

Main Course: Roast Loin of Pork, Sautéed Rosemary Potatoes, Applesauce, Wilted Kale with Sesame Dressing

Dessert: Chocolate Fudgie Brownies with Ice Cream

Menu V

Hors d'oeuvres: Roasted Garlic, Guacamole, Stuffed Mushrooms

First Course: Cream of Tomato Soup with Rice

Main Course: Broiled Salmon with Mustard and Tarragon, White *or* Wild Rice, Steamed Brussels Sprouts *or* Asparagus

Dessert: One-Bowl Cocoa Fudge Cake with Fudge Frosting

Menu VI

Hors d'oeuvres: Crudités and Pita Bread with Spicy Hummus, Wrapped Shrimp, Ham and Asparagus Roll-Ups

First Course: Lemon-Scented Angel Hair Pasta with Prosciutto Ham and Thyme *or* Green Salad with Classic Vinaigrette Dressing

Main Course: Broiled Butterflied Leg of Lamb *or* Roast Rack of Lamb, White Rice *or* Rice Pilaf with Mushrooms, Baked Acorn Squash

Dessert: Chocolate Mousse *or* Fruit and Cheese

Menu VII (meatless)

Hors d'oeuvres: Herb and Cheese Gougères, Roasted Garlic (with crackers or pita bread), Not-So-Royal Potatoes (with chives)

First Course: Tomato and Basil Bruschetta

Main Course: Green Salad with Classic Vinaigrette Dressing, Quick Three-Bean No-Meat Chili

Dessert: Lemon Bars and Ice Cream *or* Strawberry Shortcake

Thanksgiving Menu

Hors d'oeuvres: Crudités and Pita Bread with Spicy Hummus

First Course: Green Salad with Classic Vinaigrette Dressing

Main Course: Roast Turkey, Gravy, Sweet Potato Casserole, Nana's Egg Noodle Stuffing, Creamed Spinach, Cranberry Sauce

Dessert: Lily Vail's Famous Old-Fashioned Apple Pie *or* Baked Pears

Casual Entertaining at a Cookout

A cookout is probably the easiest way to cook for company. You don't need a porch or patio; a city terrace can accommodate a small grill (assuming this is okay with the fire department and/or building code). People love the smell of grilled food. The pre-heating coals emit a tempting aroma that make guests thrilled to be invited for dinner.

What Is It?

Flavor chips are fuel nuggets that give intense flavor to barbecued foods. You can buy them in bags at supermarkets and specialty cookware stores. Varieties include mesquite, apple wood, and hickory.

Cookouts are casual, so tell your guests to dress accordingly. Use casual plates and utensils and stack them near the table. Guests can fill and carry their own tableware.

You can precook some foods to be grilled, such as spareribs. You can make slowly cooked foods such as turkey by the indirect heat of a grill. Many other items can be cook extremely quickly on a grill—hamburgers, grilled steaks, and marinated chicken cutlets, for example. When you plan a cookout, serve salads or other types of pre-prepared dishes on the side.

In addition to the food items, you may need charcoal briquettes for a cookout. Because foods cook better over very hot coals, be sure to preheat the grill, and make sure the coals are ash-white before you begin to cook the food. You can enhance the flavor of grilled foods by adding some *flavor chips* to the fire. Follow these additional tips for successful cookouts:

➤ Wear an apron to protect your clothes.

➤ Take the chill off foods to be grilled by removing them from the refrigerator about 30 minutes before cooking.

➤ Grease the grill to prevent food from sticking, or use foods that have been marinated.

➤ Remove excess fat from the food to prevent fire flare-ups.

➤ Use tongs to turn the food.

➤ Keep your grill clean; the food will taste better.

➤ Have extra napkins on hand. Grilled foods can be messy, especially if they are the kind you eat with your hands.

Some Menu Suggestions for Cookouts

When planning a cookout, consider these simple cookout menus. All the recipes can be found in Part 6.

Menu I

Grilled Marinated Chicken Breasts

Lentil Salad with Mustard Vinaigrette Dressing

Green Salad with Classic Vinaigrette Dressing *or* Sliced Tomatoes with Dressing* *or* Buttermilk Herb Slaw

Blueberry Crumb Pie

Spiced Apple Iced Tea

* See the "Something Simple" sidebar in Chapter 7, "You Only Think You Hate Vegetables."

Menu II

Grilled Steak *or* Broiled Butterflied Leg of Lamb

Potato Salad with Lemon-Oregano Dressing

Spicy Tomato Salad

Poached Fruit

Sweet Lassi

Menu III

Broiled or Grilled Swordfish

Corn and Barley Salad

Green Salad with Classic Vinaigrette Dressing

Lily Vail's Famous Old-Fashioned Apple Pie

Spiced Coffee Shake

Menu IV

Southern-Style Barbecued Chicken

Rice and Pea Salad

Sliced Tomatoes with Dressing *or* Spicy Tomato Salad

Lemon Bars and Sherbet or Strawberry Shortcake

Spiced Apple Iced Tea

Menu V

Grilled Hamburgers

Baked Beans *or* Lentil Salad with Mustard Vinaigrette

Buttermilk Herb Slaw

Plain Sliced Tomatoes and Bermuda Onions

Chocolate Fudgie Brownies and Ice Cream

Lemonade

The Least You Need to Know

➤ Offer easy-to-eat finger foods with cocktails.

➤ Buy lots of ice and have nonalcoholic beverage choices at a cocktail party.

➤ Plan a dinner party with enough time to prepare for unexpected occurrences.

➤ Make sure you grease the grill, preheat it, and take the chill off the food to be cooked.

Part 6

Recipes

Once you know how to cook, you face the dilemma of what to cook. This is something we all think about. What you decide has to do with several things: your mood ("Do I feel like eating pasta? Meat?"), your schedule ("Do I have time to prepare roast chicken?"), your energy level ("Do I feel like fussing or should I just make something quick and simple?"), your confidence level ("Should I be adventurous and try something new?"), and, of course, your diet ("Is there something delicious and low-fat that I can make today?").

The following recipe sections offer you a broad range of choices. You will find something to make for a meal no matter what your mood, schedule, and circumstances. Some of the recipes are for basic, familiar favorites. But I've also included recipes for dishes that call for more up-to-date or unusual ingredients.

The recipes marked "Easy" speak for themselves; even beginners are capable of cooking these. The "Intermediate" recipes entail an extra step or so, or include a technique that a beginner may find worrisome. The "Challenging" recipes either have several steps or include techniques that require more attention—you can make mistakes if you're not careful.

Hors d'oeuvres and First Courses

Hors d'oeuvres

The literal translation of hors d'oeuvre is "outside the work" and comes from old-time restaurant notions about the pecking order among the kitchen help. Chefs and their staff were considered too important to make hors d'oeuvres; their "work" was the main meal. It was up to the serving people to prepare the little predinner morsels for diners who awaited the real food. Today, hors d'oeuvres are still outside the work—that is, you serve them before dinner. But they are by no means unimportant. Everyone looks forward to them.

Sweet and Pungent Tropical Dip

A refreshing dip—with a bite!

Level: Intermediate

Yield: about 4 cups

Can be done completely ahead

2 ripe papayas

1 ripe mango

1 ripe avocado

1 fresh jalapeño pepper

½ tsp. grated lime peel

¼ cup lime juice

¼ cup chopped fresh cilantro, or
flat leaf Italian parsley

salt to taste

corn chips

Peel the papayas, scoop out the seeds, and cut the flesh into chunks. Peel the mango and avocado and remove their flesh from the pits. Cut the flesh into chunks. Place the papaya, mango, and avocado chunks in the work bowl of a food processor. Remove the stem and seeds from the jalapeño pepper and cut the pepper into smaller pieces. Place the pieces in the food processor. Add the lime peel, lime juice, and cilantro. Process the ingredients, using the pulse feature, until the pieces are small. (Alternately you may chop the fruits and pepper by hand, place them in a bowl, and mix in the other ingredients.) Taste the dip for seasoning and add salt to taste. Serve the dip with corn chips.

Spicy Hummus

A lively version of this perennial favorite.

Level: Easy

Yield: about 1½ cups

Can be done completely ahead

1 (l–lb., approximately) can
chick peas (garbanzo beans)

½ cup fresh lemon juice

½ cup tahini

¼ cup olive oil

4–6 large cloves garlic

1 tsp. paprika

¾ tsp. cayenne pepper

½ tsp. ground cumin

½ tsp. salt, or salt to taste

pita bread, cut into wedges

Drain the beans but reserve the liquid from the can. Place the beans, 2 TB. of the reserved liquid, the lemon juice, tahini, olive oil, garlic, paprika, cayenne pepper, cumin, and salt in the work bowl of a food processor or in a blender. Process until the ingredients are a smooth puree. (Stop the machine once or twice to scrape down the sides of the bowl with a rubber spatula.) Taste for seasoning and add salt to taste. Serve the hummus with the pita wedges.

What Is It?

Tahini is sesame seed paste. It is available at many supermarkets.

Roasted Garlic

Garlic is rather tame when you roast it. Try this ultra-easy dish and see for yourself.

Level: Easy

Yield: 4–6 servings

Can be done completely ahead

1 large whole head of garlic
1 TB. olive oil
¼ tsp. salt
⅛ tsp. freshly ground black pepper

2 tsp. minced fresh herbs (any kind), or ½ tsp. dried (optional)
crackers or cut-up raw vegetables

Preheat the oven to 350°F. Remove the loose papery peel from the outside of the garlic head. Put the head on a small sheet of aluminum foil and drizzle it with the olive oil. Sprinkle with salt, pepper, and herbs. Wrap the garlic completely in the foil. Bake 1½–2 hours or until the garlic is soft when pierced with the tip of a sharp knife. Remove the garlic. Slice a piece from the top of the garlic to expose the flesh. To serve, let the garlic cool and have guests scoop some from the head; alternatively, they can use their fingers to take a clove of the cooled garlic and squeeze it onto a cracker or cut-up vegetable.

Kitchen Clue

You can roast garlic without wrapping it in foil if you use a special terra-cotta "garlic baker."

Guacamole

One of America's favorite dips! Serve leftovers on grilled chicken breasts or with fajitas.

Level: Intermediate

Yield: about 2 cups

Can be done completely ahead

1 large tomato

1 jalapeño pepper (or use 1–2 TB. chopped bottled jalapeño peppers)

2 medium avocados

3 TB. lemon or lime juice

¼ cup minced onion

1 medium clove garlic, minced

2 tsp. minced fresh cilantro (optional)

¾ tsp. salt, or salt to taste

corn chips

Cut the tomato in half crosswise, squeeze out the seeds, and chop the pulp into small pieces. Remove the stem, the fleshy white part, and the seeds from inside the jalapeño pepper and chop it into small pieces. Peel the avocados, slice the flesh all the way down to and around the pit, and put the flesh in a medium-sized bowl. Add the lemon or lime juice and mash the ingredients. Stir in the chopped tomato and jalapeño pepper, onion, garlic, cilantro, and salt. Mix well. Use a food processor or blender if you'd rather have a smoother guacamole. Serve with corn chips.

Warnings

Be careful when working with hot peppers. Use disposable gloves, if possible. Be sure to wash your hands thoroughly after you're done and don't touch your skin or eyes for a while.

Tomato and Basil Bruschetta

Very refreshing—and you can also serve it as a first course.

Level: Easy

Yield: about 18 pieces

*Can be done ahead up to the * in the instructions*

1 lb. plum tomatoes (about 7–8)

1 large clove garlic, minced

⅓ cup olive oil

⅓ cup coarsely chopped fresh basil

pinch of cayenne pepper

pinch of salt

1 loaf of French bread

Preheat the oven to 400°F. Cut the tomatoes in half crosswise and squeeze out the seeds. Chop the tomatoes and place them in a bowl. Stir in the garlic, 2 TB. of the olive oil, basil, cayenne pepper, and salt.

Slice the bread into ½"-thick slices. Brush both sides lightly with the remaining oil. Place the bread on a cookie sheet and bake the slices 3–4 minutes or until they are slightly crispy but not browned.

* Spread equal amounts of tomato mixture on top of bread pieces.

Second Thoughts

Fresh herbs are important in bruschetta. If you can't find fresh basil, substitute 1½ tsp. fresh thyme, oregano, or marjoram leaves. If you can't find any of these, substitute 4 slices of crumbled crispy bacon.

Ham and Asparagus Roll-Ups

Simple and stunning. Set the pieces on doilies for even greater visual effect.

Level: Easy

Yield: about 2½ dozen

Can be done completely ahead

4 medium- to large-thickness asparagus, cooked (or packaged frozen asparagus spears)

lightly salted water

4 slices boiled ham

6 oz. softened cream cheese, or herb-flavored cream cheese

½ lemon

2 TB. chopped fresh chives (or the green part of scallion)

freshly ground black pepper

Cut the woody, purplish bottoms off the asparagus. Peel the asparagus if desired. Cook the asparagus until they are fork tender (see Section 6, "Vegetables") and drain them under cold water. Wipe the asparagus dry with paper towels. (If you use frozen asparagus, cook them until they are tender.) Wipe the ham slices dry and spread each slice with an equal amount of cream cheese. Place a cooked asparagus spear down the length of the slice of ham. Squeeze the lemon over each asparagus spear. Sprinkle with the chives, and grind some fresh pepper over the ingredients. Roll the ham jelly-roll style to make one long roll. Place the roll seam side down on a plate in the refrigerator (cover the plate with plastic wrap). Chill for at least 30 minutes. Slice each roll into 8 sections.

Stuffed Mushrooms

Everyone loves stuffed mushrooms. You can freeze these for about a month.

Level: Easy

Yield: 16

Can be done completely ahead

16 large common white mushrooms

1½ TB. melted butter

4 oz. sweet Italian-style sausage meat

1 clove garlic, minced

¼ cup grated mozzarella cheese

2 TB. plain dry bread crumbs

1 TB. grated Parmesan cheese

1½ tsp. minced fresh oregano, or ½ tsp. dried

Preheat the oven to 350°F. Rinse and dry the mushrooms. Cut off and discard a thin slice from the bottom of each stem. Remove the stems, chop them, and set them aside. Brush the outside of the caps with the melted butter. Cook the sausage in a skillet over moderate heat for 2–3 minutes, breaking the pieces into smaller pieces as you cook them. Add the garlic and the chopped mushroom stems, and continue to cook the mixture 2–3 minutes, or until the meat is well browned. Remove the pan from the heat and drain off any excess fat. Combine the meat mixture in a bowl with the mozzarella cheese, bread crumbs, Parmesan cheese, and oregano. Mix ingredients well and use the mixture to stuff each mushroom cap. Place the filled caps on a cookie sheet. Bake for 15 minutes or until they are hot and the cheese bubbles.

* If you freeze these, thaw them before baking (they take about 30–40 minutes to thaw).

Kielbasa en Croûte

A glamorous frank-in-blanket, this hors d'oeuvre is always a best seller at a party.

Level: Intermediate

Yield: 1 roll, serving 8–10 people

Can be done ahead up to the * *in the instructions*

1 sheet packaged frozen puff pastry	1 piece of kielbasa (about ½ lb.)
1 TB. Dijon mustard	1 large egg, beaten

Preheat the oven to 400°F. Let the sheet of frozen puff pastry thaw for 15 minutes, then roll it slightly thinner on a floured surface. Spread the mustard down the center of the pastry sheet. Lay a piece of kielbasa on top of the mustard, leaving a 1" margin at each end. Wrap the pastry around the kielbasa and seal the edges of dough by pinching it together. (The edge should have an overlap no wider than ½ inch. Cut away any excess dough.) If you do not cook the roll now, place it in the refrigerator.

* Place the kielbasa roll seam side down on a cookie sheet. Brush the entire surface of the pastry with some of the beaten egg. Bake the roll 25 minutes or until it is lightly browned. To serve, slice the roll into bite-size pieces with a serrated knife. (If you prefer, serve the roll with the knife next to it and allow guests to cut their own slices.)

Second Thoughts

To make this hors d'oeuvre more visually appealing, cut out fancy shapes with scraps of dough left from the original sheet used to wrap the kielbasa. Place the shapes on top of the roll and brush them with more of the beaten egg before you bake the roll.

Wrapped Shrimp

These are glamorous and beautiful. Use fancy toothpicks to skewer them.

Level: Easy

Yield: 12

*Can be done ahead up to the * in the instructions*

12 extra-large raw shrimp (about ½ lb.)

2 TB. olive oil

2 TB. lemon juice

1 TB. minced fresh dill, or 1 tsp. dried

6 slices thin-sliced bacon

Preheat the broiler or grill. Shell and devein the shrimp as described in Chapter 13, "A Compendium of the Top 100+ Cooking Terms." Rinse the shrimp and dry them with paper towels. Mix the olive oil, lemon juice, and dill in a nonreactive dish. Add the shrimp and coat them well with the liquid. Let the shrimp marinate for 30 minutes. Cut each piece of bacon in half to make two shorter strips, and wrap each shrimp with a piece of bacon.

* Grill or broil the shrimp about 6 inches from the heat source for 2–3 minutes per side, or until the bacon is crispy and the shrimp are pink.

Kitchen Clue

Most fish markets will shell and devein shrimp for you if you call ahead. That phone call saves you lots of time.

Royal and Not-So-Royal Potatoes

You can serve this elegant and lavish dish to your most important company.

Level: Intermediate

Yield: 12–18

Can be done completely ahead

12–18 small "new" yellow or Red Bliss potatoes
¼ cup dairy sour cream
3 ounces of any type caviar

Wash the potatoes, and then steam them (or cook them in lightly salted water) for 10–15 minutes or until they are tender. Drain the potatoes under cold water. Let the potatoes cool. Peel the potatoes and cut a thin slice from the bottom of each one so that it can stand up straight. With the tip of a spoon or melon-baller, scoop a small amount of potato from each potato top to make a crater. Fill each crater with sour cream and top the sour cream with a small amount of caviar.

* For Not-So-Royal Potatoes, substitute 2 TB. chopped chives or 3 slices crumbled crispy bacon for the caviar. For variety, serve all three kinds of potatoes.

Second Thoughts

You may substitute low-fat or nonfat sour cream, plain yogurt, or créme fraîche for the sour cream.

Herb and Cheese Gougères
(Choux Puffs)

These pastries are incredibly versatile: Use them as is, or cut them in half and fill them with salad, dip, or another filling. You can freeze these, too! Without the herb and cheese, the dough can be used to make cream puffs; add 1–2 tsp. sugar to the dough, make them larger, and cook them 7–10 minutes longer.

Level: Challenging

Yield: 4 dozen

Can be done completely ahead

1 cup minus 2 TB. water

¼ lb. unsalted butter, cut into chunks

1 cup all-purpose flour, sifted

¾ tsp. salt

4 eggs

1½ TB. chopped fresh mixed herbs, or 1½ tsp. dried

½ cup grated Parmesan or Gruyère cheese

dash of cayenne pepper

egg glaze: 1 egg mixed with 2 tsp. water, optional

Preheat the oven to 400°F. Cook the water and butter over moderate heat in a medium-size saucepan. When the butter has melted, add the flour and salt, all at once. Stir vigorously with a wooden spoon until the mixture is well blended and begins to come away from the sides of the pan. Remove pan from the heat and let it cool for 2–3 minutes. Beat the eggs, one at a time, and add them one at a time to the dough, blending well after each addition. Add the herbs, cheese, and cayenne pepper and blend them thoroughly into the dough.

Butter and flour a baking sheet. Drop mounds of about 1" of dough from a teaspoon onto the sheet. Leave at least 1" space between the mounds. If you like a shiny surface on the puffs, lightly brush the tops of the mounds with some of the egg wash. Place the baking pan in the oven and raise the heat to 425°F. Bake about 18–20 minutes or until the puffs are lightly browned and crispy. Lower the heat to 300°F and bake another 5–6 minutes. Turn off the heat. Pierce the puffs with the tip of a sharp knife and return them to the oven for 3–4 minutes. Serve hot or at room temperature.

Second Thoughts

Let the puffs cool and split them in half. Remove any moist, uncooked dough. Stuff the bottom portions with savory fillings such as egg, shrimp or chicken salad, dip, or other goodies (such as bruschetta or bottled salsa).

First Courses

Most of the time you won't serve a first course for dinner. But it is welcome occasionally, and is particularly suitable for company. A first course sets a slower pace for your meal so that you and your guests can relax at the table. It also allows you to show off your culinary skills and hear everyone's praise and applause.

Shrimp Cocktail

This is one of the easiest first courses to make, especially if you have the fish merchant shell and devein the shrimp for you. Although it's simple, it's still impressive.

Level: Easy

Yield: 4 servings

Can be done completely ahead

24 extra-large raw shrimp (about 1 lb.)

water

1 slice lemon, ¼" thick

bottled cocktail sauce or lemon and dill-flavored mayonnaise

Shell and devein the shrimp as described in Chapter 13. Rinse the shrimp under cold water. Fill a 3-quart saucepan ⅔ full with water and bring the water to a boil. Add the lemon slice and let it cook 30 seconds. Remove the pan from the heat. Immerse the shrimp in the water. Cover the pan. Let the shrimp stand in the water for 5 minutes or until they are pink and firm. Drain the shrimp under cold water. Refrigerate them approximately 30 minutes or until they are cold. Arrange the shrimp on a plate or around the edges of a "cocktail cup" (you may use a dessert bowl). Garnish the dish with a dollop of sauce (or place the sauce in the cocktail cup) and some lemon slices.

Second Thoughts

To make an easy lemon and dill-flavored mayonnaise for the shrimp, mix ¾ cup mayonnaise with 2 TB. lemon juice and 2 TB. freshly minced dill.

Lemon-Scented Angel Hair Pasta with Prosciutto Ham and Thyme

This unusual dish comes from taste memories of a similar pasta dish served at a restaurant in Philadelphia named Alouette.

Level: Intermediate

Yield: 4 servings

*Can be done ahead up to the * in the instructions*

½ lb. angel hair pasta or thin spaghetti

4 TB. olive oil

2–3 oz. prosciutto ham
(or any other flavorful cured ham)

1 stalk lemongrass
(or 1½ tsp. freshly minced lemon peel)

1 shallot, chopped

1 clove garlic, minced

¾ tsp. fresh thyme leaves
or ¼ tsp. dried

¼ tsp. salt, or salt to taste

¼ tsp. freshly ground black pepper

Cook the pasta until it is *al dente*. Drain the pasta under cool water. Toss the pasta with 1 TB. of the olive oil and set it aside. Chop the ham into tiny pieces and set it aside. Remove and discard the tough outer husk of the lemongrass and the tough bottom portion. Mince the remaining inside core and set it aside. Heat 1 TB. of the olive oil in a skillet large enough to hold the pasta. Add the shallot and garlic, and cook over low to moderate heat 1–2 minutes or until the vegetables have wilted. Add the lemongrass, ham, and thyme leaves, and cook another 2 minutes.

* Add the pasta, salt, pepper, and remaining 2 TB. olive oil. Toss ingredients and continue cooking another 3–4 minutes or until pasta is hot and ingredients are evenly distributed.

Kitchen Clue

You can buy prosciutto ham in Italian specialty markets and at the deli counter of many supermarkets.

Mushroom Risotto

You can't hurry risotto. It takes time, constant stirring, and careful watching, but this tender, creamy dish is worth the effort.

Level: Challenging

Yield: 6 servings

Can be done ahead up to the * in the instructions

4 TB. olive oil

10 oz. mushrooms, any kind, coarsely chopped

salt and black pepper to taste

1 onion, chopped

1 medium clove garlic, chopped
        12 oz. arborio rice (approx. 1¾ cups)

5–6 cups canned or homemade vegetable or chicken broth or stock

½ cup dry white wine

3 TB. chopped parsley

½ cup freshly grated Parmesan cheese

Heat 2 TB. of the olive oil in a skillet. Add the mushrooms, sprinkle them with salt and pepper, and cook over moderate heat, stirring occasionally, 4–5 minutes or until they have softened and the pan juices have evaporated. Set the pan aside.

* Heat the remaining 2 TB. olive oil in a saucepan. Add the onion and cook over moderate heat, stirring occasionally, 2–3 minutes. Add the garlic and cook another minute. Stir in the rice and cook 1 minute. Pour in 1½ cups of the boiling stock. Cook over moderate heat, stirring constantly with a wooden spoon, until the liquid has been absorbed. Pour in the wine. Cook, stirring gently, until the liquid has been absorbed. Add the remaining stock, ½ cup at a time, stirring after each addition until the liquid has been absorbed. The rice is ready when the grains are soft and the mixture is creamy, about 25 minutes. Stir in the mushrooms, parsley, and Parmesan cheese. Taste for seasoning and add salt and pepper to taste.

Kitchen Clue

You may keep risotto warm for about 30 minutes; stir in an extra half-cup of stock, and then put a lid on the pan. Keep the pan over the lowest flame possible (on an electric range, over the turned-off burner).

Salad Greens with Pignoli Nuts and Shaved Parmesan Cheese

An extra easy but impressive first course.

Level: Easy

Yield: 4–6 servings

*Can be done ahead up to the * in the instructions*

a variety of greens such as Bibb, Oakleaf, and Boston lettuces, Frisée, and so on (or use store-bought mesclun)

½ cup olive oil

¼ cup balsamic vinegar

1 shallot, minced

1 tsp. powdered mustard

1 tsp. minced fresh thyme leaves, or ½ tsp. dried

salt and black pepper to taste

¼ cup lightly toasted pignoli nuts

shavings of Parmesan cheese

Wash and dry the lettuce leaves thoroughly. Break them into pieces with your hands and put them into a bowl. Combine the olive oil, balsamic vinegar, shallot, mustard, thyme, salt, and pepper, and whisk them vigorously for 15–20 seconds or until they are well blended.

* Toss the greens with some of the dressing (use as much as you like). Place the dressed greens on serving plates. Sprinkle with the pignoli nuts. Shave Parmesan cheese on top.

Soups and Salads

Soups

Did you know that the first restaurant in history (opened in Paris in 1765) served only soup? The owner of the place, a man named Boulanger, understood that a hearty soup had the power to restore a person's energy. In fact, the word "restore" influenced the new word for a public eating place: "restaurant." There are many different kinds of soup: light versions that you use as a first course and more rib-sticking ones that you can serve for supper. Soup is one course that's so versatile you can make a different one every day and not run out of recipes for years.

Old-Fashioned Chicken Soup

You guessed it, the familiar old "penicillin," this version is fragrant with dill for extra flavor.

Level: Intermediate

Yield: 8 servings

Can be done completely ahead

1 stewing hen or roasting chicken	1 large onion, left whole but peeled
water	small bunch of fresh dill, or 1 TB. dried
4 carrots, peeled	1 TB. salt, or salt to taste
3 stalks celery, peeled	6–8 whole black peppercorns
1 parsnip or small turnip, peeled	

Wash the chicken inside and out and place it in a soup pot. Pour enough water in the pot to cover the chicken by 1". Bring the liquid to a boil, lower the heat, and for the next several minutes, remove any scum that rises to the surface. Add the remaining ingredients. Cover the pan partially and simmer the soup for 2½ hours or until the chicken meat is very soft when pierced with the tip of a sharp knife. Pour the soup through a strainer or colander into a large bowl or a second pot. Set the chicken and vegetables aside. Remove the fat from the surface of the liquid with a spoon or fat-skimming tool or by patting paper towels on the surface. For best results, refrigerate the strained soup; when it is cold, the fat will rise to the surface and harden and you can scoop it off. (Refrigerate the vegetables and the chicken separately.) Serve the soup plain or with the vegetables (cut them up) and chicken (remove the meat from the bones and cut it up).

Kitchen Clue

This soup is terrific when served with cooked white rice or cooked egg noodle flakes or alphabets. Although the soup freezes well, do not freeze the cooked chicken or vegetables with it. Eat them separately or make chicken salad with the chicken.

Old-Fashioned Carrot Soup

A light but satisfying soup that is superb as a first course.

Level: Easy

Yield: 8–10 servings

Can be done completely ahead

2 TB. butter

2 TB. vegetable oil

1 medium onion, coarsely chopped

2 lbs. carrots, coarsely chopped

2 medium all-purpose potatoes, peeled and coarsely chopped

¼ cup chopped parsley

2 TB. chopped fresh dill, or 2 tsp dried

1½ tsp. salt, or salt to taste

⅛ tsp. freshly ground black pepper

7 cups canned or homemade chicken or vegetable stock

pinch of sugar

1 cup cream, any kind

Heat the butter and vegetable oil together in a soup pot. When the butter has melted and looks foamy, add the onion and cook over moderate heat 3–4 minutes or until softened. Add the carrots, potatoes, parsley, dill, salt, and pepper and cook 3–4 minutes, stirring occasionally. Add the stock and sugar. Bring the soup to a simmer. Cook, partially covered, 45 minutes. Purée the soup in portions in a food processor or blender. Return the soup to the pan. Stir in the cream. Heat the soup through and serve.

Thick-As-Fog Pea Soup

You'll find this a great treat when the weather turns cold.

Level: Easy

Yield: 8–10 servings

Can be done completely ahead

1 lb. dried green split peas

10 cups cold water

1 meaty ham bone or 2 ham hocks or a 1-lb. chunk of corned beef

3 carrots, chopped

2 stalks celery, chopped

2 medium onions, chopped (about 1 cup)

3 sprigs fresh parsley

1 bay leaf

1½ tsp. fresh marjoram, or ½ tsp. dried (or use oregano)

¼ tsp. freshly ground black pepper

Place all the ingredients in a soup pot and bring the liquid to a boil. Reduce the heat and cover the pan. Simmer for 2 hours. Discard the bay leaf. Remove the bone and reserve it. You may purée the soup in a blender if you wish and then return it to the saucepan. Remove the meat from the ham bone or hocks (or chop the corned beef) and add the pieces to the soup. Heat the soup through and serve.

Second Thoughts

To make a creamier, thinner soup, add cream or buttermilk to taste (begin with one cup, taste the soup, and add more if desired). To give the soup some pizzazz, serve it with croutons.

Cream of Tomato Soup with Rice

This velvety soup is fine for lunch or as a first course at dinner.

Level: Easy

Yield: 6–8 servings

Can be done completely ahead

2 TB. vegetable oil

1 medium onion, coarsely chopped

1 carrot, coarsely chopped

1 stalk celery, coarsely chopped

3 TB. all-purpose flour

3 cups canned or homemade chicken or vegetable stock

2 (28-oz.) cans of whole tomatoes, not drained

2 tsp. sugar

1 tsp. salt, or salt to taste

1 tsp. fresh thyme leaves, or ¼ tsp. dried

½ tsp. freshly ground black pepper

⅓ cup white raw rice

1 cup cream, any kind

Heat the vegetable oil in a soup pot. Add the onion, carrot, and celery, and cook the vegetables over low-moderate heat 3–4 minutes or until they have softened. Stir in the flour. Cook another 2 minutes. Stir in the stock. Add the tomatoes, sugar, salt, thyme, and pepper. Cook the soup, partially covered, over moderate heat for 1 hour. Purée the soup in portions in a food processor or blender. Return the soup to the pan. Add the rice and cover the pan. Cook 30 minutes or until the rice is tender. Stir in the cream and cook the soup a minute or so to reheat it.

Andalusian Gazpacho

This is a refreshing summer soup. Make sure you buy fresh, ripe, fragrant summer tomatoes.

Level: Intermediate

Yield: 6 servings

Can be done completely ahead

4 slices of home-style white bread, diced

2 large cloves garlic

1 medium onion, coarsely chopped

5 TB. olive oil

1 cup water

1½ tsp. salt, or salt to taste

5 tomatoes, de-seeded and cut into chunks

1 cucumber, peeled, de-seeded, coarsely chopped

1 green pepper, de-seeded, coarsely chopped

¼ cup red-wine vinegar

3 cups tomato juice

2 cups packaged or homemade croutons

Optional garnishes:

½ cup chopped green pepper

½ cup chopped cucumber

3–4 chopped scallions

Place the bread, garlic, onion, and olive oil into the work bowl of a food processor or into a blender. Whirl ingredients until they are finely minced, scraping down the sides of the processor bowl once or twice during the process. Add the water and salt and process them briefly. Add the tomatoes, cucumber, and green pepper and process for 10–20 seconds or until it reaches the desired consistency (you may want a true purée or you may want something chunkier). Pour the soup into a bowl and stir in the wine vinegar and tomato juice. Refrigerate for at least 1 hour. Taste for seasoning and add salt as needed. Serve the soup with croutons. To make the dish more authentic, serve it with the garnishes. (Prepare them the same way and at the same time as the other vegetables, but set them aside in separate bowls.)

Turkey Bean Soup

This hearty soup is a terrific way to use leftovers from Thanksgiving.

Level: Intermediate

Yield: 8–10 servings

Can be done completely ahead

20-oz. bag of loose mixed dried beans (such as pinto, navy, black, red, or kidney)

water

leftover turkey carcass, meat scraps, and bones

1 (2-lb., 3-oz.) can Italian-style plum tomatoes, drained and chopped into bite-size pieces

2 stalks celery, sliced into ¼"-thick pieces

1 medium onion, sliced

2 cloves garlic, chopped

1 TB. Cajun blackening spices (or use chili powder)

2 tsp. salt, or salt to taste

a sprig of fresh rosemary, thyme, or marjoram, or ½ tsp. dried (optional)

½ cup raw white rice

1 cup freshly grated Parmesan cheese (optional)

Rinse the beans under cold water and place them in a soup pot. Cover the beans with water, bring the water to a boil over high heat, and boil the beans for 2 minutes. Remove the pan from the heat, cover the pan, and let the beans rest for one hour. Drain the beans and return them to the pot. Add 2 quarts of water, the turkey carcass, meat scraps, and bones. Bring the soup to a simmer. Add the tomatoes, celery, onion, garlic, blackening spices, salt, and fresh herbs (if used). Simmer, partially covered, for about 2 hours. Stir in the rice and cook, partially covered, for about 45 minutes. Taste the soup for seasoning and add salt to taste. Remove the herb sprigs and turkey carcass. Serve soup with fresh Parmesan cheese, if desired.

Kitchen Clue

While almost any kind of good sherry will do with the following French Onion Soup recipe, an Oloroso has the best flavor for this recipe. Do not use cooking sherry.

French Onion Soup

This soup isn't hard to make, but it involves a few extra steps. The croutes are further work, but they give this classic soup style as well as fabulously rich flavor and a delightfully chewy texture on top.

Level: Challenging (easy if you don't make the croutes)

Yield: 8 servings

Can be done completely ahead

2 TB. butter

2 TB. olive oil

2 lbs. yellow onions, sliced

¾ tsp. salt, or salt to taste

½ tsp. sugar

1½ TB. flour

6 cups heated canned or homemade beef broth or stock

¼ cup sherry

bread and cheese croutes (optional)

Heat the butter and olive oil in a soup pot or large saucepan. When the butter has melted and looks foamy, add the onions, salt, and sugar. Cook the onions over low-moderate heat, stirring occasionally, for about 30 minutes or until onions have softened and become caramel-colored. Add the flour and mix ingredients together for 3 minutes. Gradually add the beef stock, stirring gently as you pour it into the soup. Cook the soup, partially covered, 35 minutes. Add the sherry. Cook another 5 minutes. Serve the soup as is or topped with bread and cheese croutes.

Bread and Cheese Croutes

8 (1"-thick) slices of French bread

2 TB. olive oil

1 clove garlic, cut in half

1¼ cups freshly grated Swiss cheese

2 TB. freshly grated Parmesan cheese

Preheat the oven to 350°F. Bake the bread on a cookie sheet for 15 minutes. Brush the bread tops with the olive oil and rub the surface of the bread with the cut side of the garlic. Turn the bread slices over and bake them another 15 minutes. Just before serving the soup, place the soup in oven-proof bowls and top each with 1 slice of the bread. Sprinkle the cheeses evenly over the bread. Place bowls on a cookie sheet and bake the soup for 12–15 minutes, or until the cheese melts and bubbles.

Homemade Stock and Bouillon

It's somewhat time-consuming to make your own homemade stock and bouillon, but it's worth it. Stock is the basis for many soups and sauces, and bouillon comes in handy for a multitude of recipes. When you make your own, you control the level of salt, fat, and flavor. You can freeze stock in small containers to use as needed. You can also freeze bouillon in a container or as cubes.

Level: Challenging

Yield: 10 cups of stock; 1½ cups concentrated bouillon

Can be done completely ahead

1 (4–5 lb.) stewing hen or 4 to 5 lbs. chicken necks, backs, or giblets

16 cups water

1 large onion, peeled and cut in half

2 carrots, peeled

2 stalks celery, rinsed

2 unpeeled cloves garlic

2 bay leaves

3 sprigs fresh parsley

2–3 sprigs fresh thyme or 4 sprigs fresh dill, or 1 tsp. dried

1 tsp. salt (optional)

8 whole black peppercorns

To make the stock, place the hen in a soup pot and add enough water to cover it by about 1". Bring the water to a boil, lower the heat, and for the next several minutes, remove any scum that rises to the surface. Add the remaining ingredients. Be sure there is enough liquid to cover all ingredients, adding more water if necessary. Cook the ingredients, partially covered, for 2½–3 hours. Pour the stock through a strainer or colander into a large bowl or second pot. Remove the fat from the surface of the liquid with a spoon or fat-skimming tool or by patting paper towels on the surface. For best results, refrigerate the strained stock; when it is cold, the fat will rise to the surface and harden and you can scoop it off. Discard the vegetables. You can use the chicken for chicken salad.

* To make the stock into bouillon, cook the degreased stock over low heat for several hours or until it has reduced to 1½ cups. Pour the liquid into 16 ice cube tray sections or into small plastic containers. Refrigerate for several hours or until firm. When dissolved in 1 cup boiling water, each cube will make 1 cup bouillon to which you may add salt as needed. You can freeze bouillon cubes in little plastic bags.

Kitchen Clue

You can make beef or veal stock and bouillon the same way, using 5 pounds of bones and meat instead of chicken. To make brown (dark) meat stock, roast the bones and meat first for about 20 minutes in a preheated 450°F oven.

Salads

Salads are among the more refreshing foods you can make. They are handy, too, because you can prepare them ahead. There are scads of different types; green salads, potato salad, and macaroni salad are familiar to most of us, but there are also interesting salads you can make from grains, starches, and legumes such as barley, beans, and rice. Here's a hint to bear in mind: Salads always taste better at room temperature or slightly chilled, but not cold.

Potato Salad with Lemon-Oregano Dressing

This tangy salad is perfect for picnics and cookouts.

Level: Easy

Yield: 4–6 servings

Can be done completely ahead

2 lbs. small red potatoes
lightly salted water
¼ cup olive oil
¼ cup fresh lemon juice
2 scallions, finely chopped

1 TB. minced parsley
1½ TB. minced fresh oregano,
    or 1½ tsp. dried
¾ tsp. salt, or salt to taste
freshly ground black pepper to taste

continues

continued

Place the potatoes in a saucepan, cover them with lightly salted water, and bring the water to a boil. Lower the heat and cook the potatoes at a simmer 15–20 minutes or until they are tender. Drain the potatoes under cold water and peel them. Cut into bite-size pieces and place them in a large bowl. Pour in the olive oil and lemon juice, and add the scallions, parsley, oregano, salt, and pepper. Toss gently. Let rest at least 1 hour before serving.

Second Thoughts

For a more intense flavor, add 1 minced garlic clove. You may leave the potatoes un-peeled if you wish.

Buttermilk Herb Slaw

The tangy buttermilk makes this coleslaw superbly refreshing.

Level: Easy

Yield: 4–6 servings

Can be done completely ahead

⅔ cup buttermilk

2 TB. mayonnaise

1 TB. cider vinegar

1 TB. sugar

2 TB. minced fresh chives (or the green part of scallion)

2 TB. minced parsley

1 TB. minced fresh dill, tarragon, or savory, or 1 tsp. dried

½ tsp. salt, or salt to taste

⅛ tsp. cayenne pepper

3 cups shredded cabbage

½ cup shredded snow peas

Mix the buttermilk, mayonnaise, vinegar, sugar, chives, parsley, herb, salt, and cayenne pepper in a medium-sized bowl. In a large bowl, combine the cabbage and snow peas and toss them together. Pour the dressing over the vegetables. Toss ingredients to coat the vegetables with the dressing. Let the salad stand for at least 30 minutes before serving.

Second Thoughts

If you don't have cider vinegar, use 1 TB. white vinegar plus 1 TB. apple juice.

Spicy Tomato Salad

This salad is especially terrific in the summer when you can get fabulous summer tomatoes.

Level: Intermediate

Yield: 6 servings

Can be done completely ahead

4 large ripe tomatoes

6 Sichuan peppercorns

½ tsp. freshly ground black pepper

1 TB. chopped fresh hot chili pepper
(such as a jalapeño)

3 TB. olive oil

1½ TB. red wine vinegar

1 TB. minced parsley

½ tsp. fresh thyme leaves, or ¼ tsp. dried

¼ tsp. salt, or salt to taste

Chop the tomatoes into bite-size pieces and place them in a bowl. Crush the Sichuan peppercorns (put them in a plastic bag and bang them with a pan or roll them with a rolling pan) and add them to the tomatoes with the black pepper, chili pepper, olive oil, vinegar, parsley, thyme, and salt. Toss ingredients and let them stand at least 30 minutes before serving.

Second Thoughts

For a tangier-tasting salad, add 2–3 tsp. of chopped fresh coriander. For a less hot version, substitute 2 TB. canned green chili peppers for the fresh hot chili pepper.

251

Kitchen Clue

You can buy Sichuan peppercorns in stores that carry Asian food products and in some supermarkets.

Easy Tuna and White Bean Salad

This is a classic Tuscan dish. Serve it with crusty Italian bread.

Level: Easy

Yield: 4 servings

Can be done completely ahead

2 cans of tuna in oil, each about 6–7 oz.

2 cans of white beans, about 1 lb. each

3 scallions, chopped

⅓ cup chopped parsley

6 TB. olive oil

2 TB. red wine vinegar

2 tsp. lemon juice

1 TB. chopped fresh oregano,
  or 1 tsp. dried

¼ tsp. freshly ground black pepper

Drain most of the oil from the tuna. Put the fish in a bowl. Rinse the beans under cold water and drain them in a strainer. Add the beans, scallions, and parsley. Toss the ingredients gently. Mix the olive oil, red-wine vinegar, lemon juice, oregano, and black pepper. Pour the dressing over the fish and beans. Let the salad stand at least 10 minutes before serving.

Second Thoughts

Substitute 12 oz. cooked shrimp for the tuna.

Rice and Pea Salad

A tasty alternative to potato or macaroni salad.

Level: Easy

Yield: *4–6 servings*

Can be done completely ahead

3 cups cooked, cooled white rice	1 tsp. Dijon mustard
¾ cup thawed frozen peas	¾ tsp. salt, or salt to taste
¾ cup diced boiled ham	¼ tsp. freshly ground black pepper
⅓ cup olive oil	3–4 TB. mayonnaise
1½ TB. red-wine vinegar	

Mix the rice, peas, and ham in a bowl. Mix the olive oil, wine vinegar, Dijon mustard, salt, and pepper in a second bowl. Pour the dressing over the rice. Toss the ingredients. Add 3 TB. of mayonnaise and stir it into the salad. If you like a more moist salad, stir in the remaining mayonnaise.

Second Thoughts

You can leave out the ham if you wish. Whether or not you do, try a few of these ingredients:

- ➤ ½ chopped red pepper
- ➤ 8 cooked, cut-up shrimp
- ➤ 1 cup thawed frozen corn kernels
- ➤ 1 chopped, de-seeded tomato

Corn and Barley Salad

This novel salad is worth a try; it's colorful, beautiful, and delicious.

Level: Intermediate

Yield: 4–6 servings

Can be done completely ahead

1 cup barley (sometimes packaged as pearled barley)

1 medium tomato

1 cup cooked or thawed frozen corn kernels

2 scallions, finely chopped

3 TB. finely chopped parsley

2 tsp. minced fresh oregano or marjoram, or ¾ tsp. dried

¾ tsp. salt, or salt to taste

¼ tsp. freshly ground black pepper

½ cup olive oil

3 TB. red wine vinegar

1 TB. Dijon mustard

Place the barley in a saucepan, add enough cold water to cover by 1", and let it stand 1 hour. Drain the barley and return it to the saucepan. Pour in 2 cups of water. Bring the water to a boil, lower the heat, cover the pan, and cook the barley about 30 minutes or until all the liquid has been absorbed. While the barley is cooking, cut the tomato in half crosswise, squeeze out the seeds, and chop the pulp into small pieces. When the barley is cooked, put it into a bowl and add the tomato, corn, scallions, parsley, oregano, salt, and pepper. Mix the ingredients. In a small bowl, whisk the olive oil, red wine vinegar, and mustard. Pour this over the barley salad and toss the ingredients. Let the salad stand at least 30 minutes before serving.

Second Thoughts

You may use 1 cup thawed frozen peas in addition to or instead of the corn in the Corn and Barley Salad.

The Easiest Chicken Salad in the World

The apple and nuts give crunch and flavor to this version of classic chicken salad.

Level: Easy

Yield: 4 servings

Can be done completely ahead

3 cups diced cooked chicken

1 large tart apple (such as a Granny Smith), peeled, cored, and diced

½ cup chopped almonds

¾ cup mayonnaise

freshly ground black pepper

Mix all the ingredients together in a bowl. If you like a more moist salad, add slightly more mayonnaise. Chill the salad slightly, but do not serve it ice cold.

Second Thoughts

Experiment with The Easiest Chicken Salad in the World by trying these alternatives:

➤ Use turkey instead of chicken

➤ Use toasted almonds or walnut pieces instead of plain almonds

➤ Use chopped pear instead of apple

➤ Season the salad with 1–2 tsp. curry powder

➤ Use less mayonnaise (½ cup) and add plain yogurt

Chicken Salad Provençale

This salad looks gorgeous, so consider serving it to company for lunch or as a light dinner during warm weather.

Level: Challenging

Yield: 4 servings

*Can be done ahead up to the * in the instructions*

several pieces of leafy lettuce such as
 Oakleaf lettuce

4 cups diced cooked chicken

1 small ripe avocado (optional)

1 large red pepper

1 small red onion, sliced

18 black olives

½ cup olive oil

3 TB. red wine vinegar

1 tsp. Dijon mustard

1 tsp. fresh thyme leaves or about
 ½ tsp. dried

½ tsp. salt, or salt to taste

⅛ tsp. freshly ground black pepper

Wash and dry the lettuce leaves and arrange them on a platter. Place the chicken in a mound in the center. Peel and cut the avocado (if used) and arrange the slices around the chicken. Remove the stem and seeds from the pepper, cut it into strips, and arrange the strips near the avocado and chicken. Place red onion slices around the platter, and scatter the olives here and there. Combine the remaining ingredients in a bowl and whisk to blend them well.

* Pour the dressing over the meat and vegetables. If possible, wait about 15 minutes before you serve the salad.

Lentil Salad with Mustard Vinaigrette

A refreshing first course or buffet dish.

Level: Intermediate

Yield: 4 servings

Can be done completely ahead

1 cup lentils

2 whole cloves

1 onion, peeled but left whole

1 bay leaf

1 cup diced zucchini

1 tomato, de-seeded and chopped

3 TB. chopped shallots

5 TB. olive oil

2 TB. red wine vinegar

1 TB. Dijon mustard

1½ tsp. fresh thyme leaves or
 ½ tsp. dried

salt and freshly ground black pepper
 to taste

Rinse the lentils in a sieve under cold running water. Drain them and place them in a saucepan. Stick the cloves into the onion and put it into the pan. Add the bay leaf and enough cold water to cover the lentils by 1". Bring the water to a boil, lower the heat, and simmer the lentils for about 15–20 minutes or until they are tender. Drain the lentils. Discard the clove-stuck onion and the bay leaf. Place the lentils in a bowl. Add the zucchini, tomato, and shallots and toss the ingredients. Combine the olive oil, red wine vinegar, mustard, thyme, salt, and pepper in a small bowl and whisk these ingredients for a few seconds until they are well combined. Pour the dressing over the salad and mix.

Second Thoughts

Add 4–6 oz. chopped cooked shrimp or 1 cup of diced smoked turkey or ham.

Salad Croutons

Use these in any green tossed salad. You may also put them on top of soup.

Level: Easy

Yield: about 2 cups

Can be done completely ahead

2 TB. olive oil

1 TB. butter

2 cloves garlic, minced

2 cups ½" white bread cubes

1½ tsp. minced fresh herbs of choice, or ½ tsp. dried (optional)

Preheat the oven to 325°F. Heat the olive oil and butter in a skillet. When the butter has melted and looks foamy, add the garlic and cook it over low heat 3–4 minutes. Add the bread cubes and herbs (if used). Toss the bread around the pan to coat the cubes with oil and butter. Place the coated cubes on a cookie sheet. Bake the cubes 12–13 minutes or until lightly browned and crispy. Store croutons in an airtight container.

Kitchen Clue

Homemade croutons are tender and absorb flavorful dressings better than firm packaged croutons. You may use whole wheat or Italian bread; trim the crusts of any bread you choose.

Fish and Shellfish

A generation or so ago, most people bought the same familiar fish they'd always eaten. Today, there is a staggering assortment available from all over the world. Your meals will be more interesting if you try several types, alternating between lean and fatty fish, mild and robustly flavored varieties, and fillets, steaks, and whole fish.

Menu suggestions for dishes to accompany fish and shellfish appear in Section 5, "Pastas, Rice, and Grains," and Section 6, "Vegetables."

Broiled or Grilled Swordfish

Great on the grill or in the oven broiler, this is a "meaty fish" that's filling and satisfying. It's wonderful with a bunch of colorful vegetables: spinach, beets, corn, and cauliflower, or with Pasta with Sun-Dried Tomatoes and Pignoli Nuts or Wild Rice Fritters.

Level: Easy

Yield: 4 servings

Can be done ahead up to the * in the instructions

4 swordfish steaks, about 1¼" thick

6 TB. lemon juice

6 TB. olive oil

½ tsp. freshly ground black pepper

1½ TB. Dijon mustard

2 TB. minced fresh basil or dill, or 2 tsp. dried

1 TB. minced fresh savory, oregano, marjoram, or thyme, or 1 tsp. dried

Place the steaks in a glass, ceramic, stainless-steel, or other nonreactive dish. Combine the remaining ingredients in a small bowl. Pour the mixture over the fish. Let the fish marinate in the refrigerator about 1 hour, turning the fish after 30 minutes.

* Preheat the broiler or grill. Place the broiler pan or grill rack about 6 inches from the heat source. Broil or grill the steaks 5 minutes. Turn them over and broil or grill them another 4–6 minutes or until fish is just cooked through.

Kitchen Clue

You may substitute fresh tuna, monkfish, or halibut steak. You may also vary this versatile dish by using lime juice instead of lemon or by adding a large minced shallot to the marinade.

Easy Shrimp Scampi

A luxurious dish for special family or company dinners, this version has a surprise ingredient. Perfect with cooked white rice and any green vegetable.

Level: Intermediate

Yield: 4 servings

Can be done ahead up to the * in the instructions

1¾ lbs. large or extra-large raw shrimp	3 cloves garlic, minced
6 TB. melted, cooled butter	1 TB. minced shallot
⅓ cup olive oil	2 TB. chopped parsley
4 TB. cream sherry	¼ tsp. salt, or salt to taste

Preheat the broiler. Shell and devein the shrimp as described in Chapter 13, "A Compendium of the Top 100+ Cooking Terms." Rinse the shrimp under cold water, dry them in paper towels, and cut into the deveined area of each one, deep enough so you can flatten or "butterfly" the shrimp. (To butterfly them, gently press down on the curvy, deveined side with the palm of your hand.) Do not cut through completely. Place the shrimp, cut side up, in a baking dish. Combine the remaining ingredients in a small bowl and pour this mixture over the shrimp.

* Place the dish in the broiler with the rack set about 6 inches below the heat source. Broil the shrimp, without turning them, 5–7 minutes or until they are pink and firm.

Fein on Food

Typically, Shrimp Scampi recipes call for dry sherry. This version originated when there was no dry sherry in our house and Harvey's Bristol Cream came to the rescue. The sweet, cream sherry has been the family's first choice for Shrimp Scampi and other shellfish ever since.

Broiled Salmon with Mustard and Tarragon

This dish looks good and tastes as if you really fussed—but it is amazingly easy and only takes 5 minutes to prepare. Serve it with cooked white or wild rice and steamed asparagus or Brussels sprouts.

Level: Easy

Yield: 4 servings

*Can be done ahead up to the * in the instructions*

4 salmon steaks, about 1¼" thick

2 TB. olive oil

2 TB. Dijon mustard

2 TB. lime juice

2 TB. chopped fresh tarragon leaves, or 2 tsp. dried

¼ tsp. freshly ground black pepper

Preheat the broiler. Place the salmon steaks in a heatproof pan. Mix the olive oil, mustard, lime juice, tarragon, and black pepper. Spoon some of this mixture over the salmon. Turn the salmon over and spoon remaining sauce over the fish.

* Broil the salmon 5 minutes. Turn the steaks and broil another 4–5 minutes, basting with the pan juices once or twice, or until fish is just cooked through.

Sole Meuniére

This dish is a classic, and though it is extremely simple to make, it is one of the most elegant dishes you can serve company. Excellent with steamed new potatoes or wild rice, and steamed asparagus, snow peas, or sautéed spinach.

Level: Easy

Yield: 4 servings

Cannot be done ahead

¼ cup all-purpose flour

½ tsp. salt, or salt to taste

¼ tsp. freshly ground black pepper, or pepper to taste

4 fillets of sole

3½ TB. butter

1 TB. vegetable oil

2 TB. lemon juice

2 TB. chopped parsley

Preheat the oven to 140°F. Combine the flour, salt, and pepper in a plate. Dredge the fish fillets in the flour and shake off the excess. Heat the vegetable oil and 2 TB. of the butter in a skillet over moderate heat. When the butter has melted and looks foamy, add the fish to the pan. Cook the fillets over moderate heat 4–5 minutes, turning them once with a rigid spatula, or until they are delicately browned. Transfer the fillets to a plate and keep them warm in the oven. Add the remaining 1½ TB. butter and the lemon juice to the pan and mix ingredients until the butter melts. Pour the sauce over the fish. Sprinkle the fish with the parsley and serve.

Roasted Chilean Sea Bass with Bacon and Hazelnuts

Monkfish and cod are good substitutes here. This dish is wonderful with cooked white rice, Broccoli with Garlic and Lemon, Sautéed Zucchini, Pepper and Corn, or sautéed spinach.

Level: Easy

Yield: 4 servings

*Can be done ahead up to the * in the instructions*

1½ to 2 lbs. Chilean sea bass	1 TB. olive oil
3 slices of bacon	1½ tsp. grated lemon peel
2 TB. chopped shallots	3 TB. ground hazelnuts
2 TB. Dijon mustard	salt and pepper

Preheat the oven to 450°F. Place the fish in a shallow baking pan. Fry the bacon in a skillet until the pieces are very crispy. Crumble the bacon into fine pieces and set aside in a bowl. Discard most of the bacon fat from the skillet. Add the shallots to the skillet and cook over low to moderate heat for about 2 minutes, or until they have softened. Add the shallots to the bacon. Stir in the mustard, olive oil, lemon peel and hazelnuts and mix thoroughly. Spread the mixture over the fish. Sprinkle with salt and pepper.

* Roast for 10–12 minutes or until fish is just cooked through.

Crunchy Crusted Trout

Oatmeal gives this dish a faintly sweet taste and a crunchy crust. Try this dish with mashed potatoes and Wilted Kale with Sesame Dressing.

Level: Intermediate

Yield: 4 servings

*Can be done ahead up to the * in the instructions*

4 TB. olive oil	¼ tsp. freshly ground black pepper
1½ TB. lemon juice	4 trout fillets
1 tsp. Dijon mustard	1 cup uncooked quick oatmeal
2 TB. chopped chives (or the green part of scallion)	vegetable oil
½ tsp. salt, or salt to taste	lemon wedges

Mix the olive oil, lemon juice, mustard, chives, salt, and pepper in a glass, ceramic, stainless-steel, or other nonreactive dish large enough to hold the trout fillets. Place the fillets in the dish and coat them with the mixture. Let the fish rest 10 minutes. Crush the oats on a flat plate. Dredge the fillets in the oats. Let the oat-coated fillets rest 15 minutes or longer.

* Heat ¼" vegetable oil in a skillet. Add the fillets and sauté them over moderate heat about 3 minutes per side, or until the fillets are lightly browned. Serve with lemon wedges.

Second Thoughts

If you prefer not to fry the fish, preheat the oven to 375°F and bake the fish on a cookie sheet about 12 minutes or until lightly browned.

Baked Bluefish

The tomatoes and celery in this recipe flavor the fish and help keep it juicy. The dish goes well with baked or mashed potatoes, white rice, green beans, broccoli, or any other green vegetable.

Level: Easy

Yield: 4 servings

*Can be done ahead up to the * in the instructions*

4 bluefish fillets

¼ cup lemon juice

2 TB. olive oil

freshly ground black pepper to taste

2 tomatoes, coarsely chopped

2 stalks celery, cut into ½" slices

2 TB. minced fresh dill or 2 tsp. dried

¼ cup fine, dry plain bread crumbs

Preheat the oven to 375°F. Place the bluefish fillets in a baking dish. Sprinkle the fish with the lemon juice, olive oil, and black pepper. Place the tomatoes and celery on top of the fish. Sprinkle the vegetables with the dill and bread crumbs.

* Bake the fish about 20 minutes, or until the bread crumbs are browned and the fish is cooked through.

Kitchen Clue

If you peel the celery, it will be less stringy and more digestible. Peel from the thin end using a vegetable peeler. Pull any strings that don't come off. You can make the recipe for Baked Bluefish with mackerel, snapper, shad, pompano, or grouper.

Warm Open-Face Fresh Tuna "Sandwich" on Garlic Toast

Tuna sandwiches will never seem the same after you've tried this. If you like your grilled tuna rare, be sure to cook the fish for the minimum time specified. Fine for lunch or dinner, serve it with any kind of green salad, potato salad, or potato chips.

Level: Intermediate

Yield: 4 servings

*Can be done ahead up to the * in the instructions*

Vinaigrette dressing, plain or herb (see Section 7, "Sauces and Gravies")

1½ lbs. fresh tuna steak, 1¼" thick

5 TB. olive oil

salt and pepper

8 slices Italian or French bread, cut into ½" thick slices

1 clove garlic, cut in half

2 large tomatoes, sliced

1 medium red onion, sliced

Preheat the broiler or grill. Mix the dressing ingredients and set them aside.

* Brush the tuna with 1 TB. of the olive oil and sprinkle with salt and pepper. Place the broiler pan or grill rack about 6 inches from the heat source. Broil or grill the steaks for 4–5 minutes. Turn them over and broil or grill them another 4–6 minutes or until fish is cooked as desired. While the tuna cooks, rub the slices of Italian bread with the cut side of the garlic and brush with the remaining olive oil. Toast the bread lightly. Place two slices of toast on each of four plates. Slice the tomato and onion and arrange them on top of the toast. Slice the tuna and place the slices over the onion. Pour some dressing over the sandwich, using as little or as much of it as you wish.

Crabcakes with Hot Salsa

Crabcakes are versatile: Use them as a first course or main course, or stuff them inside crusty French bread slathered with Hot Salsa (recipe below) or mayonnaise, or make them smaller to serve as hors d'oeuvre. They're terrific with French fries.

Level: Intermediate

Yield: 4 servings

Can be done completely ahead

1 lb. flaked crabmeat	¼ tsp. Cajun blackening spices
1 egg	2 TB. minced parsley
1 tsp. powdered mustard	¼ cup milk
½ tsp. salt, or salt to taste	2 TB. cracker crumbs or flour
¼ tsp. cayenne pepper	¼ cup vegetable oil, approx.

Combine the crabmeat, egg, mustard, salt, cayenne pepper, Cajun blackening spice, and parsley in a medium-size bowl. Mix in the milk. Add the cracker crumbs and blend ingredients thoroughly. Shape the mixture into 8 patties about ½" thick. Heat the vegetable oil in a skillet. Fry the crabcakes a few at a time over moderate heat about 3 minutes per side, or until both sides are browned and crispy. Add more oil to the pan if necessary to prevent sticking. Drain crabcakes on paper towels. Serve plain or on plates cloaked with Hot Salsa.

Hot Salsa

¼ cup prepared white horseradish	2 TB. minced parsley
¼ cup lemon juice	½ tsp. salt, or salt to taste
¼ cup minced red bell pepper	black pepper to taste
2 scallions, minced	½ cup olive oil
½ stalk celery, minced	hot pepper sauce
2 cloves garlic, minced	

Combine horseradish, lemon juice, red pepper, scallions, celery, garlic, parsley, salt, and pepper in a bowl. Gradually whisk in the olive oil. Season to taste with hot pepper sauce.

Kitchen Clue

Remember that when you reheat fried foods, you must put them in a preheated oven at 400°F in a single layer on a cookie sheet. Put the food on a rack if possible for even better results.

Fannie Daddies with Red Pepper Mayonnaise

These crispy morsels with the old-fashioned name are fried clams. Serve them as hors d'oeuvres or as an entrée stuffed inside a crusty roll. This recipe works with soft-shell crabs and sea scallops, too. Good with French fries or potato chips.

Level: Intermediate

Yield: 4 servings

Can be done completely ahead

The Clams

24 shucked cherrystone or top neck clams

½ cup flour

2 eggs, beaten

¾ cup cracker crumbs

½ tsp. salt, or salt to taste

¼ tsp. paprika

freshly ground black pepper to taste

3 cups vegetable oil, approx.

Pat the clams dry on paper towels and dredge them in the flour. Dip the floured clams in the eggs. Mix the cracker crumbs, salt, paprika, and black pepper and coat the clams with this mixture. Set the clams aside on a rack for about 15 minutes. Heat enough of the vegetable oil in a deep skillet to cover the clams completely. When the oil reaches about 365°F (a crumb of bread will sizzle quickly), deep-fat fry the clams a few at a time, for about 2 minutes, or until they are nicely browned. Drain on paper towels. Serve with Red Pepper Mayonnaise.

Red Pepper Mayonnaise

1 cup mayonnaise

1 TB. drained capers

2 TB. chopped red bell pepper

Mix ingredients together.

1 TB. chopped dill pickle

1 chopped scallion

¼ tsp. cayenne pepper, or to taste

Kitchen Clue

The coatings on fried foods adhere better if you let the ingredients air dry on a rack for about 15 minutes after coating them.

Baked Scallops and Tomatoes

This recipe makes a great quick dinner. Serve it with steamed new potatoes or cooked white rice, cauliflower, broccoli, corn, or green beans.

Level: Easy

Yield: 4 servings

Cannot be done ahead

1¼ lbs. large scallops

salt and freshly ground black pepper
    to taste

3 TB. chopped parsley

3 TB. chopped fresh basil

2 tsp. chopped fresh oregano

2 tomatoes, chopped

1 small onion, chopped

¼ cup olive oil

¼ cup fresh lemon juice

Preheat the oven to 425°F. Rinse and drain the scallops and place them in a baking dish. Sprinkle with salt, pepper, parsley, basil, and oregano. Add the tomatoes and onion, pour in the olive oil and lemon juice and toss the ingredients to coat the scallops and tomatoes evenly with the flavorings. Bake 12–15 minutes or until scallops are cooked through.

Meat and Poultry

In the United States, we are fortunate to have a huge variety of high-quality meats and poultry, so dinner never has to be boring. We're also lucky that there are so many different cuts of meats and types of chicken. If you don't have the time to cook a large roast beef, you can quickly grill some chicken breasts. You can prepare a pot roast a few days ahead of serving time or a last-minute Veal Marsala. With so many choices, you'll never be stuck without an idea for dinner.

Menu suggestions for dishes to accompany meat and poultry recipes appear in Section 5, "Pastas, Rice, and Grains," and Section 6, "Vegetables."

How to Make Great Hamburgers

Simple dishes like hamburgers take more thinking than complicated ones. Don't worry, though—this page covers the tricks of the trade. Accompaniments? The usual suspects: Baked Beans, and any kind of potato salad or French fries.

Level: Easy

Yield: makes 4 (5-oz.) burgers

Cannot be done ahead

1¼ lbs. ground beef round, chuck, or sirloin (or a mixture of all three)

½ tsp. salt, or salt to taste

⅛ tsp. ground pepper

1 tsp. Worcestershire sauce (optional)

4 hamburger rolls

thinly sliced Vidalia, Bermuda, or Spanish onion

thinly sliced tomato

slices of dill pickle

ketchup, mustard, or mayonnaise

Mix the meat, salt, pepper, and Worcestershire sauce, if used. Shape the meat into four patties about 4"–5" in diameter. Preheat a broiler, grill, or a skillet set over high heat. (If you panfry the burgers in the skillet, brush the bottom of the pan with a film of butter or vegetable oil.) Broil, grill, or fry the patties for 1 minute per side. Reduce the heat to moderate and cook the burgers, turning them once, another 3–4 minutes, depending on the degree of rareness you like. Serve the burgers on buns, topped with onion, tomato, and pickle. Spread the roll with the condiment of your choice.

Kitchen Clue

Here are some tips for better burgers:

➤ If you like your burgers very rare, mix 1 TB. of ice shavings into each patty to keep the meat cold.

➤ Never press down on a burger when it cooks; this releases necessary natural fluids.

➤ Turn the burgers with a rigid spatula for easier handling.

How to Prepare a Steak

Some people just need a hunk of steak every once in awhile. Here's how to satisfy that craving. Serve it with a green salad or Spicy Tomato Salad and Baked Potatoes.

Level: Easy

Yield: 8–12 oz. (serves 1 person)

Cannot be done ahead

steak for grilling, such as New York strip, sirloin, T-bone, porterhouse, rib, Delmonico, club, shell, or filet mignon

salt and freshly ground black pepper

garlic powder (optional)

Preheat a broiler, grill, or a skillet set over high heat. (If you panfry the steaks in the skillet, brush the bottom of the pan with a film of butter or vegetable oil.) Sprinkle the steak with salt, pepper, and garlic powder. Broil, grill, or fry the steak for 1 minute per side. Reduce the heat to moderate, and cook the steak on both sides, depending on the thickness of the steak and the degree of doneness you like (see hints below). When you turn the steak, use a spatula or tongs—not a fork.

Here are some handy facts about cooking steak:

➤ Total cooking times for a 1"-thick steak are 6–8 minutes for rare, 8–10 minutes for medium, and 11–12 minutes for well-done.

➤ Total cooking times for a 1½"-thick steak are 9–11 minutes for rare, 12–15 minutes for medium, and 16–18 minutes for well-done.

➤ Time depends on factors other than thickness: Frozen steaks (yes, you can cook steaks straight from the freezer!) will take twice as long; cold steaks straight from the fridge may take a little longer. Filets mignon, which can be very thick, may take longer.

Second Thoughts

Most people like their steaks plain. But if you like an extra bit of pizzazz, mix 4–5 TB. of fresh minced herbs of your choice with 1 TB. lemon juice and ½ cup softened butter. Put a spoonful of this mixture on top of each portion of finished steak.

Pearl J. Fein's Famous Standing Rib Roast

Although old-fashioned, this is still one of the most regal-looking roasts around. This version is an old family favorite: my mother-in-law's specialty. Suggested accompaniments: Baked Stuffed Potatoes and Creamed Spinach or Broccoli with Garlic and Lemon.

Level: Intermediate

Yield: makes 6–8 servings

Cannot be done ahead

1 (3-rib) standing beef rib roast	1 tsp. freshly ground black pepper
kitchen string	1–1½ tsp. garlic powder
4 tsp. paprika	water
2 tsp. salt, or salt to taste	

Preheat the oven to 450°F. If the butcher hasn't done this for you, remove the strings that tie the ribs to the bones, if there are any. Carve the meat from the bone as close to the bone as you can so that you are left with a boneless roast and L-shaped rib bones. Tie the meat back onto the bones with kitchen string. Place the paprika, salt, pepper, and garlic powder in a small bowl and add enough water to make the mixture a bit thinner than ketchup. Brush the mixture on the surface of the roast, including the bones. Place the roast, bones down, in a roasting pan. Roast the beef 20 minutes. Lower the heat to 350°F and cook 15–20 minutes more per pound, depending on whether you like the meat rare, medium, or well done. A meat thermometer inserted into the middle of the meat will read 120–135°F for rare, 135–145°F for medium, and 145°F+ for well-done.

Let the roast beef stand 15 minutes before carving it. To carve the meat, remove the strings and place the now-boneless roast on a carving board. Carve the meat into slices of equal thickness, depending on how many people you will be serving.

Kitchen Clue

Cutting the meat from the bone and tying it back on with string before roasting makes it easier to carve when it's cooked. Ask the butcher to do this for you. Or, you can roast the meat without carving and tying it. In this case, you'll have to cut the meat from the bone, after cooking is complete, to make it a "boneless" roast.

Hot and Spicy Pot Roast

This isn't just any ordinary pot roast—it's hot and spicy. You can make it milder or even more fierce, if you want. This is a good dish to serve with Mashed Potatoes or Polenta and steamed carrots.

Level: Intermediate

Yield: 6–8 servings

Can be done completely ahead

1 (3–4 lb.) beef roast for pot roast such as brisket, rump, or bottom round

2 TB. vegetable oil

2 large onions, cut into large chunks

1 (28-oz.) can Italian style plum tomatoes, drained

1 cup canned or homemade beef broth or stock

2 tsp. paprika

1 tsp. salt, or salt to taste

½ tsp. freshly ground black pepper

1½ tsp. minced fresh oregano, or ½ tsp. dried

1½ tsp. minced fresh thyme, or ½ tsp. dried

½ tsp. powdered mustard

½ tsp. cayenne pepper

Wipe the meat dry with paper towels. Preheat a Dutch oven or fireproof casserole over moderate heat. Add the vegetable oil to the pan. Put the meat in the pan and cook it 12–15 minutes, turning it occasionally, until all sides are darkly colored. Pour off excess fat from the pan. Add the onions, tomatoes, and broth. In a small bowl, combine the paprika, salt, black pepper, oregano, thyme, mustard, and cayenne pepper. Sprinkle the mixture over the ingredients. Reduce the heat, cover the pan and cook at a bare simmer about 2–2½ hours, or until meat is tender.

Second Thoughts

To make traditional pot roast, sprinkle the meat with salt, pepper, and paprika. Brown it as described in the recipe. Add the onions, tomatoes, and broth (or use red wine, beer, or water as a substitute); then proceed with the recipe.

What Is It?

A **Dutch oven** is a large heatproof, short-handled casserole or pan.

Chili con Carne

Everyone's got a favorite recipe for chili. This one's moderately spicy and thick with ground meat. Serve with a green salad.

Level: Easy

Yield: 4 servings

Can be done completely ahead

1½ TB. vegetable oil

1 large onion, chopped

2 cloves garlic, minced

1 lb. ground sirloin or round

1 (28-oz.) can Italian style plum tomatoes, drained and chopped

1 (6-oz.) can tomato paste

1¾ cups canned or homemade beef broth or stock

2 TB. chili powder

2 tsp. dried oregano

1½ tsp. ground cumin

1½ tsp. salt, or salt to taste

½ tsp. red pepper flakes

½ tsp. freshly ground black pepper

2 bay leaves

1 (15-oz.) can red kidney beans, drained

Heat the vegetable oil in a large, deep skillet. Add the onion and garlic and cook over moderate heat for 3–4 minutes or until the vegetables have softened. Add the meat and cook 5–6 minutes or until the meat turns brown. Break up the meat with a wooden spoon as it cooks. Add the tomatoes, tomato paste, beef broth, chili powder, oregano, cumin, salt, red pepper flakes, black pepper, and bay leaves. Bring the mixture to a boil, lower the heat, and simmer the mixture for 25 minutes. Add the beans and cook another 15–20 minutes, or until most of the liquid has evaporated and the meat is surrounded by sauce as thick as gravy.

Taco Meatloaf

If you're bored with regular meatloaf, try this version with a spicy Southwestern taste. The classic meatloaf accompaniment is Mashed Potatoes. Add a green vegetable to round out the meal.

Level: Easy

Yield: 6 servings

Can be done completely ahead

2 lbs. ground round or chuck

2 tsp. salt, or salt to taste

¼ tsp. freshly ground black pepper

2 eggs, beaten

½ cup bread crumbs

½ cup plain yogurt

½ cup grated cheddar cheese

1 small onion (about ½ cup), chopped

3 TB. tomato paste

2 tsp. chili powder

a dash or two of hot pepper sauce

Preheat the oven to 350°F. Combine all the ingredients in a large bowl. Put the mixture in a 9" × 5" × 3" loaf pan. Bake it about 50–60 minutes, or until the meatloaf is well browned and begins to pull away from the sides of the pan. If you don't have a loaf pan, you can make a free-standing meatloaf: Shape the meat into an oval and bake it in a jelly roll pan.

Second Thoughts

For traditional meatloaf, combine the meat (or use a combination of 1 lb. ground round or chuck, ½ lb. ground pork, and ½ lb. ground veal) with the salt, pepper, eggs, and breadcrumbs. Stir in ½ cup ketchup, a small, chopped onion and 2 tsp. Worcestershire sauce and proceed with the recipe.

Roast Rack of Lamb

This dish can be expensive, but it's a rich, lavish-tasting treat and incredibly easy to make. A great company dish. Side dish suggestions include: Tuscan Style White Beans with Tomato Sauce or Wild Rice Fritters and any steamed vegetable.

Level: Easy

Yield: makes 4–5 servings

Can be done ahead up to the * in the instructions

2 racks of lamb	2 TB. olive oil
salt and black pepper to taste	2 TB. minced, fresh rosemary,
2 large cloves of garlic, minced	or 2 tsp. dried, crushed rosemary
3 TB. Dijon mustard	¼ cup dry, plain bread crumbs

Preheat the oven to 450°F. Trim most of the excess fat from the meat. Sprinkle the meat lightly with salt and pepper. Mix together the garlic, mustard, olive oil, and rosemary and brush this on the top surface of the meat. Sprinkle with the bread crumbs.

* Place the meat in a roasting pan. Roast 10 minutes. Reduce the heat to 350°F and continue to roast the meat 20–40 minutes, depending on how well done you like your meat; a meat thermometer will read 120–125°F for rare and 135–140°F for medium. Let the roast stand about 10 minutes before you serve it.

What Is It?

A **rack of lamb** is a strip of uncut rib chops.

Broiled Butterflied Leg of Lamb

You're in luck if you have an outdoor grill because it gives the lamb the smoky flavor of charcoal. Otherwise, use your oven broiler. Try this with Baked Beans or Boiled Corn on the Cob, or any of these: Potato Salad with Lemon-Oregano Dressing, Corn and Barley Salad or Lentil Salad with Mustard Vinaigrette.

Level: Easy

Yield: 6 servings

*Can be done ahead up to the * in the instructions*

3 lb. boneless leg of lamb

¼ cup Dijon mustard

2 TB. olive oil

3 TB. lemon juice

2 cloves garlic, minced

2 tsp. fresh thyme, or ½ tsp. dried

¼ tsp. salt, or salt to taste

¼ tsp. freshly ground black pepper

Place the lamb in a glass, ceramic, stainless-steel, or other nonreactive dish. Combine the remaining ingredients in a small bowl and mix them well. Pour the mixture over the meat. Let the meat marinate in the liquid 15 minutes (or as long as 2 hours).

* Preheat the broiler or grill. Place the meat on a rack in the broiler pan (or on the grill grids) and set about 4–6 inches away from the heat source. Cook 8–12 minutes. Use tongs to turn over the meat and cook it another 8–12 minutes, or until it is cooked to your liking.

Roast Loin of Pork

Try this dish with Sautéed Rosemary Potatoes or Bulgur Wheat and Lentil Pilaf, along with and a leafy green vegetable such as kale or spinach.

Level: Easy

Yield: 6 servings

*Can be done ahead up to the * in the instructions*

1 (4-lb.) boneless loin of pork

¾ tsp. salt, or salt to taste

½ tsp. freshly ground black pepper

1 small onion, minced

1 large clove garlic, minced

1 TB. Dijon mustard

1 TB. olive oil

Preheat the oven to 450°F. Wipe the meat dry with paper towels and place it in a roasting pan. Combine the remaining ingredients in a small bowl. Spread this mixture on the top surface and part of the sides of the meat.

* Roast the meat about 15 minutes. Lower the heat to 350°F and roast another hour, or until juices run clear when the roast is pierced with a sharp knife. A meat thermometer inserted into the thickest part of the meat should read about 150°F. Let the roast stand 10–15 minutes before carving it.

Second Thoughts

This basic dish can stand all sorts of variations. Try adding 2 tsp. caraway seeds to give the pork an unusual flavor and crunchy texture. You might also include 1½ tsp. of chopped fresh rosemary (or ½ tsp. dried) in the seasoning mixture or spread ¼ cup orange marmalade or apricot jam on the roast for the last 15 minutes of cooking.

Stuffed Pork Chops

The apples and raisins in this dish harmonize deliciously with the pork, which has its own faintly sweet flavor. Lovely with Mashed Potatoes or Sweet Potato Casserole, Cranberry Sauce (see Section 7, "Sauces and Gravies"), and steamed Brussels sprouts.

Level: Easy

Yield: 4 servings

*Can be done ahead up to the * in the instructions*

1 TB. butter

1 medium tart apple, cored, peeled
   and finely chopped

¼ cup raisins

¼ cup chopped nuts, preferably cashews
   or almonds

¼ tsp. salt

⅛ tsp. ground ginger

⅛ tsp. cinnamon

8 thick pork chops, cut with a pocket

Preheat the oven to 350°F. Heat the butter in a skillet over moderate heat. When the butter has melted and looks foamy, add the apple and raisins and cook 2–3 minutes, or until the fruit has softened. Remove the pan from the heat and stir in the nuts, salt, ginger, and cinnamon. Set the mixture aside to cool (about 15 minutes). Place equal amounts of the mixture inside the pockets of the pork chops.

* Put the pork chops in a baking pan. Bake them 35 minutes or until they are cooked through.

Kitchen Clue

You can have the butcher cut the pocket into the chop for you, or do it yourself: With the tip of a sharp knife, make a cut into the side of the chop, and then cut through to almost cut the chop in half, leaving about ½" around the edges.

Texas Ribs with Orange-Scented Barbecue Sauce

These ribs are both tangy and sweet. Eat them with corn on the cob, baked beans, Potato Salad with Lemon-Oregano Dressing (Section 2, "Soups and Salads"), and maybe a hunk of cornbread.

Level: Challenging

Yield: 4 servings

Can be done completely ahead

3½ –4 lbs. regular pork spareribs
   (you can also use country-style ribs)

½ cup molasses

½ cup ketchup

1 TB. soy sauce

⅓ cup orange juice

1 medium onion, finely chopped

1 TB. freshly grated orange peel

1½ TB. butter

1 large clove garlic, minced

1 tsp. powdered mustard

½ tsp. ground ginger

¼ tsp. ground cloves, or 4 whole cloves

pinch of salt (optional)

1 TB. white vinegar

½ tsp. hot pepper sauce

Cut the ribs into sections of 3–4 ribs. Bring a soup pot half filled with water to a boil over high heat. Lower the heat. Immerse the ribs in the liquid. Cook the ribs at a bare simmer for 25 minutes. Remove the ribs and set them aside. Preheat the oven to 350°F. While the ribs are cooking, combine the remaining ingredients in a saucepan and stir until well blended. Bring the mixture to a boil over high heat. Lower the heat and simmer the sauce 5 minutes. Place the ribs in a roasting pan and brush most of the sauce over them. Cook 25–30 minutes, brushing more sauce onto the ribs, and turning them frequently during the cooking process. Use all the sauce on the ribs.

Second Thoughts

If you prefer, grill the ribs on an outdoor grill. Cook them over indirect moderate heat for 25–30 minutes, turning them often and brushing with sauce until all the sauce has been used.

Veal Marsala

This is an old-fashioned favorite that everyone still loves. Serve it with Steamed Broccoli, Polenta, and Sautéed Mushrooms.

Level: Easy

Yield: 4 servings

Cannot be done ahead

4 TB. flour

½ tsp. salt, or salt to taste

⅛ tsp. freshly ground black pepper

1¼ lbs. veal cutlets

2 TB. butter

2 TB. olive oil

½ cup Marsala wine

Preheat the oven to 140°F. Combine the flour, salt, and pepper on a plate. Dredge the veal cutlets in the flour mixture and shake off the excess. Heat half the butter and olive oil in a large skillet over moderate heat. When the butter has melted and looks foamy, add some of the cutlets. Cook 3–5 minutes, turning the meat once, or until the cutlets are cooked through. Repeat with the remaining butter and olive oil and the remaining cutlets. As you finish cooking the cutlets, put them on a dish and keep them warm in the oven. When all the cutlets are cooked, add the wine to the skillet and stir the ingredients with a wooden spoon to release any browned bits and particles that may have stuck to the bottom of the pan. Cook a minute or so, and then pour the sauce over the veal and serve.

How to Broil or Grill Chicken

This is one of the more basic recipes in a home cook's repertoire, and you can keep changing it to create endless recipes. Serve with any green or yellow vegetable, wild rice, or Rice Pilaf with Mushrooms.

Level: Easy

Yield: 4 servings

*Can be done ahead up to the * in the instructions*

1 (2½–4 lb.) broiler-fryer chicken, cut up

2 TB. vegetable oil or melted butter

salt, black pepper, garlic powder (or garlic salt), and paprika

Preheat the broiler or grill. Wash and dry the chicken parts. Place the parts on a rack in a broiler pan. Rub the surfaces with the vegetable oil or melted butter. Sprinkle the chicken with salt, pepper, garlic powder (or garlic salt), and paprika. You don't need to measure these ingredients; just dust the surface with them. If you use garlic salt, use slightly less regular salt in the recipe.

* Place the broiler pan and rack (or grill rack) about 6 inches below the heat source. Broil or grill the pieces 30–35 minutes, turning them occasionally with tongs or until the juices run clear when the thigh is pricked with the tip of a sharp knife. Baste the chicken two or three times.

Second Thoughts

Consider these variations:

➤ Sprinkle the chicken with 2 TB. chopped, fresh rosemary or 2 tsp. dried, crushed rosemary.

➤ Coat the chicken with 2 TB. Dijon mustard along with the other ingredients.

➤ Before broiling, marinate the chicken parts in vinaigrette dressing for 30 minutes.

➤ Marinate the chicken in 1 cup plain yogurt plus 1 tsp. ground ginger, ½ tsp. cinnamon, ½ tsp. ground cumin, ½ tsp. salt, and 1 minced garlic clove before broiling.

Southern-Style Barbecued Chicken

This dish is tangy and rich: A perfect choice for a summer cookout, yet hearty in winter as well. Accompaniments are the same as for spareribs.

Level: Easy

Yield: 4 servings

Can be done completely ahead

1 (2½–4 lb.) broiler-fryer chicken, cut up	1 TB. chili powder
2 TB. olive oil	1½ tsp. powdered mustard
salt and black pepper to taste	½ tsp. ground ginger
⅓ cup ketchup	1 clove garlic, minced
¼ cup vinegar	1 TB. butter
¼ cup brown sugar	¼ lemon
1½ TB. Worcestershire sauce	

Wash and dry the chicken pieces, rub them with olive oil, and sprinkle them with salt and pepper. Combine all the remaining ingredients in a small saucepan. Cook the sauce over moderate heat 10 minutes. Discard the lemon quarter. Preheat the broiler or grill. Place the broiler pan and rack (or grill rack) about 6 inches below the heat source. Broil or grill the pieces, turning them occasionally with tongs and basting the parts often with the barbecue sauce, for 30–35 minutes, or until the juices run clear when the thigh is pricked with the tip of a sharp knife.

How to Sauté Chicken

This is another basic recipe that you can change in numerous ways. You'll be amazed at how easy and how versatile this dish is! Use the pan juices as gravy for cooked rice of any kind. Sautéed chicken goes well with almost any starch or vegetable.

Level: Easy

Yield: 4 servings

Can be done completely ahead

1 (2½–4 lb.) broiler-fryer chicken, cut up	salt, black pepper, garlic powder (or garlic salt), and paprika
1 TB. vegetable oil	½ cup white wine, or canned or homemade chicken broth or stock
1 TB. butter	

Wash and dry the chicken parts. Heat the vegetable oil and butter in a skillet over moderate heat. When the butter has melted and looks foamy, add the chicken parts. Sprinkle the chicken with salt, pepper, garlic powder (or garlic salt), and paprika. You don't need to measure these spices, just dust the surface with them. If you use garlic salt, use slightly less regular salt in the recipe. Cook the chicken 15 minutes or until the pieces are lightly browned on all sides. Discard excess pan fat. Pour the white wine or broth into the pan. Lower the heat, cover the pan, and cook the chicken at a simmer about 25 minutes or until the parts are cooked through.

Like most other chicken dishes, this one is so versatile that you can experiment with an endless assortment of variations:

➤ After you brown the chicken, remove it from the pan temporarily and add a chopped onion and 4 peeled and cut-up carrots to the pan. Cook them 2–3 minutes, return the chicken to the pan, and proceed as above.

➤ After you brown the chicken, temporarily remove it from the pan and add a chopped onion, a green pepper cut into strips, and a red pepper cut into strips. Cook them 2–3 minutes, return the chicken to the pan, and proceed as above.

➤ Add 8 oz. fresh mushrooms to the pan with the wine or stock.

How to Roast Chicken

So simple, yet so impressive. Roast chicken is suitable for family or company meals. Like other chicken dishes, this one goes well with almost any vegetable or starch, but try it with Wild Rice Fritters, Nana's Egg Noodle Stuffing, or Rice and Fruit Stuffing.

Level: Easy

Yield: 6 servings

*Can be done ahead up to the * in the instructions*

1 (4½–7 lb.) roasting chicken

2 TB. vegetable oil or melted butter

salt, black pepper, garlic powder (or garlic salt), and paprika

Preheat the oven to 400°F. Remove the plastic bag of giblets from inside the bird. Wash the giblets and put them in the roasting pan, if you want to eat them. Otherwise, freeze them for when you want to make stock. (See the "Soups and Salads" recipe section for a stock recipe.) Wash the chicken inside and out. Place the chicken on a rack in the roasting pan. Rub the surface with the vegetable oil or melted butter. Sprinkle the chicken with salt, pepper, garlic (or garlic salt), and paprika. You don't need to measure these ingredients; just dust the surface with them. If you use garlic salt, use slightly less regular salt in the recipe. Place the chicken breast side down on the rack.

* Just before you put the chicken in the oven, lower the heat to 350°F. Roast the bird 45–60 minutes, basting once or twice during that time. Turn the chicken breast side up. Continue to roast the chicken until a meat thermometer inserted into the thickest part of the thigh registers 165–180°F, or when the juices run clear when the thigh is pricked with the tines of a fork. (See Chapter 16, "Timing Is Everything: Creating Your First Masterpiece," for temperature suggestions and USDA recommendations.) After you have turned the chicken breast side up, baste only during the next 15–45 minutes (depending on the size of the chicken). Do not baste for the last 25–30 minutes of roasting time. After you take the chicken out of the oven, let it stand 15 minutes before you carve it.

Kitchen Clue

Generally speaking, chicken takes about 22 minutes per pound to roast all the way through.

Lemon-Oregano Roasted Chicken

This is but one of many variations on roasted chicken, perfect with Mashed Potatoes or cooked white rice, steamed sugar snap peas or broccoli.

Level: Intermediate

Yield: 6 servings

*Can be done ahead up to the * in the instructions*

1 (4½–7 lbs.) roasting chicken
⅓ cup lemon juice
¼ cup olive oil
1 large clove garlic, minced
1 TB. minced fresh oregano, or 1 tsp. dried

2 tsp. minced fresh basil
   or ⅓ tsp. dried
¾ tsp. salt, or salt to taste
¼ tsp. freshly ground black pepper

Preheat the oven to 400°F. Remove the plastic bag of giblets from inside the bird. Wash the giblets and put them in the roasting pan if you want to eat them. Otherwise, freeze them for when you want to make stock. (See the "Soups and Salads" recipe section for a stock recipe.) Wash the chicken inside and out. Place the chicken breast side down on a rack in a roasting pan. Combine the remaining ingredients in a small bowl and pour the mixture over the chicken.

* Just before you put the chicken in the oven, lower the heat to 350°F. Roast the bird 45–60 minutes, basting once or twice during that time. Turn the chicken breast side up. Continue to roast the chicken until a meat thermometer inserted into the thickest part of the thigh registers 165–180 degrees, or until the juices run clear when the thigh is pricked with the tines of a fork. (See Chapter 16 for temperature suggestions and USDA recommendations.) After you have turned the chicken breast side up, baste only during the next 15–45 minutes (depending on the size of the chicken). Do not baste for the last 25–30 minutes of roasting time. After you take the chicken out of the oven, let it stand 15 minutes before you carve it.

Lily Vail's (My Mother's) Fried Chicken

You may think it sounds nutty to make fried chicken at home when you can buy it in all sorts of fast food places, but no fast-food fried chicken tastes like this. Family and friends ask for the recipe all the time. Best accompaniments: French fries, Potato Salad with Lemon-Oregano Dressing, Buttermilk Herb Slaw, Baked Beans, steamed green beans, or any other vegetable.

Level: Intermediate

Yield: 4 servings

Can be done completely ahead

⅔ cup all-purpose flour

1 tsp. salt, or salt to taste

½ tsp. paprika

¼ tsp. garlic powder (or garlic salt)

a few grindings of black pepper

1 (2½–4 lb.) broiler-fryer chicken, cut into 8 pieces (or use 3–4 lbs. chicken parts)

vegetable oil

Combine the flour, salt, paprika, garlic powder (or garlic salt), and black pepper in a plastic bag. If you use garlic salt, use slightly less regular salt in the recipe. Wash the chicken parts and put them in the bag. Shake the bag to coat the chicken with the flour mixture. Remove the chicken pieces and place them on a cake rack or broiler rack for 30 minutes to "air dry."

There are two ways to deep-fat fry the chicken:

➤ Heat enough vegetable oil in a deep pan to cover the chicken pieces. When the oil reaches about 365°F (a crumb of bread will sizzle quickly), deep-fat fry the chicken a few pieces at a time. Do not crowd the pan. Cover the pan. Cook the chicken 8–10 minutes. Remove the chicken pieces with a large strainer, slotted spoon, or tongs, and keep them out of the hot oil for one minute. Return the pieces to the pan and continue to cook them another 8–10 minutes or until they are cooked through. (Pierce the thigh or drumstick in the thickest part with the tip of a sharp knife. If the juices run clear, the chicken is done.) Drain on paper towels.

➤ Heat enough vegetable oil in a deep skillet to come halfway up the sides of the chicken. When the temperature reaches about 365°F, fry the chicken a few pieces at a time. Do not crowd the pan. Cover the pan. Cook the chicken 20–25 minutes, turning the pieces occasionally. Uncover the pan for the last 4–5 minutes. Drain the fried chicken on paper towels.

Roasted Rock Cornish Hens with Curry Stuffing

This dish takes several steps and some time. It is a stunning dish for company, though, so you might want to save this one for special occasions. Serve it with a plain, steamed, or sautéed vegetable.

Level: Challenging

Yield: 6–9 servings

Can be done ahead up to the * in the instructions

5 TB. butter	2 tsp. fresh lemon juice
2½ tsp. curry powder	dash of cayenne pepper
1 medium onion, chopped	½ cup chopped almonds
1 tart apple such as a Granny Smith, cored, peeled, and chopped	6 rock Cornish hens
	salt and freshly ground black pepper to taste
½ cup raisins	
3 cups cooked white rice	

Melt 2 TB. of the butter with ½ tsp. of the curry powder and set this mixture aside. Melt the remaining butter in a skillet. Add the onion, apple, and raisins and cook them over moderate heat for 3–4 minutes. Add the rice, lemon juice, remaining curry powder, cayenne pepper, and nuts; toss ingredients until they are well combined. Remove the pan from the heat. Let the stuffing cool in the refrigerator at least 30 minutes. Wash the hens inside and out. If giblets are packed inside, wash and roast them with the birds or freeze them for when you want to make stock. (See the "Soups and Salads" recipe section for a stock recipe.)

* Preheat the oven to 400°F. Fill the hens with the stuffing. Truss the cavities closed (as described in Chapter 13, "A Compendium of the Top 100+ Cooking Terms"), if desired. Brush the hens with the reserved butter-curry mixture and sprinkle them with some salt and pepper. Place the hens breast side down on a rack in a roasting pan. Just before you put the birds into the oven, lower the heat to 350°F. Roast the hens 40 minutes, basting them once or twice during that time. Turn over the hens and roast them another 35–40 minutes, or until the juices run clear when the thigh is pricked with the tip of a sharp knife. Let the birds rest 10 minutes before you carve them.

Kitchen Clue

Serve the hens whole, or cut each in half and place the halves on a platter with the stuffing tucked beneath the meat.

Grilled Marinated Chicken Breasts

You'll love how fast this dish cooks! Eat it as is or in a sandwich. Slice it and put it on top of a salad, serve it with Sautéed Zucchini, Pepper, and Corn or use it for fajitas.

Level: Easy

Yield: 4 servings

*Can be done ahead up to the * in the instructions*

4 boneless, skinless chicken breast halves

2 TB. vegetable oil

2 TB. lemon juice

2 tsp. Dijon mustard

1 shallot or scallion, minced

1 clove garlic, minced

2 tsp. fresh thyme leaves, or ½ tsp. dried

¼ tsp. salt, or salt to taste

⅛ tsp. freshly ground black pepper

If you wish, place the chicken breasts between two pieces of waxed paper and pound them with a meat mallet, the flat side of a cleaver, or a pot bottom to a thickness of about ¼". (This step makes the cooking more even, but it isn't essential.) Place the chicken in a glass, ceramic, stainless-steel, or other nonreactive dish. Combine the remaining ingredients in a small bowl and whisk them together to make a marinade. Pour the marinade over the chicken and let the meat marinate at least 1 hour. Turn the chicken once or twice during this time. Preheat the broiler. Remove the chicken from the marinade.

* Place the chicken on a rack in the broiler pan (or on the grill grids), set about 4–6 inches away from the heat source. Broil or grill the pieces 3 minutes per side, or until they are cooked through.

Baked Honey-Mustard Chicken Breasts

Really easy to prepare and enticingly sweet, this chicken recipe goes with almost any vegetable or starch, but try it with Rice Pilaf with Mushrooms.

Level: Easy

Yield: 4 servings

*Can be done ahead up to the * in the instructions*

4 whole boneless, skinless chicken
    breast halves

⅓ cup orange juice

1 TB. Dijon mustard

1 TB. honey

1 tsp. Worcestershire sauce

salt and freshly ground black pepper
    to taste

Preheat the oven to 350°. Place the chicken breast halves in a baking dish. Combine the orange juice, mustard, honey, and Worcestershire sauce and pour the liquid over the chicken. Sprinkle the chicken with salt and pepper.

* Bake for 20–25 minutes or until breasts are cooked through.

Stir-Fried Chicken and Peanuts

This Chinese dish is spicy-hot! Cut down on the chili peppers if you wish. Serve with fried or cooked white rice and stir-fried spinach.

Level: Intermediate

Yield: 2–4 servings

*Can be done ahead up to the * in the instructions.*

The sauce

2 TB. soy sauce

1 TB. Shaohsing sherry or Chinese
    rice wine

½ tsp. white vinegar

1 TB. sugar

dash of salt

1 tsp. sesame seed oil

The chicken

3 TB. vegetable oil

4 boneless, skinless chicken breast halves,
    cut into bite-size chunks

4 dry red chili peppers

4 chopped scallions

1 tsp. minced fresh ginger

½ cup roasted peanuts

1 tsp. cornstarch mixed with 2 tsp. water

Mix the sauce ingredients and set it aside.

* Heat 2 TB. of the vegetable oil in a wok, stir-fry pan, or skillet over high heat. Add the chicken and stir-fry for about 2 minutes, or until the pieces have turned white. Remove

the chicken to a bowl and set aside. Heat the remaining vegetable oil in the pan. Add the chili peppers, scallions, and ginger and cook briefly, until the peppers turn dark. Return the chicken to the pan and stir the ingredients until well mixed. Add the sauce and peanuts and stir-fry briefly. Stir the cornstarch mixture and pour it into the pan. Stir-fry until the sauce has thickened and all pieces are thoroughly coated. Remove to a serving dish. Serve immediately.

How to Roast a Turkey

When you see how simple it is to roast a turkey, you'll be the first to volunteer for Thanksgiving dinner duty. The standard accompaniments are Sweet Potato Casserole (see Section 6, "Vegetables"), Mashed Potatoes, Cranberry Sauce (see Section 7, "Sauces and Gravies"), Nana's Egg Noodle Stuffing, or Chestnut and Sausage Stuffing, and a vegetable.

Level: Intermediate

Yield: Depends on the size of turkey; the general rule is 1 lb. turkey per person (an 8-lb. turkey will feed 8 people, for example)

Can be done ahead up to the * in the instructions

1 turkey

salt, freshly ground black pepper, garlic powder (or garlic salt), and paprika

1 cup orange juice, apple juice, white wine, or chicken stock

2 TB. butter or olive oil (optional)

Preheat the oven to 325°F. Remove the plastic bag of giblets from inside the turkey. Wash the giblets and set them aside. Wash the inside of the turkey thoroughly. Wash the skin and remove any obvious hairs and pinfeathers. If the turkey legs are tied or locked with a plastic device, you may have to untie the legs or remove them from the plastic lock to wash the inside of the bird. Retie the legs. Dispose of the plastic lock before roasting the turkey. Place the turkey breast side up on a rack in a roasting pan. Sprinkle with salt, pepper, garlic powder (or garlic salt), and paprika. You don't need to measure these spices, just dust the surface with them. If you use garlic salt, use slightly less regular salt in the recipe. Turn over the turkey and sprinkle the back with the seasonings. Keep the turkey breast side down.

* Roast the turkey 35–55 minutes, depending on the size of the bird. Baste with pan juices and orange juice (or whatever else you use). You may also place the butter or olive oil in the pan to add to the basting juices. Roast another 35–55 minutes. Baste the turkey and turn it breast side up. Roast the turkey until a meat thermometer inserted into the thickest part of the thigh registers 165–180°F, or when the juices run clear when the thigh is pricked. (See Chapter 16 for temperature suggestions and USDA recommendations.) For cooking times see the chart that follows. After you turn the turkey breast side up, baste it every 15–20 minutes, but stop about ½ hour before you expect the turkey to be done.

USDA Guidelines for Total Cooking Time for Turkey

Weight	Stuffed	Unstuffed
8–12 lb.	3–3½ hours	2¼–3 hours
12–14 lb.	3½–4 hours	3–3¾ hours
14–18 lb.	4–4¼ hours	3¾–4¼ hours
18–20 lb.	4¼–4¾ hours	4¼–4½ hours
20–24 lb.	4¾–5¼ hours	4½–5 hours

Many people discard the giblets, but others like to eat them. If you're one of the latter, season the giblets with the turkey seasonings and place them in the roasting pan to bake, or use the giblets for stock or gravy. (See Section 2, "Soups and Salads," for a stock recipe, and Section 7, "Sauces and Gravies," for a gravy recipe.)

Kitchen Clue

If you stuff the turkey, do so just before you roast it. (See Chapter 6, "The Meat Market," for information on stuffing poultry.) Tie the legs together with kitchen string. Do *not* put a foil tent over the turkey—this steams the meat instead of roasting it. Be sure turkey stuffing cooks to 165°F on a meat thermometer before you eat it. Let the turkey rest 15 minutes before carving.

Kitchen Clue

Fresh turkey has a superior flavor to frozen turkey. If you use frozen turkey, thaw it in the refrigerator. This may take a couple of days. You can speed the process by putting the turkey (in its wrapper) in a sink full of cold water and changing the water occasionally.

Turkey Cutlets with Chili Pepper and Cheese

This dish is spicy but not fiercely hot. The avocado and tomatoes give it a refreshing quality; it works nicely with Polenta and a green salad.

Level: Intermediate

Yield: 4 servings

Can be done ahead up to the jalapeño in the instructions

1 jalapeño or other hot pepper

¼ cup all-purpose flour

½ tsp. salt, or salt to taste

¼ tsp. freshly ground black pepper

20–24 oz. turkey cutlets

3 TB. olive oil or vegetable oil

1 large tomato, sliced

1 small avocado, peeled and sliced

1½ cups shredded Monterey Jack cheese

2 TB. freshly grated Parmesan cheese

Preheat the oven to 375°F. Remove the stem, the fleshy white part, and the seeds from the jalapeño pepper and chop it into small pieces. Combine the flour, salt, and pepper and dredge the turkey cutlets in this mixture. Shake off excess flour. Heat the olive oil in a skillet and sauté the turkey cutlets over moderate heat, 2–3 minutes per side or until lightly browned. Place the cutlets in a baking dish. Place the tomato slices over the cutlets. Sprinkle the tomato slices with the hot pepper. Place the avocado slices on top of the tomato. Scatter the shredded Monterey Jack cheese and Parmesan cheese on top.

* Bake the dish 10–15 minutes, or until cheese is hot and bubbly and beginning to brown lightly.

Second Thoughts

You can prepare this dish with veal or chicken cutlets, and substitute Havarti or Muenster cheese for the Monterey Jack.

Pastas, Rice, and Grains

Pasta and grain dishes have become big favorites. They are a healthy, nutritious alternative to meat and make ideal side dishes, too, because of their varied tastes and textures. Most people are familiar with several shapes of pasta and with white rice. But there is much more to consider: bulgur wheat, wild rice, beans, and so on. Anyone who wants to add a little pizzazz to everyday or company meals can learn how to use these ingredients to make delicious food without too much fuss.

Crunchy Crusted Macaroni and Cheese

This is a treasured old family recipe. Its unique crunchy crust keeps the macaroni moist.

Level: Easy

Yield: 4–6 servings

*Can be done ahead up to the * in the instructions*

1½ cups elbow macaroni

2 TB. butter

2 TB. flour

2 cups milk

½ tsp. salt

¼ tsp. freshly ground black pepper

⅛ tsp. freshly grated nutmeg

2 cups grated cheese, preferably cheddar
   or American

1½ cups crispy rice cereal (optional)

2 TB. melted butter (optional)

continues

continued

Preheat the oven to 350°F. Cook the macaroni until it is *al dente*. Drain the macaroni. While the macaroni is cooking, heat the butter in a saucepan over low heat. When the butter has melted and looks foamy, add the flour and cook, stirring constantly (preferably with a whisk), 2–3 minutes. Stir the milk gradually into the flour mixture, until the sauce is smooth. Add the salt, pepper, and nutmeg. Add the cheese and continue to cook, stirring with the whisk or a wooden spoon, 4–5 minutes or until the cheese has melted and the sauce is smooth. Pour the sauce over the cooked macaroni and mix thoroughly. You may eat the dish like this, but if you prefer it baked, place the mixture into a buttered baking dish. Combine the crispy rice and butter (if used) and sprinkle this over the cheese-coated macaroni.

* Bake about 30 minutes or until the top is crispy.

Second Thoughts

Corn flakes make a good substitute for the crispy rice.

Gillian's Ziti Casserole

This recipe was created by our daughter and goes over in a big way at parties. Serve it with a green salad and Italian bread.

Level: Easy

Yield: 4 servings

*Can be done ahead up to the * in the instructions*

5–6 large fresh shiitake mushrooms (or substitute 12 common white mushrooms)

1 TB. olive oil

1 lb. ziti

1 (15-oz.) container ricotta cheese (or nonfat ricotta)

1 cup oil-packed sun-dried tomatoes, drained and cut up

1 cup black olives, cut in half

1½ cups shredded mozzarella cheese

1 TB. chopped fresh basil, or 1 tsp. dried

3–4 TB. freshly grated Parmesan cheese

Preheat the oven to 350°F. Rinse and dry the mushrooms and cut them into bite-size pieces. Discard the tough inedible stems. Heat the olive oil in a small pan. Add the mushrooms and cook over moderate heat 3–4 minutes. Set the mushrooms aside. Cook the ziti until it is *al dente*. Drain the ziti. Combine the ziti with the ricotta cheese, mushrooms, sun-dried tomatoes, olives, ½ cup of the mozzarella cheese, and the basil. Mix ingredients well. Place the mixture in a deep casserole dish. Top with the remaining mozzarella cheese and sprinkle with the Parmesan cheese.

* Bake the casserole 20–25 minutes or until cheese is bubbly.

Meredith's Pasta with Eggplant Sauce

One of the easiest, freshest-tasting dishes you can whip up in a hurry, this recipe was created by our daughter for her college friends—but everyone loves it.

Level: Easy

Yield: 4 servings

*Can be done ahead up to the * in the instructions*

1 small eggplant	2 tsp. capers, drained (optional)
6 plum tomatoes	2 TB. chopped fresh basil, or 2 tsp. dried
½ cup olive oil	pinch of salt and pepper
8–10 black olives, sliced	1 lb. pasta, preferably penne or ziti

Cut off and discard the stem of the eggplant. Cut the eggplant into bite-size pieces and set it aside. Cut the plum tomatoes into pieces. Heat the olive oil in a skillet. Add the eggplant, tomatoes, olives, capers, basil, salt, and pepper. Stirring occasionally, cook over moderate heat about 10 minutes or until the vegetables have softened.

* Either keep the sauce warm over low heat or reheat it when you make the pasta. Cook the pasta until it is *al dente*. Drain the pasta. Top it with the sauce and serve.

Kitchen Clue

Some people salt eggplant because they think the vegetable is bitter. If you think so, put the cut-up eggplant in a colander, sprinkle it with salt, and let it stand for 30 minutes. Then wipe the pieces off with paper towel and proceed with the recipe.

Pasta with Sun-Dried Tomatoes and Pignoli Nuts

This dish is such a favorite that people eat it hot, warm, or cold, and it can even be reheated without losing its flavor.

Level: Easy

Yield: 4 servings

Can be done ahead up to the * in the instructions

1 lb. pasta, preferably bow-shaped farfalle

½ cup olive oil

⅓ cup pignoli nuts

2 cloves garlic, minced

⅔ cup coarsely chopped sun-dried tomatoes

1 TB. coarsely chopped fresh basil, or 1 tsp. dried

¼ tsp. salt, or salt to taste

¼ tsp. freshly ground black pepper

Cook the pasta until it is *al dente;* then drain it. While the pasta is cooking, heat 2 TB. of the olive oil in a skillet over moderate heat. Add the pignoli nuts and cook them, stirring occasionally, 3–4 minutes or until the nuts are lightly toasted. Add the garlic, sun-dried tomatoes, and basil and cook another 1–2 minutes to heat them. Add the remaining olive oil.

* Cook another minute or until ingredients are hot. Add the pasta. Toss the ingredients to coat them completely and cook another 3–4 minutes or until the pasta is hot. Taste the dish for seasoning and add salt and pepper to taste.

Second Thoughts

This dish also is excellent if you add a cup of diced smoked turkey or baked ham. If you decide to use these ingredients, add them with the sun-dried tomatoes.

Kitchen Clue

If you like good old-fashioned spaghetti with tomato sauce, check out the "Sauces and Gravies" recipe section where you'll find a recipe for marinara sauce and several variations.

How to Cook White Rice

Every good cook should know this recipe. White rice goes with practically every entrée and can be the basis of many wonderful main dishes, as well.

Level: Easy

Yield: 3 cups cooked rice; 4–6 side dish servings

Can be done completely ahead

1 cup raw long grain white rice, *not* converted
1¾ cups water

Place the rice in a 2–3 quart saucepan and cover it with the cold water. Bring the mixture to a boil over high heat. Let the mixture boil 1 minute. Remove the pan from the heat. Stir the rice mixture with a fork. Cover the pan and let the rice stand (off the heat) 1 minute. Return the pan of rice to the heat and turn the heat to the lowest temperature. Cook the rice without lifting the cover for 18 minutes or until grains are fluffy and all the liquid has been absorbed. Remove the pan from the heat and let the rice stand, covered, for about 10 minutes before serving.

Need some interesting but simple ideas to spruce up rice? Try these:

➤ Use canned or homemade chicken, beef, or vegetable stock instead of water to cook the rice.

➤ Dissolve ½ tsp. saffron threads in 1 TB. boiling water and add it to the cooking water.

➤ Add the juice of one large lemon and 3–4 TB. chopped fresh parsley to the cooked rice.

➤ Add 3–4 TB. olive oil and 1 cup cooked corn kernels and/or peas to the cooked rice.

➤ Add 4–5 TB. lightly toasted pignoli nuts to the cooked rice.

Rice Pilaf with Mushrooms

This is the kind of dish that looks and tastes as if you fussed a lot—but it's not at all difficult to make.

Level: Intermediate

Yield: 4–6 servings

Can be done completely ahead

2 TB. vegetable oil

1 TB. butter (optional)

1 medium onion, finely chopped
(about ½ cup)

6–8 oz. mushrooms, sliced

1 cup raw long grain white rice,
not converted

2 TB. chopped parsley

1 tsp. salt, or salt to taste

¼ tsp. freshly ground black pepper

1¾ cups canned or homemade beef,
chicken, or vegetable stock

Heat the oil and butter in a deep skillet. When the butter has melted and looks foamy, add the onion and cook over moderate heat 2–3 minutes or until the vegetable has wilted slightly. Add the mushrooms and cook another 1–2 minutes, stirring once or twice. Add the rice, parsley, salt, and pepper and cook, stirring frequently, for 2–3 minutes or until the rice grains are hot and thoroughly coated with oil. Pour in the stock. Bring the mixture to a boil. Let the mixture boil 1 minute. Remove the pan from the heat. Stir the rice mixture with a fork. Cover the pan and let the rice stand (off the heat) 1 minute. Return the pan of rice to the heat and turn the heat to the lowest temperature. Cook the rice without lifting the cover for 18 minutes or until grains are fluffy and all the liquid has been absorbed. Remove the pan from the heat and let the rice stand, covered, for about 10 minutes before serving.

Second Thoughts

You may change this basic pilaf in numerous ways. Try one of these options:

➤ Add a minced garlic clove with the onion.

➤ Add ½ cup chopped sweet red pepper with the onion.

➤ Use wild mushrooms instead of common white mushrooms.

➤ Sprinkle 1 tsp. fresh thyme leaves (or about ½ tsp. dried thyme) on the rice before you stir and cover it.

➤ Add 1 cup diced leftover chicken or turkey with the mushrooms.

Fried Rice

This colorful dish makes a delightful addition to a buffet table. It's also suitable as a brunch food or a side dish, especially with other stir-fried foods.

Level: Intermediate

Yield: 4–6 servings

Can be done completely ahead

2½ TB. vegetable oil

2 large eggs, beaten

3 scallions, chopped into ½" pieces

⅔ cup diced boiled ham or
    barbecued pork

½ cup thawed frozen peas or blanched fresh peas

6–8 canned water chestnuts,
    cut into small chunks (about ¼ cup)

3 cups cold cooked rice

¾ tsp. salt, or salt to taste

Heat ½ TB. of the vegetable oil in a wok or skillet. Add the eggs and fry them, without stirring, over moderate heat about 1 minute. Turn them over to cook on the reverse side. If you are using a wok, you will have to move the egg as it cooks to make sure raw egg slides to the bottom of the pan. Cook the eggs on the reverse side 30–45 seconds or until they have set. Remove the cooked eggs, chop them into pieces, and set them aside. Heat the remaining vegetable oil in the wok or skillet. Add the scallions and stir-fry over high heat 30–45 seconds. Add ham, peas, and water chestnuts; stir-fry 1 minute. Add the rice and stir-fry 2–3 minutes. Add the salt and egg and stir-fry 1 minute. Dish out the fried rice and serve.

301

Second Thoughts

Many people are used to fried rice that is brown. In Hong Kong and many parts of mainland China, traditional fried rice is white. However, if you prefer the brown color, add 2–3 TB. of soy sauce when you add the rice, but then do not use as much salt. You also can add numerous ingredients when you add the ham or pork to make "many precious" fried rice, for example: ½ cup cut-up cooked shrimp, ½ cup diced cooked lobster meat, ½ cup diced cooked chicken, 1 cup bean sprouts, and/or ¼ cup chopped, soaked, and softened dried shiitake mushrooms.

How to Cook Wild Rice

With its chewy texture and nut-like flavor, wild rice is a perfect accompaniment to roasted or grilled fish, meats, or poultry.

Level: Easy

Yield: 3 cups cooked rice; 4–6 servings

Can be done completely ahead

1 cup wild rice
water
½ tsp. salt, or salt to taste
⅛ tsp. freshly ground black pepper

1 cup water or canned or homemade
    chicken, beef, or vegetable broth or stock
½ cup additional water
1 small bay leaf

Place the wild rice in a saucepan and add enough cold water to cover the rice by 1 inch. Bring the mixture to a boil over high heat and boil the mixture for 5 minutes. Drain the rice. Return the rice to the pan and add the salt, pepper, stock, water, and bay leaf. Bring the mixture to a boil. Lower the heat, cover the pan, and cook 30–35 minutes or until the rice is tender and all the liquid has been absorbed. Discard the bay leaf.

Fein on Food

Wild rice isn't rice at all, nor is it related to rice. It is the seed of a marsh grass. Early English settlers in this country called it rice because its narrow, tapering shape bears a superficial resemblance to rice. Before the English colonized Minnesota, where wild rice has its origins, the French fur trappers who lived in the region called wild rice "crazy oats." But wild rice isn't related to oats, either. Wild rice is chewy, quite unlike the soft textures of cooked rice or oats.

Wild Rice Fritters

An outstanding choice to serve with the Thanksgiving turkey.

Level: Challenging

Yield: 6–8 servings

Can be done completely ahead

1½ cups cooked, cooled wild rice
1½ cups cooked, cooled white rice
1 large onion, minced
3 large eggs

5 TB. all-purpose flour
1 tsp. salt, or salt to taste
¼ tsp. freshly ground black pepper
vegetable oil for panfrying

Mix the wild rice, white rice, and onion in a large bowl. Beat the eggs and add them to the rice mixture. Stir the mixture to combine the ingredients. Stir in the flour, salt, and pepper. Heat about ¼ inch of vegetable oil in a large skillet. When the oil is hot enough to make a tiny piece of bread sizzle around the edges, drop some of the wild rice mixture into the pan to form "pancakes" about 2–4 inches wide, depending on the size fritters you want. Fry the fritters over moderate heat about 2–3 minutes per side or until they are crispy and golden brown. Drain on paper towels.

Kitchen Clue

Remember that when you reheat fried foods, you must put them in a single layer on a cookie sheet and bake in a preheated 400°F oven. For even better results, place the food on a rack.

Tuscan-Style White Beans with Tomato Sauce

This dish is a perfect accompaniment to grilled poultry and meats.

Level: Easy

Yield: 4 servings

Can be done completely ahead

3 TB. olive oil

1 clove garlic, minced

1 TB. minced fresh sage,
    or 1 tsp. dried; *or* 2 tsp. fresh
    thyme leaves, or ½ tsp. dried

¼ tsp. freshly ground black pepper

2 cups canned white beans
    (rinsed under cold water and drained)

1 cup canned crushed tomatoes

Heat the olive oil in a saucepan. Add the garlic and cook over low heat for 1 minute, stirring often. Add the sage and pepper, stir briefly, and add the beans and crushed tomatoes. Cook the beans 10–12 minutes until the flavors have had a chance to blend.

Quick Three-Bean No-Meat Chili

A popular vegetarian dish. For extra nourishment, serve it with cooked rice.

Level: Easy

Yield: makes 6 servings

Can be done completely ahead

¼ cup olive oil

2 onions, chopped

2 cloves garlic, chopped

2 carrots, chopped

3 cups canned tomato sauce

2 cups water

2 TB. tomato paste

1 (15-oz.) can garbanzo beans, drained

1 (15-oz.) can red kidney beans, undrained

1 cup lentils

2 all-purpose potatoes, peeled and cut into bite-sized pieces

2 TB. chili powder

1 (4-oz.) can chopped mild green chili peppers

1 tsp. dried basil

Heat the olive oil in a large skillet. Add the onions and garlic and cook them over moderate heat 3–4 minutes or until they have softened. Add the carrots, tomato sauce, water, tomato paste, garbanzo beans, kidney beans, lentils, potatoes, chili powder, chili peppers, and basil. Bring the ingredients to a boil over high heat. Lower the heat and simmer 15 minutes, covered. Remove the cover and cook another 20 minutes, or until sauce surrounding the beans has thickened to a gravy-like consistency. Stir occasionally during this time.

Kitchen Clue

If you prepare this dish a day or two ahead, the beans may absorb some of the moisture in the sauce. When you reheat it, stir in about ½ cup water.

Baked Beans

This recipe may spoil you. Once you taste homemade baked beans, you may never want to eat the canned kind again.

Level: Intermediate

Yield: 6–8 servings

Can be done completely ahead

continues

continued

1 lb. dried white beans (such as Navy, Great Northern, or pea)

6 cups water

1 medium onion, finely chopped (about ½ cup)

6 oz. salt pork

⅔ cup molasses

¼ cup brown sugar

1 TB. powdered mustard

½ tsp. salt, or salt to taste

¼ tsp. freshly ground black pepper

⅛ tsp. ground cloves, or 2 whole cloves

Rinse and drain the beans. Place them in a large saucepan, cover them with water, and bring the water to a boil over high heat. Boil 2 minutes. Remove the pan from the heat, cover the pan, and set it aside 1 hour or more. Return the pan to the heat and bring the mixture to a simmer over moderate heat. Cook the beans 45 minutes. Preheat the oven to 300°F. Add the onion to the beans and stir. Remove and discard the rind from the salt pork, if there is one. Cut the pork into bite-size chunks and add it, and the remaining ingredients, to the beans. Stir the beans to blend ingredients. Pour the mixture into a casserole, cover, and bake 3–4 hours, stirring the beans occasionally, until they are tender and the sauce has thickened to a gravy-like consistency. Peek at the beans once in awhile. If they become too dry during cooking time, add water ¼ cup at a time.

Second Thoughts

For more gently flavored beans, substitute ¾ cup maple syrup for the molasses and sugar. This recipe is a "New England-style" version. You may substitute lima beans and add an 8-ounce can of tomato sauce to make Pennsylvania-style beans.

Polenta

Polenta is not a meal-in-a-minute kind of dish and it requires some watching and stirring. But it is worth the effort. Not only is it a tasty, culinary relief from the same old side dishes, it also lends itself to endless variation.

Level: Intermediate

Yield: 4 servings

Can be done completely ahead

4–4½ cups water, stock, or milk

1 tsp. salt, or salt to taste

1 cup cornmeal

2 TB. butter, optional

Pour the water into a saucepan, using the larger amount if you prefer softer polenta. Add the salt and bring to a boil. Turn the heat to low. Gradually add the cornmeal as you stir the ingredients with a wooden spoon. Continue to cook, stirring occasionally, for 15–20 minutes, depending on whether you prefer soft, creamy polenta or a firmer version. At 20 minutes, the mixture will begin to come away from the sides of the pan. Stir in the butter, if desired.

Second Thoughts

Polenta is fine served plain, but consider topping the dish with:

➤ Crumbled Gorgonzola cheese or freshly grated Parmesan cheese

➤ Sautéed mushrooms

➤ Marinara sauce

➤ Sautéed sausage and peppers

If you make firm polenta, you may pour it into a greased loaf pan, chill it, slice it, and fry the slices until they're crispy. Serve them with gravy or any savory sauce with dinner or with maple syrup for breakfast.

Kitchen Clue

Although you may make polenta ahead, it's better if you serve it immediately. If you do prepare it ahead, cover the pan; add water ¼ cup at a time to reheat and stir to the proper consistency.

Bulgur Wheat and Lentil Pilaf

You may use this side dish as stuffing for chicken, turkey, or crown roast of pork.

Level: Challenging

Yield: 6 servings

Can be done completely ahead

1 cup lentils

3 cups water

2 TB. olive oil

1 TB. butter

3 TB. pignoli nuts or
  coarsely chopped almonds

1 medium onion, finely
  chopped (about ½ cup)

1 cup bulgur wheat

½ cup currants or raisins

2 cups canned or homemade chicken
  or vegetable broth or stock

¾ tsp. salt, or salt to taste

freshly ground black pepper to taste

Place the lentils and water in a saucepan and bring them to a boil over high heat. Lower the heat and simmer for 10 minutes. Drain the lentils and set them aside. Heat the olive oil and butter in a large skillet. When the butter has melted and looks foamy, add the pignoli nuts and cook them over moderate heat 2 minutes or until they begin to color lightly. Add the onion and cook 6–8 minutes or until it is lightly browned. Add the bulgur wheat and cook 3–4 minutes. Add the lentils, currants, stock, salt, and pepper. Bring the mixture to a boil. Turn the heat to low, cover the pan, and cook 25–30 minutes or until all the liquid in the pan has been absorbed. Taste for seasoning and add salt and pepper to taste.

Kitchen Clue

You can find bulgur wheat in many supermarkets. It is also available in health food stores and specialty shops.

Nana's Egg Noodle Stuffing

Nana called this egg noodle "filling"—which it is, because no one can stop eating it.

Level: Easy

Yield: 6–8 servings

Can be done completely ahead

1 lb. barley-shaped egg noodle pasta
    (or use acini pepe or orzo-shaped pasta)

2 TB. vegetable oil

1 large onion, sliced

3 stalks celery, sliced into ¼" slices

10–12 oz. mushrooms, sliced

4 TB. melted butter

2 large eggs

1 tsp. salt, or salt to taste

¼ tsp. freshly ground black pepper

Preheat the oven to 375°F. Cook the egg noodle pasta until it is *al dente*. Drain the pasta and set it aside. Heat the vegetable oil in a skillet over moderate heat. Add the onion and celery and cook 3–4 minutes or until the vegetables have wilted. Add the mushrooms and cook another 5 minutes or until the mushrooms have softened and most of the water has evaporated from the pan. Add the vegetable mixture to the egg noodle pasta. Stir in the melted butter. Beat the eggs and add them. Add the salt and pepper. Stir to blend the ingredients. Put the mixture into a baking dish. Bake for 40–50 minutes or until it is crispy and browned on top.

Rice and Fruit Stuffing

This simple dish is a super side dish as well as a stuffing for roasted chicken or rock Cornish hens.

Level: Intermediate

Yield: enough for 1 roasting chicken or 6 Cornish hens; makes 4–6 side dish servings

Can be done completely ahead

½ cup butter

1 medium onion, chopped
    (about ½ cup)

1 stalk celery, chopped

3 cups cooked white rice

2 tart apples, peeled and chopped

1 cup chopped dried fruit, such as
    apples, apricots, prunes, and peaches

½ cup raisins

½ cup broken cashew nuts or
    toasted chopped almonds

1 tsp. salt, or salt to taste

1 TB. fresh thyme leaves or 1 tsp. dried

continues

continued

Heat the butter in a skillet. When the butter has melted and looks foamy, add the onion and celery and cook over moderate heat 3–4 minutes or until the vegetables have softened. Remove the pan from the heat. Add the remaining ingredients and stir gently to distribute the solid ingredients throughout the rice. Cool completely before you use this to stuff poultry.

Chestnut and Sausage Stuffing

This rich stuffing is suitable for the Thanksgiving table. The sherry gives it a lively flavor.

Level: Challenging

Yield: about 8 cups

Can be done completely ahead

1 lb. Italian style sweet sausage, not in casing or with the casing removed

2 TB. olive oil

1 large onion, finely chopped (about ¾ to 1 cup)

2 stalks celery, sliced into ¼" thick pieces

10–12 oz. mushrooms, coarsely chopped or sliced

1 TB. fresh thyme leaves, or 1 tsp. dried

1½ tsp. chopped fresh sage leaves or ½ tsp. dried

2 cups coarsely cut up bottled or canned chestnuts (about 10 oz.)

6 cups of ½" bread cubes

⅓ cup half and half cream

4 TB. melted butter

¼ cup sherry wine

Fry the sausage meat in a skillet over moderate heat for 12–15 minutes, breaking the pieces into smaller bits, or until the meat is thoroughly browned and lightly crispy. Drain the fat from the pan, remove the meat, and set it aside. Heat the olive oil in the skillet and add the onion and celery. Cook over moderate heat, stirring occasionally, for 2–3 minutes or until the vegetables have wilted. Add the mushrooms and cook another 3–4 minutes or until mushrooms have softened and most of the liquid has evaporated from the pan. Remove the pan from the heat. Add the sausage to the vegetables and sprinkle the ingredients with the thyme and sage. Break the chestnuts into pieces using your hands, and add them and the bread cubes to the mixture. Toss ingredients so that they are evenly distributed in the pan. Pour in the cream, melted butter, and sherry wine and toss ingredients thoroughly. Store the stuffing in the refrigerator until you are ready to stuff a bird. If you will be baking the stuffing separately, put it into a large casserole, preheat the oven to 375°F, and bake for 40–50 minutes or until it is crispy and browned on top.

Kitchen Clue

You can find bottled or canned chestnuts in many supermarkets or in specialty food stores. Be sure to buy the plain ones, not those packaged in sugar syrup. Most people use dry sherry for stuffing, but sweet sherry offers an unusual and delicious surprise.

Vegetables

Years ago when cookbooks recommended boiling vegetables to death, foods like spinach, cabbage, broccoli, green beans, and even the more accepted carrot developed bad reputations. Mushy canned vegetables were even worse. In recent times, we have learned to prepare vegetables that look and taste better. We keep them colorful and satisfyingly crunchy. They are more nutritious this way, too. In addition, the variety of vegetables available today, even at your local supermarket, has grown considerably. Fresh zucchini, eggplants, and sugar snap peas were barely known to most people a generation or two ago, but they now supplement the more familiar choices. As a result, more and more people appreciate vegetables.

How to Boil and Steam Vegetables

Here are instructions for the simplest ways to serve fresh vegetables. After you cook the vegetables, serve them plain, or with a bit of butter and lemon juice, or a sprinkling of freshly grated cheese—or cool them and coat them with vinaigrette dressing.

To boil: Bring lightly salted water (about ½ tsp. salt for every quart of water) to a boil. Add the vegetables a few at a time to keep the water at an even temperature. Cover the pan if cooking hard vegetables such as beets or potatoes; keep the pan uncovered for more tender vegetables such as snow peas. Lower the heat slightly so that the vegetables cook at a slow boil, rather than a full, rolling boil. In the chart below, the times suggested are calculated to begin when the water returns to a boil after adding the vegetable.

To steam: Pour enough lightly salted water into a steamer or saucepan (with a steamer insert) so that it will not evaporate during cooking time. The water level should be at least 1 inch below the container that holds the vegetable. Bring the water to a boil, place the vegetable into the container and cover the steamer or saucepan.

Vegetable	Minutes to Boil	Minutes to Steam
asparagus	4–8	7–10
green beans	7–10	10–15
beets	20–50	not recommended
broccoli (cut up)	5–6	6–8
Brussels sprouts	8–10	10–15
carrots (1½" slices)	12–15	15–20
cauliflower (cut up)	5–8	12–15
potatoes ("new")	15–20	about 25
snow peas	1	4–6
zucchini (1" slices)	1–2	6–8

Baked Acorn Squash

This is a wonderful choice for Thanksgiving or other holiday dinners.

Level: Easy

Yield: 4 servings

Can be done completely ahead

2 acorn squash

½ tsp. salt, or salt to taste

¼ cup finely chopped nuts

¼ cup golden raisins

2 TB. brown sugar

1½ TB. softened butter

Preheat the oven to 425°F. Cut the squash in half, cutting perpendicular to the ridges. Slice a small piece from the bottom of each half so that the squash can stand up straight in a baking dish. Scoop the seeds and stringy flesh from inside the cavity and sprinkle the orange flesh with salt. Lightly grease a baking dish. Place the squash cut side down on the baking dish. Prick the shell in three or four places with the tines of a fork. Bake 20–25 minutes. Combine remaining ingredients. Remove the squash from the oven and turn it cut-side up. Fill the cavities with the nut mixture. Return the squash to the oven and bake it another 10–20 minutes or until the flesh is tender when pierced with the tip of a sharp knife.

Boiled Corn on the Cob

Corn is America's first choice vegetable. Be sure to buy corn with the husks still on.

Level: Easy

Yield: 6 servings

The flavored butters can be done completely ahead of time; the corn cannot

6 ears fresh corn with medium-size kernels

4 quarts water

1 cup milk

Remove the husks and silk from the ears of corn. Bring a large pan of water (about 4 quarts) to a boil. Add the milk. Let the liquid return to a boil. Immerse the corn and cover the pan. Turn off the heat. Let the corn stand in the milk/water for 5–10 minutes, or until tender. Use tongs to remove the corn. Serve with plain butter or one of the suggested flavored butters.

* To make any of the flavored butters, simply blend the ingredients with a whisk in a small bowl.

Flavored Butters for Cooked Corn (each recipe is enough for 6 ears of corn)

Chili butter

4 TB. softened butter

1 tsp. chili powder

Curry butter

4 TB. softened butter

1 tsp. curry powder

Marjoram butter

4 TB. softened butter

1 TB. freshly minced marjoram, or ½ tsp. dried

Scallion butter

4 TB. softened butter

2 TB. finely minced scallion

Zesty butter

4 TB. softened butter

1 TB. Dijon mustard

2 tsp. prepared white horseradish

Lemon-herb butter

4 TB. softened butter

1 TB. fresh lemon juice

½ tsp. freshly grated lemon peel

2 tsp. minced fresh chives (or the green part of scallion)

2 tsp. minced fresh basil, or ½ tsp. dried

315

Kitchen Clue

Milk is used as a mild sweetener. If you don't wish to make the corn with milk, you may add a teaspoon of sugar to the cooking water instead.

Broccoli with Garlic and Lemon

Peeling the broccoli stems makes the vegetable delightfully tender.

Level: Intermediate

Yield: 4 servings

*Can be done ahead up to the * in the instructions*

1 bunch broccoli (2 to 3 stalks)

2 TB. olive oil

2 large cloves garlic, sliced in half

¼ tsp. salt, or salt to taste

⅛ tsp. freshly ground black pepper

juice of half a lemon (about 2 TB.)

Remove the florets from the broccoli stalks by cutting them with a paring knife. Cut the florets into bite-size pieces. Cut a ½" slice from the bottom of each stem. Peel the stems by using a paring knife to pull back a thin layer of the skin, starting at the cut end. (Or use a vegetable peeler to peel the stems.) Cut the broccoli stems into bite-size pieces. Steam the broccoli in a steamer insert or in a vegetable steamer for 6–8 minutes or until barely tender. Drain the broccoli under cold running water and set it aside.

* Heat the olive oil in a skillet. Cook the garlic over moderate heat 1 minute or until it is just beginning to brown. Discard the garlic. Add the broccoli pieces to the pan, sprinkle them with salt and pepper, and cook 1–2 minutes or until they are hot, stirring occasionally. Remove the broccoli to a serving dish, sprinkle it with the lemon juice, and serve.

Classic Creamed Spinach

This opulent dish makes a spinach lover of everyone.

Level: Intermediate

Yield: 4 servings

Can be done completely ahead

2 (10-oz.) pkgs. frozen chopped
    spinach, thawed

2 TB. butter

2 TB. flour

1 cup half and half cream, or milk

salt to taste

⅛ tsp. freshly grated nutmeg

freshly ground black pepper

½ cup grated Swiss or Gruyère cheese, optional

2–3 TB. freshly grated Parmesan cheese, optional

Squeeze as much water out of the spinach as possible. Set it aside. In a saucepan, melt the butter over moderate heat. When the butter looks foamy, add the flour and blend it in. Lower the heat and cook for about 2 minutes, without letting the flour brown. Gradually add the cream or milk, and blend the ingredients thoroughly using a whisk. Be sure to reach the corners of the pan where the flour tends to stick. Cook for a minute or so until the sauce has thickened. Stir in the spinach and seasonings and the cheeses if used. Cook another 1–2 minutes to heat thoroughly.

Wilted Kale with Sesame Dressing

This dish is delicious, unique, and healthy.

Level: Easy

Yield: 4 servings

Cannot be done ahead

1–2 TB. sesame seeds

1 large bunch of fresh kale, leaves left whole

lightly salted water

2 TB. vegetable oil

Place the sesame seeds in an ungreased frying pan and cook them over moderate heat 3–4 minutes or until they are lightly toasted. (You may also toast them in an oven or toaster-oven preheated to 350°F.) Set the seeds aside. Wash the kale leaf by leaf to rid it of all sand. Remove any extra-large stems. Bring a large soup pot of lightly salted water to a boil. Add the kale to the boiling water and cook 4–6 minutes or until the leaves have wilted and the stems have softened. Remove the kale, drain it into a strainer or colander, and squeeze out as much of the liquid as possible. Toss the kale with the vegetable oil and sprinkle it with the toasted sesame seeds.

Second Thoughts

As an alternative to sesame seeds, sprinkle the kale with 1–2 TB. lemon juice or balsamic vinegar.

Sautéed Dill-Scented Carrots

This is the most requested vegetable dish in the Fein household.

Level: Easy

Yield: 4 servings

Can be done completely ahead

1 lb. carrots	½ tsp. sugar
lightly salted water	¼ tsp. salt, or salt to taste
3 TB. butter	1 TB. minced fresh dill, or 1 tsp. dried

Peel the carrots and cut them into bite-size chunks. Place the carrots in a saucepan and cover them with lightly salted water. Bring the water to a boil, lower the heat, and simmer the carrots 12–15 minutes or until they are fork tender. Drain the carrots. Heat the butter in the pan. When the butter has melted and looks foamy, add the carrots, sugar, salt, and dill. Toss the ingredients to heat them through and serve.

Second Thoughts

Here's another way to serve these carrots: Purée the cooked carrots, add the remaining ingredients plus 3–4 TB. cream. Taste for seasoning and add salt and pepper to taste. Reheat this dish in a preheated 350°F oven for 6–10 minutes or in a saucepan over moderate heat for 3–4 minutes. Stir frequently to prevent sticking.

Sautéed Sugar Snap or Snow Peas

This is an easy, well-liked dish suitable for family or company.

Level: Easy

Yield: 4 servings

Can be done ahead up to the * in the instructions

½ lb. sugar snap or snow peas	1 TB. vegetable oil
lightly salted water	½ tsp. sugar
1 TB. butter	pinch or two of salt

Wash the peas. Remove the top "string" by cutting a tiny piece from the curvy tip and pulling backwards. Bring about 2 quarts of lightly salted water to a boil. Add the peas and cook 45 seconds. Drain the peas. Rinse them thoroughly under cold water.

* Heat the butter and vegetable oil in a skillet. When the butter has melted and looks foamy, add the peas, sprinkle them with the sugar and salt, and sauté them 1–2 minutes over moderate heat or until they are hot.

Sautéed Zucchini, Pepper, and Corn

This dish is so colorful, it looks grand next to almost any meat or poultry dish.

Level: Intermediate

Yield: 4 servings

Cannot be done ahead

1 red bell pepper	1 cup frozen corn kernels, thawed
4 TB. olive oil	¼ tsp. salt, or salt to taste
1 small onion, finely chopped	⅛ tsp. freshly ground black pepper
2 cloves garlic, minced	3 TB. minced fresh basil or 1 tsp. fresh thyme leaves
3 small zucchini, sliced into ⅛" pieces	

Remove the stem from the pepper. Cut the pepper in half and remove the seeds and any extra white membrane that clings to the inside. Chop the pepper into bite-size pieces. Heat the olive oil in a skillet. Add the onion, garlic, and red pepper, and cook over moderate heat 2–3 minutes or until the vegetables have softened. Add the zucchini and corn and stir the ingredients. Sprinkle in the salt, pepper, and basil and cook 3–4 minutes or until vegetables are tender.

Second Thoughts

Add a cup of thawed frozen peas or blanched fresh peas for extra bulk, texture, and color.

Sautéed Mushrooms

Sautéed mushrooms work well with Veal Marsala and many other sautéed, grilled, or roasted meat and poultry dishes.

Level: Easy

Yield: 4 servings

Can be done completely ahead

1 lb. fresh mushrooms, any kind

2 TB. olive oil

2 TB. butter

3–4 TB. chopped parsley

salt and pepper to taste

Clean and dry the mushrooms and cut them into bite-size pieces. Heat the olive oil and butter in a skillet. When the butter has melted and looks foamy, add the mushrooms and cook over moderate heat for 4–8 minutes, or until the mushrooms begin to brown and the liquid in the pan has evaporated. Sprinkle with the parsley, salt, and pepper.

How to Make Baked Potatoes

Centuries ago, when Spanish conquistadors discovered Inca tribesmen baking potatoes in hearth fires, they knew the dish was a winner and took the recipe back to Europe. We still love baked potatoes today, and they are among the easiest foods to prepare.

Level: Easy

Yield: makes 4 servings

Cannot be done ahead

4 large russet baking potatoes

Preheat the oven to 400°F. Scrub the potatoes thoroughly. Do NOT wrap them in foil. Do *not* brush the skin with vegetable oil. Bake the potatoes 10 minutes. Prick the potato skin in 2 or 3 places with the tines of a fork. Continue to bake another 35–45 minutes or until the potatoes are tender all the way through when pierced with the tip of a sharp knife.

Kitchen Clue

You pierce the potato to prevent steam that builds up in the flesh from causing the potato to explode. You don't wrap the potatoes because wrapping causes the potato to "steam" rather than to bake, which results in poor potato texture as well as soggy skin. Oiling the skin also causes slight steaming, and it adds unnecessary calories.

Baked Stuffed Potatoes

This is the ideal company dish; you can make it a day ahead and it tastes and looks great.

Level: Easy

Yield: 4 servings

Can be done completely ahead

4 large russet baking potatoes	½ tsp. salt, or salt to taste
2 TB. softened butter	freshly ground black pepper to taste
2 TB. softened cream cheese	6–8 TB. milk
3 TB. minced fresh chives or parsley	paprika

Preheat the oven to 400°F. Scrub the potatoes thoroughly. Do not wrap them in foil. Do not brush the skin with vegetable oil. Bake the potatoes 10 minutes. Prick the potato skin in 2 or 3 places with the tines of a fork. Continue to bake the potatoes another 35–45 minutes or until they are tender all the way through when pierced with the tip of a sharp knife. When the potatoes are cool enough to handle but still warm, split them in half lengthwise. Scoop the flesh into a bowl but reserve the skins. Add the butter, cream cheese, chives, salt, and pepper. Blend the ingredients with a fork or mash them with a potato masher; do not use a food processor or the mixture will acquire a glue-like consistency. Add 6 TB. milk and stir the potatoes briefly until the mixture is smooth. If the mixture seems dry, add the remaining milk and stir it in. Place the potato mixture into the hollowed potato skins. Dust the top lightly with paprika. Bake the potatoes 12–15 minutes or until they are lightly crispy on top.

Second Thoughts

For a low-fat version of baked stuffed potatoes, try this: Substitute 1 cup low-fat cottage cheese and ½ cup skim milk or buttermilk for the butter, cream cheese, and milk.

Mashed Potatoes, Basic and Beyond

Is there anyone who doesn't love mashed potatoes? Smooth or lumpy, this is the ultimate comfort food.

Level: Easy

Yield: 6 servings

Can be done completely ahead

2 lbs. all-purpose or Yukon gold potatoes

lightly salted water

4–5 TB. butter ½ cup hot milk

1 tsp. salt, or salt to taste

freshly ground black pepper to taste

Peel the potatoes and cut them into chunks. Place them in a saucepan and add enough lightly salted water to cover them. Bring the water to a boil, lower the heat, and simmer the potatoes 15–20 minutes or until they are fork tender. Drain the potatoes. In the saucepan or a bowl, mash the potatoes with a potato masher, fork, electric mixer, or handheld beater set on low speed. Do not use a food processor or the mixture will acquire a glue-like consistency. Add the butter in chunks and continue to mash until the mixture is free of lumps. Add the milk, salt, and pepper, and stir briefly with a wooden spoon until ingredients are smooth and thoroughly blended. Taste for seasoning and add salt and pepper to taste. To reheat this dish, preheat the oven to 350°F, spoon the potatoes into a baking dish, and bake 15–20 minutes.

Kitchen Clue

Many cooks use russet potatoes for this dish. I believe the texture is better—denser and more opulent—with all-purpose or Yukon gold potatoes.

Second Thoughts

Mashed potatoes are so versatile you can change the recipe easily to suit your own tastes. Here are a few suggestions:

➤ For super-rich mashed potatoes, add 3–4 TB. softened cream cheese and/or ½ cup dairy sour cream when you add the butter.

➤ For lower-fat mashed potatoes, use 3 TB. diet margarine and ½ cup low-fat cottage cheese instead of the butter. Use skim milk.

➤ For garlic mashed potatoes, boil and mash the potatoes with 6 whole, peeled garlic cloves.

➤ For mashed potatoes with an Irish accent, add ¼ cup more milk plus 2 cups of chopped cooked kale or cabbage.

Sweet Potato Casserole

This is a traditional Thanksgiving dish, but there's no need to wait for a holiday to have it.

Level: Easy

Yield: 8–10 servings

Can be done completely ahead

6 large sweet potatoes	½ cup orange or apple juice
lightly salted water	1½ tsp. salt, or salt to taste
4 TB. butter or margarine	1 tsp. cinnamon
½ cup maple syrup or honey	½ tsp. freshly grated nutmeg

Peel the sweet potatoes and cut them into chunks. Place them in a saucepan and add enough lightly salted water to cover them. Bring the water to a boil, lower the heat, and simmer the potatoes 15–20 minutes or until they are fork tender. Drain the potatoes. In the saucepan or a bowl, mash the potatoes with a potato masher, fork, electric mixer, or handheld beater set on low speed. Do not use a food processor or the mixture will acquire a glue-like consistency. Add the butter in chunks and continue to mash until the mixture is free of lumps. Add the maple syrup, orange or apple juice, salt, cinnamon, and nutmeg, and stir ingredients 1–2 minutes or until they are smooth and thoroughly blended. Taste for seasoning and add salt to taste. To reheat this dish, preheat the oven to 350°F, spoon the potatoes into a baking dish, and bake 20–30 minutes.

Second Thoughts

Some people sprinkle marshmallows on sweet potato casserole. While some folks say this is terribly unsophisticated, others claim it's the only way to eat sweet potatoes. If you like marshmallows, put them on top of the casserole after you have baked it for 15 minutes (20 minutes if the casserole was cold). Bake an additional 12–15 minutes or until the marshmallows are lightly browned.

Sautéed Rosemary Potatoes

You better make lots of these; they go like wildfire. You can reheat extras to serve with eggs for breakfast.

Level: Easy

Yield: makes 4–6 servings

Can be done completely ahead

16–18 "new" or small red bliss potatoes

lightly salted water

2 TB. butter

2 TB. vegetable oil

½ tsp. salt, or salt to taste

¼ tsp. freshly ground black pepper

1½ TB. minced fresh rosemary,
    or 1½ tsp. dried, crushed rosemary

Place the potatoes in a large saucepan and cover them with lightly salted water. Bring the water to a boil, lower the heat, and simmer the potatoes 15–20 minutes or until they are fork tender. Drain the potatoes and peel them when they are cool enough to handle. Heat the butter and vegetable oil in a large skillet. When the butter has melted and looks foamy, add the potatoes to the pan. Sprinkle the potatoes with the salt, pepper, and rosemary. Sauté the potatoes over moderate heat for 15–20 minutes, shaking the pan occasionally, or until the potatoes are browned on all sides and are lightly crispy.

How to Roast a Red Pepper

Roasted red peppers are versatile; use them as an hors d'oeuvre or part of an antipasto, or slice them into salad or pasta.

Level: Intermediate

Yield: 1 pepper makes 2–3 servings

Can be done completely ahead

1 sweet red pepper

1 brown paper bag (preferred) or 1 plastic bag

Preheat the oven broiler. Be sure the rack is 4–6 inches from the heat source. Put the red pepper on the rack and broil it 2–3 minutes or until the surface is lightly scorched. Turn the pepper and repeat this process until all sides are scorched. Remove the pepper and put it in the paper bag. Let it cool at least 10 minutes. When the pepper is cool enough to handle, remove it from the bag. The skin will peel off easily. Pull out the stem, cut the pepper in half, and pull out the seeds. The pepper will seem "wet." When you have removed the stem, seeds, and skin, carve the pepper into thick or narrow strips, as desired.

Second Thoughts

Roasted red peppers are delicious when served with their natural juices. You may also sprinkle them with a few drops of olive oil and/or balsamic vinegar, or sprinkle some freshly chopped basil on top.

Sauces and Gravies

The art of sauce making has always had an honored place in culinary history because a great sauce can enhance any ingredient and provide a fabulous finishing touch for a dish. Some sauces are pourable liquids, some are thick and viscous, some are chunky. (For more information on sauces, see Chapter 14, "A Compendium of Catchwords Used in Recipes.")

Marinara Sauce

Make a double batch and freeze leftovers to use for dinner when you're in a hurry.

Level: Easy

Yield: 2 cups (enough for 1 lb. of pasta)

Can be done completely ahead

1 (2-lb. 3-oz.) can Italian plum tomatoes, drained

3 TB. olive oil

1 small onion, chopped

4 large cloves garlic, minced

2 TB. minced fresh basil, or 1½ tsp. dried

½ tsp. salt, or salt to taste

¼ tsp. freshly ground black pepper

Drain and chop the tomatoes. Heat the olive oil in a saucepan over low to moderate heat and add the onion and garlic. Cook 3 minutes or until the vegetables have softened. Add the tomatoes, basil, salt, and pepper. Simmer 45 minutes, taste for seasoning, and add salt and pepper to taste. Serve the sauce chunky or purée it in a food processor or blender.

continues

continued

Here are some variations on marinara sauce:

➤ **Puttanesca:** Add 12 sliced pitted green olives, 12 sliced pitted black olives, 1 TB. of drained capers, and 6 mashed anchovy fillets to the sauce after it has cooked for 30 minutes.

➤ **Mushroom:** Sauté 1 cup of sliced mushrooms with the onion and garlic.

➤ **Amatriciana:** Add 4 slices chopped pancetta or bacon to the olive oil. Cook until lightly crispy. Discard all but 3 TB. fat from the pan. Continue with the recipe adding ½ tsp. red pepper flakes with the tomatoes.

Barbecue Sauce

This all-purpose barbecue sauce can be used for almost any kind of meat or poultry but is especially good with chicken or pork.

Level: Easy

Yield: about 3 cups

Can be done completely ahead

⅓ cup vegetable oil

1 TB. butter, optional

1 medium onion, finely chopped
(about ½ cup)

2 cloves garlic, minced

1 cup ketchup

1 cup canned tomato sauce

½ cup water

⅓ cup honey

¼ cup cider vinegar

2 tsp. Worcestershire sauce

dash of hot pepper sauce

Heat the vegetable oil and butter in a saucepan over moderate heat. When the butter has melted and looks foamy, add the onion and garlic and cook 3 minutes or until the vegetables have softened. Add the remaining ingredients, stir, and simmer 40 minutes, stirring occasionally.

How to Make Gravy

Too many people have a fear of making gravy, but if you follow the steps one by one, you will be successful.

Level: Intermediate

Yield: 2 cups

Can be done completely ahead

the roasting pan fluids from a turkey, chicken, roast beef, or other roast

water, stock, or wine

2 TB. rendered pan fat, butter, or vegetable oil

2 TB. flour

salt and pepper to taste

Strain the fluids from the pan in which you cooked the roast. Reserve the strained liquid. Fat will rise to the top. Scoop the fat with a spoon or bulb baster and set 2 TB. of the fat aside. Measure the pan fluids in a large measuring pitcher. Add enough water, stock, or wine to equal 2 cups. Place the roasting pan over low heat and add the 2 TB. of the scooped fat (or use butter or vegetable oil). When the fat is hot or the butter has melted and looks foamy, sprinkle the flour evenly in the pan. Mix the ingredients with a wooden spoon, scraping up bits and pieces that have stuck to the bottom of the roasting pan. Cook 2 minutes.

Gradually add the fluids, constantly stirring the ingredients. When all the fluids have been absorbed, raise the heat to moderate and cook the gravy (stirring frequently) 1–2 minutes or until it has a uniform texture and has thickened to a gravy-like consistency. Strain the gravy if desired. Taste the gravy for seasoning and add salt and pepper as necessary. Reheat the gravy in a small saucepan or by microwave.

This recipe is for plain, medium-thick gravy. Try these variations:

➤ For thicker gravy, use 3 TB. flour; for thinner gravy use 2½ cups liquid.

➤ For giblet gravy, add chopped cooked giblets after you have cooked the flour for one minute. (You may roast the giblets with the poultry or simmer them for 30 minutes in stock or water.)

➤ For Madeira gravy, add 3–4 TB. Madeira wine to the finished gravy.

➤ For cream gravy, use 1–1½ cups fluid plus 1 cup cream.

➤ For shallot and herb gravy, add 2 chopped shallots and 1½ tsp. fresh thyme leaves (or ½ tsp. dried thyme) to the fat before you add the flour.

Classic Vinaigrette Dressing

This is one of the world's most basic sauces. Make extra—it lasts a week or more in the fridge.

Level: Easy

Yield: about ⅔ cup

Can be done completely ahead

½ cup olive oil

3 TB. red wine vinegar

1½ tsp. Dijon mustard, or ½ tsp. powdered mustard

1 medium garlic clove, minced (optional)

salt and pepper to taste

Combine the ingredients in a bowl and whisk them together until well blended, or place them in a covered container and shake them for several seconds until they are well blended. Taste the sauce for seasoning, and add salt and pepper as desired.

You may use vinaigrette as a salad dressing or marinade. It is such a versatile recipe you may change it in numerous ways to please your palate. Here are a few possibilities:

➤ **Balsamic vinaigrette:** Use 2 TB. balsamic vinegar instead of the 3 TB. red wine vinegar.

➤ **Shallot vinaigrette:** Add 1 minced shallot.

➤ **Herb vinaigrette:** Add 1 TB. minced fresh herbs such as marjoram, oregano, basil, thyme, savory, chervil, and dill, or 1 tsp. dried herbs.

➤ **Mustard vinaigrette:** Add 1½ tsp. Dijon mustard.

➤ **"French" dressing:** Add 1 TB. mayonnaise and ½ tsp. paprika.

➤ **Lemon vinaigrette:** Use lemon juice instead of vinegar.

White Sauce

Basic and versatile, this one should be a part of every cook's repertoire.

Level: Intermediate

Yield: 1¼ cups

2 TB. butter

2 TB. flour

1¼ cups hot milk

salt and ground white pepper

freshly grated nutmeg

Heat the butter in a saucepan over low heat. When the butter has melted and looks foamy, add the flour and stir the ingredients about 2 minutes, or until the ingredients look bubbly. Add the milk gradually, stirring vigorously with a whisk. Cook, stirring constantly, another minute or so. Stir in salt and pepper to taste and add a grating or two of nutmeg.

White sauce, also known as *béchamel*, is the basis for many other sauces. (See the entry in the section "Sauce" of Chapter 14.) Here are a few variations:

➤ **Velouté:** Use chicken stock instead of milk.

➤ **Mornay:** Stir ½ cup finely grated Swiss cheese into the white sauce and cook until the cheese melts.

➤ **Soubise:** Melt 3 TB. butter in a saucepan, add 3 cups of sliced onions, and cook, covered, over low heat for 25 minutes. Add the cooked onions to the white sauce, and then stir in ⅓ cup cream. Purée the ingredients in a food processor or blender.

Cranberry Sauce

You won't find a simpler cranberry sauce. But don't save it for Thanksgiving dinner; it's also super with chicken and pork.

Level: Easy

Yield: 6 servings

Can be done completely ahead

1 12-oz. package fresh whole cranberries (about 3 cups)

1½ cups sugar

3 TB. orange-flavored brandy

Preheat the oven to 350°F. Wash and drain the berries and place them in a single layer in a baking dish. Add the sugar and toss the berries to coat them. Cover the dish. Bake 45–50 minutes. Take the dish from the oven and remove its cover. Stir the berries and let them cool. Stir in the brandy. Chill at least 1 hour or until cold.

Crème Fraîche

Everyone will think you are a well-informed gourmet if you serve this marvelous, modern topping for fruit. And it's so easy to do!

Level: Easy

Yield: about 1¼ cups

Can be done completely ahead

continues

continues

1 cup whipping cream, not ultra-pasteurized

3 TB. stirred plain yogurt or buttermilk

Combine the ingredients and whisk them until well blended. Pour the mixture into a saucepan. Cook over moderate heat about 2 minutes or until the chill is off and the mixture feels almost lukewarm. Pour the ingredients into a jar. Cover the jar and let the mixture stand at room temperature 12–15 hours or until it has thickened to the consistency of stirred yogurt. Refrigerate the sauce at least 24 hours to allow the flavors to mellow.

Kitchen Clue

Crème fraîche is a gently tangy, slightly thick sauce that you can use on top of berries or chocolate cake for dessert, or that you can use to enrich soups, gravy, and dozens of other savory dishes that call for sour cream or cream. If you want a thicker sauce, whip it slightly.

Fudge Sauce

This rich, velvety sauce is the perfect topping for ice cream, poached pears, crêpes, and plain cake.

Level: Challenging

Yield: about 1 cup

12 oz. semisweet chocolate	½ cup orange juice
3 TB. butter	¼ cup orange-flavored liqueur
1½ TB. sugar	¼ cup rum
1 orange, the peel cut into strips	

Melt the chocolate in the top part of a double boiler set over near-simmering water, stirring occasionally; set it aside to cool. Heat the butter and sugar in a skillet over low-moderate heat. When the butter has melted and looks foamy, add the orange peel and cook about 4 minutes or until the sugar begins to brown slightly. Add the orange juice, stir, and discard the orange peel. Heat the liqueur and rum together in a small saucepan. Ignite them and then pour them into the orange mixture. Cook, stirring until the flames die down. Add the melted chocolate and blend it into the ingredients, stirring with a whisk until a smooth sauce has formed.

Quick Breads, Brunches, and Breakfasts

Quick Breads

Quick breads are suitable for breakfast, lunch, brunch, or dinner, for tea time and coffee breaks, and even for dessert. While they usually taste best within a day or so after you bake them, you can freeze quick breads for a few weeks.

One important note on quick breads: Don't mix the dry ingredients, particularly baking soda or baking powder, with liquids such as milk or buttermilk, until you are ready to bake the bread. If you do, the gas formed by a chemical reaction between the ingredients will dissipate, and your bread won't rise in the oven.

Buttermilk Biscuits

Best when warm, served with butter, jam, or Devonshire cream.

Level: Intermediate

Yield: 10–12 biscuits

Can be done completely ahead

2 cups all-purpose flour
2 tsp. baking powder
¾ tsp. salt
½ tsp. baking soda

½ cup chilled butter
    or shortening, or a mixture of these
⅔ cup buttermilk

continues

continued

Preheat the oven to 400°F. Lightly grease a cookie sheet. Sift the flour, baking powder, salt, and baking soda into a bowl. Cut the butter into chunks and add the chunks to the flour mixture. Work the fat into the flour mixture using your fingers, a pastry blender, or two knives until the ingredients resemble crumbs. Add the buttermilk and gather the ingredients with your hands or a large wooden spoon to make a soft ball of dough.

Lightly flour a pastry board or a clean work surface. Knead the ball of dough on the floured surface 10–12 times to make the dough slightly smoother. Press the dough or roll it to ½" thickness. Use more flour on the board if the dough sticks. Cut out 10–12 circles with a cookie cutter or the top of a glass. You will have to reroll the dough to get the last 2 or 3 circles. Place the circles on the cookie sheet 1 inch apart for crisper, darker biscuits or closer together for fluffier, lighter biscuits. Bake 20 minutes or until the biscuits have risen and are browned on top.

Kitchen Clue

Devonshire cream is a thick, clotted cream. Specialty stores sell it in jars; look in the refrigerator case.

Irish Soda Bread

This densely textured loaf is wonderful with coffee or tea or as an accompaniment to soup or salad.

Level: Easy

Yield: one loaf

Can be done completely ahead

3½ cups all-purpose flour

1 TB. brown sugar

¾ tsp. salt

1 tsp. baking soda

1½ cups buttermilk

½ cup dried currants or raisins (optional)

1 tsp. caraway seeds (optional)

Preheat the oven to 350°F. Lightly grease a baking sheet. Mix the flour, brown sugar, salt, and baking soda in a bowl. Add the buttermilk, and mix the ingredients until a soft dough has formed. If you use the currants and caraway seeds, work them in with your hands. Lightly flour a pastry board or a clean work surface. Knead the ball of dough on the floured surface 18–20 times to make the dough smoother. Use more flour on the board if the dough sticks. Shape the dough into a ball, and then flatten it slightly. Cut a small X on the top with the tip of a sharp knife. Place the dough on the baking sheet and bake it 40–45 minutes or until it is golden brown.

Banana Bread

This old-fashioned bread is delicious plain but even better when spread with softened cream cheese.

Level: Easy

Yield: one loaf

Can be done completely ahead

2 cups all-purpose flour

1 tsp. baking soda

½ tsp. baking powder

½ tsp. salt

1 cup sugar

½ cup vegetable oil

2 large eggs

3 medium very ripe bananas

3 TB. milk

¾ tsp. vanilla extract

⅔ cup finely chopped nuts (optional)

Preheat the oven to 350°F. Grease a 9" × 5" × 3" loaf pan. Sift the flour, baking soda, baking powder, and salt into a bowl and set it aside. Beat the sugar and vegetable oil with a handheld or electric mixer set at moderate speed for 2–3 minutes or until the mixture is light and fluffy. Add the eggs one at a time, beating after each addition. Mash the bananas until they are mushy, then add them. Beat the mixture thoroughly to incorporate the bananas. Add the flour mixture, stirring only enough to moisten the dry ingredients and blend them in. Gently stir in the milk, vanilla extract, and nuts (if desired). Pour the batter into the prepared pan and bake the bread 1 hour or until a cake tester inserted into the center comes out clean. Cool the bread in the pan 15 minutes. Remove the bread from the pan and let it cool on a cake rack.

Kitchen Clue

Banana bread tastes better the second day. Wrap it in plastic wrap and let the flavors mellow. You may add 2 tsp. of cinnamon to the batter if you prefer banana bread with a hint of spiciness.

Blueberry Muffins

These muffins are dense and cakey.

Level: Intermediate

Yield: 12 muffins

Can be done completely ahead

5 TB. butter

1¾ cups all-purpose flour

½ cup sugar

¾ tsp. salt

1½ tsp. baking powder

½ tsp. baking soda

1 TB. freshly grated orange peel

1 cup buttermilk

1 large egg

½ tsp. vanilla extract

1 cup blueberries

Preheat the oven to 400°F. Grease 12 large muffin cups. Melt the butter and set it aside to cool slightly. Sift the flour, sugar, salt, baking powder, and baking soda into a bowl. Stir in the orange peel. Combine the buttermilk, egg, vanilla extract, and melted butter in a second bowl. Beat the liquid ingredients to form a uniformly colored mixture. Pour the liquid ingredients into the dry ones. Stir only enough to moisten all the dry ingredients. Do NOT beat into a smooth batter; this makes the muffins tough. Fold in the blueberries. Fill the muffin cups ½ to ⅔ full with the batter. Bake 20–25 minutes or until a cake tester inserted into the center comes out clean.

Second Thoughts

If you don't like the taste of orange, substitute the orange rind with 2 tsp. freshly grated lemon rind, or use ¾ tsp. cinnamon instead. (Sift it with the other dry ingredients.)

Chocolate Macadamia Nut Bread

You'll get wows when you serve this rich-tasting loaf. It's delicious even without the macadamia nuts.

Level: Challenging

Yield: one loaf

Can be done completely ahead

2 oz. unsweetened chocolate	⅓ cup vegetable shortening
1¾ cups all-purpose flour	2 large eggs
1½ tsp. baking soda	2 tsp. vanilla extract
1 tsp. salt	1¼ cups buttermilk
1¼ cups sugar	½ cup coarsely chopped macadamia nuts

Preheat the oven to 350°F. Grease a 9" × 5" × 3" loaf pan. Melt the chocolate in the top part of a double boiler set over near-simmering water, then set it aside to cool. Sift the flour, baking soda, and salt into a bowl and set it aside. Beat the sugar and shortening together with a handheld or electric mixer at moderate speed about 1 minute or until the ingredients are well blended. Add the eggs and vanilla extract and beat the mixture 1–2 minutes or until smooth and fluffy. Add ⅓ of the dry ingredients to the egg mixture and blend it in. Add ⅓ of the buttermilk and blend it in. Repeat this process two more times until all the flour and buttermilk are used. Scrape the sides of the bowl once or twice to make sure all of the batter is incorporated. Stir in the chocolate and the nuts and mix the ingredients for a short time until the color is uniform. Pour the batter into the prepared pan. Bake approximately 45 minutes or until a cake tester inserted into the center comes out clean. Cool the bread in the pan 10 minutes. Remove the bread from the pan and let it cool on a cake rack.

Breakfast and Brunch Dishes

Sometimes you want something more than a quick doughnut and a swallow of coffee for breakfast. While you may not have time for much more during the week, weekends are the ideal time to begin the day with something good to eat. If you have weekend guests, you'll surely want to serve them something tasty but easy.

How to Cook Eggs

Eggs are still favorites for breakfast. Here are several ways to cook them.

Level: Easy

Yield: makes 2 servings

Cannot be done ahead, except for hard-cooked eggs

Scrambled Eggs

4 large eggs

1 TB. milk or water

salt and black pepper to taste

1 TB. butter

Crack the eggs into a mixing bowl, add the milk or water and some salt and pepper and blend the ingredients gently (do not let them become frothy). Melt the butter in a skillet over moderate heat. When the butter looks foamy, add the eggs. Cook, without stirring, about 15 seconds. Using a large spoon or flat wooden spatula, push the eggs (which have already begun to set around the edges of the skillet) toward the center of the pan. Then stir the eggs gently to be sure that uncooked portions reach the bottom of the pan. When the eggs look creamy, not runny, they are done.

Fried Eggs Sunny Side Up and Fried Eggs Over Easy

1 TB. butter

4 large eggs

salt and black pepper to taste

To fry eggs sunny-side up, melt the butter in a skillet over moderate heat. When the butter looks foamy, crack the eggs into the pan. Cook for 3–4 minutes, piercing bubbles that appear in the whites. The eggs are done when the whites have set and look creamy with crispy brown edges. To make eggs over easy, flip over the sunny-side up eggs and cook them about 30 seconds. Sprinkle the eggs with salt and pepper.

Soft- and Hard-Cooked Eggs

water

4 large eggs

Add enough water to a saucepan to cover the eggs by at least 1 inch. Bring the water to a boil. Use a spoon to gently lower the eggs into the water. Turn the heat to low. Cook 3–6 minutes for soft-cooked eggs (time depends on the degree of softness desired) or 12–15 minutes for hard-cooked eggs.

The Best Buttermilk Pancakes You Ever Ate

These are plump, fluffy, American-style breakfast pancakes—great with melted butter and real maple syrup on top.

Level: Intermediate

Yield: 6 servings

Cannot be done ahead

3 TB. butter	1 tsp. baking powder	1 egg
2½ cups flour	1 tsp. baking soda	3 cups buttermilk
2 TB. sugar	½ tsp. salt	butter for frying the pancakes

Melt the 3 TB. of butter and set it aside to cool. Sift the flour, sugar, baking powder, baking soda, and salt into a bowl. Combine the egg, buttermilk, and melted, cooled butter in a second bowl. Beat the liquid ingredients to form a uniformly colored mixture. Add the liquid ingredients to the dry ones and stir only until all the flour is moist. Preheat a griddle or large skillet over moderate heat. Lightly butter the pan before you make each batch of pancakes. When the butter has melted and looks foamy, slowly spoon, ladle, or pour 2 TB. batter onto the griddle to make a silver-dollar size pancake, or increase the amount of batter for bigger pancakes. Leave a little space between each one. Cook the pancakes about 2 minutes or until tiny bubbles begin to appear on the surface. Flip the pancakes with a rigid spatula and cook them about a minute or until the undersides are lightly browned (lift an edge with the spatula to test for doneness).

Fein on Food

At one time, fats and eggs were forbidden during Lent, so pancakes, which include both, became traditional for Shrove Tuesday, the day preceding Ash Wednesday, when Lent begins. One Shrove Tuesday, back in 1445, a woman in Olney, England, was preparing pancakes when she heard the church bell. Realizing that she would be late for services, she ran out of the house, frying pan and all, flipping pancakes all the way. The next year the women of the town did the same thing, to mimic the woman, but the sympathetic vicar decided to make a yearly event of it. The "pancake race" has been a tradition ever since. That same tradition was adopted in Liberal, Kansas, in 1950, after someone from that town saw the Olney race.

Smoked Salmon and Onion Frittata

This omelet-like dish is colorful, flavorful and fragrant; a good choice for brunch or Sunday breakfast. And it's easier to make than an omelet.

Level: Easy

Yield: 4 servings

*Can be done ahead up to the * in the instructions*

6 eggs, beaten
¼ cup milk
2 TB. butter or margarine
1 medium onion, chopped, about ½ cup

1 cup chopped smoked salmon, about 4 oz.
2 TB. chopped fresh dill
sour cream, optional

Preheat the oven to 350°F. Mix the eggs and milk together. Melt the butter over moderate heat in a large skillet. When the butter looks foamy, add the onion and cook 4–5 minutes or until onions have wilted and are just beginning to brown. Add the smoked salmon and dill and cook another minute, stirring constantly. Turn the heat to low. Add the egg mixture. When the eggs begin to set at the edges of the pan, stir the mixture gently with a fork, bringing hardened edges toward the center to allow uncooked portions of the mixture to reach the heat at the bottom of the pan. Continue cooking and occasionally stir the eggs in this way for 3–4 minutes, then cook undisturbed for a few minutes more, until the eggs are set but still moist looking.

* Transfer the pan to the oven and cook 5–8 minutes, or until the top has set. Serve the frittata plain or topped with sour cream.

Second Thoughts

For a basic frittata, leave out the onion, salmon, and dill and follow the instructions above, adding the eggs when the butter looks foamy. You may also use other ingredients in a frittata: sautéed potatoes, cooked vegetables, crisped ham, bacon or sausage, and grated cheese are just a few examples.

Pain Perdu

This is the New Orleans version of French toast, and you are in for a scrumptious surprise with this recipe.

Level: Easy

Yield: 4 servings

*Can be done ahead up to the * in the instructions*

5 large eggs

½ cup sugar

½ cup milk

2 TB. orange-flavored brandy

1 tsp. finely grated lemon or orange peel (optional)

12 slices of French or Italian bread (approximately), ½" thick

butter for frying

Beat the eggs, sugar, milk, brandy, and lemon peel with an electric beater or whisk for 1–2 minutes, or until they are thick and foamy. Pour the mixture into a shallow dish or a pan big enough to hold the bread slices. Add the bread slices to the egg mixture, turning them occasionally. Let the slices soak 4–5 minutes or until they are thoroughly saturated.

* Preheat a griddle or large skillet over moderate heat. Lightly butter the pan (with a tsp. or two of butter) before you make each batch of bread. When the butter has melted and looks foamy, add the soaked bread slices and cook them 2–3 minutes or until the bottoms are golden brown. Flip the bread with a rigid spatula and cook the slices another 2–3 minutes or until the bottoms are golden brown.

Kitchen Clue

The number of bread slices you use depends on the width of the bread. The most tender Pain Perdu is made with wide slices of French or Italian bread.

The name *Pain Perdu* actually is a misnomer. It means "lost bread." This dish, which is similar to French toast, was invented in an effort to use up stale bread that might otherwise be lost.

Noodle Casserole

This dish is ideal for a buffet-style brunch or any informal get-together.

Level: Intermediate

Yield: 4 servings

Can be done completely ahead

⅓ cup dried mushrooms

hot water

2 TB. butter

1 small onion, chopped (about ¼ cup)

1 lb. smoked turkey or boiled ham, diced

6 sun-dried tomatoes, chopped

½ lb. egg noodles (cooked according to package directions)

¼ tsp. salt, or salt to taste

¼ tsp. freshly ground black pepper

2 large eggs, beaten

1 cup light cream or half-and-half

½ cup grated Swiss or Monterey Jack cheese

Preheat the oven to 350°F. Lightly butter a casserole. Place the mushrooms in a small bowl, cover with hot water, and let them soften for about 10–20 minutes. Rinse and drain the mushrooms and set them aside. (If you use shiitake mushrooms, cut off and discard the tough inedible stems. If you use large mushrooms, chop or slice them.) Melt the butter over moderate heat in a skillet. When the butter looks foamy, add the onion and cook it 3–4 minutes or until it has softened. Add the mushrooms, turkey or ham, and sun-dried tomatoes and cook another minute. Remove the pan from the heat and set it aside. Place the noodles in a bowl and add the meat mixture, salt, and pepper. Beat the eggs and cream separately and add them to the bowl. Stir ingredients to coat the noodles thoroughly. Pour the mixture into the prepared dish. Top with the cheese. Bake 40 minutes or until the top is crusty and golden brown.

Desserts

Some people say they would rather skip dinner and go right to dessert. Everyone knows why—dessert is pure indulgence, something to be enjoyed without focusing on nutrition or worrying about whether it's "good for you." Eating dessert means satisfying a sweet tooth, indulging in the pleasurable. Thankfully, there's an enormous variety of recipes that do just that—from homey pies to elegant mousses. You can serve a tall and stately cake or simple poached fruit. Or perhaps your choice will be a stack of cookies perfect for dunking in milk. Whatever you choose, enjoy it!

Chocolate Fudgie Brownies

Better make two recipes of these because they get gobbled up quickly.

Level: Easy

Yield: 16

Can be done completely ahead

4 squares unsweetened chocolate	½ cup all-purpose flour
⅓ cup butter	¼ tsp. salt
2 large eggs	1 tsp. vanilla extract
1 cup sugar	½ cup finely chopped nuts (optional)

Preheat the oven to 350°F. Lightly grease an 8" × 8" baking pan. Put the chocolate and butter in the top part of a double boiler set over barely simmering water. Stir for 3–4 minutes or until the ingredients have melted. Remove the top part of the double boiler from the heat.

continues

continued

Combine the eggs and sugar in a large bowl and beat them with an electric mixer set at moderate speed 2–3 minutes or until the mixture is as thick as stirred yogurt and as pale as cream-colored daffodils. Add the flour, salt, vanilla extract, and nuts, if desired, and stir them in. Add the chocolate and butter mixture and stir to blend all the ingredients thoroughly. Pour the batter into the prepared pan. Bake 30 minutes. Cool the brownies in the pan. Cut them into 16 squares.

One-Bowl Cocoa Fudge Cake with Fudge Frosting

This rich dessert creates quite a dilemma: You don't know whether to eat the cake or the frosting first, or eat both together. When you get down to your last bite, which will it be: cake or frosting?

Level: Intermediate

Yield: 8–10 servings

Can be done completely ahead

Cake

2 cups cake flour

1½ cups sugar

⅔ cup unsweetened cocoa powder

1½ tsp. baking soda

1 tsp. salt

1½ cups buttermilk (low-fat or skim)

½ cup vegetable shortening

2 large eggs

1½ tsp. vanilla extract

Frosting

12 oz. semisweet chocolate

1 cup sour cream

pinch of salt

1 tsp. vanilla extract

Preheat the oven to 350°F. Lightly grease two 9" cake pans. Sift the cake flour, sugar, cocoa powder, baking soda, and salt into a large bowl. Add the buttermilk and shortening. Beat the mixture for 2 minutes with an electric mixer set at moderate speed, scraping down the sides of the bowl occasionally with a rubber spatula. Add the eggs and vanilla extract and beat another 2 minutes, again scraping down the sides of the bowl occasionally. Pour the batter into the prepared pans. Bake 30–35 minutes or until a cake tester inserted into the middle of the cake comes out clean. Let the cake cool in the pans 10 minutes, and then invert the layers onto a cake rack to cool completely.

To make the frosting, put the chocolate in the top part of a double boiler set over barely simmering water. Stir for 3–4 minutes or until the chocolate has melted. Remove the top part of the double boiler from the heat. Add the sour cream, salt, and vanilla extract to the chocolate. Beat the ingredients vigorously with a whisk until the mixture is smooth. Let the frosting cool 15–20 minutes or until it is of spreading consistency. Spread about a half cup of the frosting between the layers and the rest on the top and around the sides of the cake. After you cut the cake, store the uneaten portions in the refrigerator.

Chocolate Mousse

This rich, dark mousse is a perennial favorite.

Level: Challenging

Yield: 4 servings

Can be done completely ahead

8 oz. semisweet chocolate

2 TB. confectioner's sugar

2 egg yolks

2 TB. rum or very strong coffee

1 TB. water

1¼ cups whipping cream

Put the chocolate in the top part of a double boiler set over barely simmering water. Stir for 3–4 minutes or until the chocolate has melted. Remove the top part of the double boiler from the heat. Whisk in the confectioner's sugar and egg yolks. Add the rum or coffee and water, and whisk them in. Set the mixture aside. Whip the cream until it stands in soft peaks. Fold all but ½ cup into the chocolate mixture. Spoon the mousse into individual serving dishes. Refrigerate at least 1 hour. Garnish with the reserved whipped cream.

Second Thoughts

For a frothier mousse, whip 2 egg whites until they stand in soft peaks and fold them into the chocolate mixture, after adding the whipped cream. (Remember, though, that eating raw eggs poses some health risks.)

Strawberry Shortcake

A favorite! The cakes are really biscuits, with a little extra sugar. Their buttery, moist interior soaks up the sweet juice of the sugared berries.

Level: Intermediate

Yield: 10–12 individual cakes

*Can be done ahead up to the * in the instructions*

continues

continued

10–12 buttermilk biscuits
    (see Section 8)

2 TB. sugar

3 TB. extra buttermilk

1 quart strawberries

¼ cup sugar

1 cup heavy cream

Preheat the oven to 400°F. Prepare the biscuits as instructed in the recipe in Section 8, but add 2 TB. sugar to the dry ingredients and 3 TB. extra buttermilk to the liquids. Bake the biscuits and let them cool. Split the biscuits in half crosswise. Slice the berries. Add all but 1 tsp. of sugar and let the fruit macerate for at least 30 minutes. Whip the cream with the remaining tsp. of sugar until it has thickened but is still pourable (the thickness of applesauce).

* Place the biscuit halves on serving plates, cooked side down, top with the berries and pour the cream on top.

What Is It?

When you **macerate** fruits, you place them in a flavored liquid, so they can absorb flavor and soften in texture. Here, the dissolving sugar and natural fluids in the fruit combine to create their own juices.

New York Cheesecake

This is the most sophisticated, velvet-textured cheesecake you will ever eat.

Level: Challenging

Yield: 8–10 servings

Can be done completely ahead

1 TB. butter

⅓ cup graham cracker crumbs

1½ lbs. cream cheese

2 TB. freshly grated orange peel

2 TB. freshly grated lemon peel

1 tsp. vanilla extract

½ cup cream, any kind

1 cup sugar

4 eggs

⅓ cup dairy sour cream or plain yogurt

Preheat the oven to 350°F. Spread the butter on the bottom and sides of a 9" springform pan. Sprinkle the inside of the pan with the graham cracker crumbs. Shake the pan to coat the bottom and sides completely. Using an electric mixer set at moderate speed, beat the cream cheese, orange peel, and lemon peel about 2 minutes—occasionally scraping down the sides of the bowl with a rubber spatula—or until the cheese has softened and is smooth. Gradually add the vanilla, cream, and sugar and beat the ingredients another 2–3 minutes, again occasionally scraping down the sides of the bowl. Add the eggs one at a time, beating after each addition. Add the sour cream and beat the batter briefly to make sure it is smooth.

Pour the batter into the prepared pan. Prepare a *bain-marie:* that is, place the springform pan inside a larger pan. Fill the larger pan with enough hot water to come at least 1 inch up the sides of the springform pan. Bake the cake in the bain-marie 70–75 minutes or until the top of the cake is lightly brown.

Remove the springform pan from the bain-marie and let the cake cool in the pan. When the cake has reached room temperature, refrigerate it at least 4 hours or until it is thoroughly chilled. To serve the cake, remove the sides of the springform pan.

Apple Brown Betty

While this is baking, your entire house will have the most wonderful perfume of apples and cinnamon.

Level: Easy

Yield: 6 servings

Can be done completely ahead

5–6 pie apples, such as Granny Smith, Rhode Island Greening, or Golden Delicious (about 5 cups of fruit)

2 TB. lemon juice

4 cups (½") diced home-style white bread, trimmed of crusts

¾ cup brown sugar

½ cup melted butter

¾ tsp. ground cinnamon

¼ tsp. freshly grated nutmeg

pinch of salt

Preheat the oven to 375°F. Peel the apples and remove the cores. Cut the apples into bite-size pieces. Sprinkle the lemon juice over the apples. Place the apples in a baking dish. Combine the diced bread, brown sugar, melted butter, cinnamon, nutmeg, and salt in a bowl. Toss the ingredients to coat the bread completely. Place the coated bread on top of the apples. Bake the Betty 50–60 minutes or until the top is golden brown and crusty.

Second Thoughts

You can make Betty with just about any fruit or mixture of fruits, such as nectarines, peaches and blueberries, or pears. Use about 5 cups of bite-size fruit pieces.

How to Poach Fruit

When you learn how to poach fruit, you can make more dessert dishes than you can imagine. Poaching is one of the most versatile cooking methods available. You can store the poached fruit in the fridge, in the poaching fluid, for 1–3 days.

Level: Intermediate

Yield: 1 whole fruit will serve 1–2 people

Can be done completely ahead

1½ cups sugar

6 cups water

3 strips of lemon peel

1 (4") piece of vanilla bean, or 1 TB. vanilla extract

fruit

Combine the sugar, water, lemon peel, and vanilla bean in a saucepan. Bring the mixture to a boil over high heat. Reduce the heat to low and cook 10 minutes. Add the fruit. The fruit must be completely immersed in the poaching liquid; using a smaller pan makes this step easier. Alternatively, you can cut large fruit such as pears or peaches in half. (Remove the seeds or pit.) Cook the fruit until it is barely fork tender. The time depends on the fruit. Remove the pan from the heat and let the fruit cool in the poaching fluid.

The best fruit choices for poaching are pears, peaches, apricots, plums, nectarines, and blueberries. You can peel fruit before you poach it, but you don't have to. The skin of peaches and pears comes off easily after the fruit is poached. To serve, peel the fruit and remove the seeds and core. Transfer the fruit to serving dishes. Strain the poaching liquid. You may serve the poaching liquid as is, on top of the fruit, or boil it down over high heat for several minutes, until it reaches a syrupy consistency. Let the liquid cool and pour it over the fruit.

You may season the poaching liquid in several delicious ways by adding one of the following to the liquid:

➤ 3" piece of cinnamon stick
➤ 1 cup red wine
➤ peel from half an orange
➤ a chunk of fresh ginger or several pieces of crystallized ginger
➤ 4–5 cracked cardamom pods

Kitchen Clue

The amount of poaching liquid in this recipe will be enough for up to 1½ lbs. of fruit. If you use vanilla extract in a recipe instead of vanilla bean, do *not* add it until you remove the pan from the heat. Heat dissipates the intensity of the extract.

Peach Melba

One of the most elegant desserts, this is just one example of what you can do once you know how to poach fruit.

Level: Intermediate

Yield: 6 servings

*Can be done ahead up to the * in the instructions*

6 poached peaches (see recipe for poached fruit), cooled
2 boxes of fresh raspberries or 1½ cups frozen berries (defrosted and drained)
2½ TB. sugar
2 TB. orange-flavored liqueur or Kirschwasser (optional)
6 scoops vanilla ice cream
⅓ cup lightly toasted chopped almonds (optional)

Peel the peaches, cut them into halves, and remove the pits. Place two halves into each of 6 dessert dishes. Crush the berries and mix them with the sugar and the liqueur (if used). Set this mixture aside. (If you use frozen, presweetened packaged berries, omit the sugar.)

* Place the scoops of ice cream on top of the peaches. Pour equal amounts of the raspberry mixture over the ice cream. Sprinkle each portion with equal amounts of the toasted almonds, if you like.

Baked Pears

Similar to baked apples, but spicier and more sophisticated.

Level: Easy

Yield: 4 servings

Can be done completely ahead

4 firm pears, preferably Comice, Bartlett, or Anjou

½ lemon

1 cup red wine

1 cup sugar

2 cinnamon sticks

6 whole cloves

pinch of salt

Amaretto cookies and/or ice cream (optional)

Preheat the oven to 350°F. Peel the pears, cut them in half, and remove the cores. Rub the fruit with the cut side of the lemon. Put the pears into a baking dish. Place the wine, sugar, cinnamon sticks, cloves, salt, and the lemon half in a saucepan. Bring the mixture to a boil over high heat. Cook 2 minutes. Pour the mixture over the pears. Cover the dish and bake the pears 20 minutes. Remove the cover and bake another 10 minutes, basting the pears once or twice during this time. Let the pears cool slightly or completely before serving them. Serve the pears with Amaretto cookies, ice cream, or both. You may spoon the baking liquid over the pears or boil it in a saucepan for a few minutes to reduce it to a syrupy consistency.

Summer Fruit Crisp

Supereasy and best when served warm, with ice cream on top.

Level: Easy

Yield: 4 servings

Can be done completely ahead

Filling

3 nectarines, sliced (or peeled peaches)

3 large plums, sliced

1 cup blueberries

½ cup sugar

½ tsp. ground cinnamon

¼ tsp. fresh grated nutmeg

2 TB. cornstarch

2 TB. lemon juice

Crust

⅔ cup brown sugar

¾ cup uncooked oats

¾ cup all-purpose flour

4 TB. butter

Preheat the oven to 375°F. Slice the fruit into a bowl and toss with the sugar, cinnamon, nutmeg, cornstarch, and lemon juice. Spoon the mixture into a baking dish. In a bowl, toss the brown sugar, oats, and flour until they are well combined. Add the butter and work into the dry ingredients until the mixture resembles coarse meal. Place the oat mixture on top of the fruit. Bake about 45 minutes or until the crust is golden brown.

Dipped Strawberries

This one is everybody's favorite!

Level: Easy

Yield: about 24

Can be done completely ahead

1-pint box of strawberries

6 oz. semisweet chocolate

1 TB. shortening

Rinse the berries quickly under cold water but do *not* remove the green hulls. Dry the berries thoroughly with paper towels. Put the chocolate and shortening in the top part of a double boiler set over barely simmering water. Stir for 3–4 minutes or until the chocolate has melted. Remove the top part of the double boiler from the heat. Dip the tips of the strawberries in the hot chocolate mixture to coat about half a berry. Place the berries on waxed paper or foil to cool. The chocolate will harden as it cools.

Second Thoughts

While dipped fruit is stunning and delicious as is, you can fancy it up even more. Put some plain or toasted ground nuts on a plate. After you dip the berries in the chocolate, roll the chocolate part in the ground nuts, and then set the berries aside to cool and harden.

How to Make Pie Crust

Don't let yourself be intimidated by pie crust. Follow the recipe step by step, and you'll see that you can do it and be successful. Try not to handle the dough too much; over-handling makes the crust tough.

Level: Challenging

Yield: enough for a two-crust, 9" or 10" pie

Can be done completely ahead

2½ cups all-purpose flour

1 tsp. sugar

¾ tsp. salt

1 tsp. freshly grated lemon peel (optional)

½ cup cold butter

⅓ cup cold vegetable shortening

4–6 TB. milk, approximately

Combine the flour, sugar, salt, and lemon peel, if desired, in a large bowl. Cut the butter and shortening into chunks and add the chunks to the flour mixture. Using your fingers, a pastry blender, or two knives, work the fat into the flour mixture until the ingredients resemble crumbs. Alternatively, you may use a food processor; if you use one, add the ingredients to the work bowl and mix with 24–36 quick, short pulses—enough for the mixture to resemble coarse meal. Add the milk, using only enough to gather pastry into a soft ball of dough. (Start by using 4 TB. of the milk.) If you use a food processor, add 4 TB. milk and process the ingredients for several seconds until the mixture forms a ball of dough. Add the remaining milk, if necessary, to help shape the dough. Cut the dough in half and flatten each half to make a disk shape. Wrap the dough in plastic wrap and let it stand at least 30 minutes.

Here are some interesting facts about pie dough:

➤ You can refrigerate pie dough for several days, or you can freeze it for up to 2 months. Put the wrapped dough in a plastic bag for freezing.

➤ The less liquid you use to make the dough, the more tender and flaky the crust will be.

➤ The addition of lemon peel gives the dough a pleasant fragrance that is particularly nice for fruit pies. You can use ½ tsp. cinnamon in addition to or instead of the lemon peel.

➤ You can use another liquid instead of milk. Most recipes call for ice water. Milk is more enriching and provides a better color. You may also use fruit juice (which is especially good for fruit pie), melted vanilla ice cream, plain yogurt, or—if you like a really rich dough—sour cream.

➤ The dough should rest after you prepare it in order to let the flour gluten relax. If you skip this step, the dough may be tough. This step is particularly important for food processor dough.

➤ Although you may halve the dough (for a streusel-top pie, for example), why not prepare a full recipe and use the other half for a second pie?

Lily Vail's Famous
Old-Fashioned Apple Pie

My mom's best! It's simple, lightly seasoned, and not overly sweet.

Level: Challenging

Yield: 8 servings

Can be done completely ahead .

3 lbs. pie apples, peeled, cored,
    and sliced (about 8–9 apples)

½ cup sugar

2 TB. lemon juice

¾ tsp. ground cinnamon

2 TB. all-purpose flour

1 recipe pie dough

1 TB. butter

Preheat the oven to 375°F. Combine the apple slices, sugar, lemon juice, cinnamon, and flour in a large bowl. Toss the ingredients to coat all the apple slices. Lightly flour a pastry board or a clean work surface. With a rolling pin, roll one half of the dough on the floured surface into a circle about ⅛" thick, making sure the circle is larger than the pie pan by about 1 inch. If the dough sticks, use more flour on the board. Place the dough in a 9" or 10" pie pan. Pour the apple filling into the dough-lined pan. Cut the butter into small pieces and dot the top of the filling with it. Roll out the remaining dough and place it over the filling. Gently press the bottom and top crusts together along the flared edge of the pie pan. For a fluted rim, press your thumb and index finger against the outside of the rim, or crimp it with the tines of a fork or the blunt side of a knife. (If the edge seems too thick, trim some of the dough.) Cut steam vents in the top crust with the tip of a sharp knife, or use the tines of a fork. Bake the pie 50–60 minutes or until the crust is golden brown.

Here are some interesting facts about apple pie:

➤ The best apples to use for pie are Rhode Island Greening, Granny Smith, Gravenstein, Newton Pippin, Northern Spy, Golden Delicious, Idared, Stayman Winesap, Baldwin, Jonagold, and Braeburn.

➤ You need only the simplest seasoning; otherwise, you may overwhelm the delicate flavor of the apples. If you prefer additional flavoring, add ½ tsp. nutmeg or 1 tsp. freshly grated lemon peel.

➤ For a change you can add 1 cup raisins or other cut-up dried fruit or 1 cup cranberries. (If you include cranberries, increase the sugar to 1 cup.)

➤ You can freeze apple pie for several months. Double wrap it in plastic wrap. Thaw the pie completely, and then warm it in a preheated 375°F oven for about 15 minutes to freshen the crust. If you make the pie in a glass pan, you can defrost it in a microwave.

➤ You can top pie with a streusel crust instead of pie dough. See the following recipe for Blueberry Crumb Pie.

Blueberry Crumb Pie

A light, refreshing summer pie.

Level: Intermediate

Yield: 8 servings

Can be done completely ahead

Streusel crust	Filling	
¾ cup flour	5 cups blueberries	¼ tsp. salt
⅓ cup sugar	½ cup sugar	2 TB. fresh lemon juice
6 TB. butter	5 TB. all-purpose flour	1 pie shell, unbaked (homemade or store-bought frozen, 9")
	¾ tsp. ground cinnamon	

Preheat the oven to 375°F. To make the streusel crust, combine the flour and sugar in a mixing bowl. Using your fingers, a pastry blender, or two knives, work the butter into the flour mixture until the ingredients resemble crumbs. If you use a food processor, add the ingredients to the work bowl and mix using 18–24 quick, short pulses—enough for the mixture to resemble coarse meal. Set aside the streusel. Mix the blueberries, sugar, flour, cinnamon, salt, and lemon juice in a large bowl. Pour the blueberry filling into the pie shell. Cover the top with the streusel. Bake the pie 50–60 minutes or until top is golden brown.

Kitchen Clue

You can use two 1-pint boxes of blueberries in this recipe. Although a liquid pint equals 2 cups, a dry pint of blueberries from most markets is about 2½ cups. You can freeze this pie for 3–4 months.

Pumpkin Ice Cream Pie in Graham Cracker Crust

Suitable for Thanksgiving dinner or in the spring when you're not expecting "pumpkin" anything.

Level: Easy

Yield: 8 servings

Can be done completely ahead

1½ cups packaged graham cracker crumbs

6 TB. melted butter

1 quart softened vanilla ice cream

1 cup plain mashed pumpkin (canned is fine, but do NOT use "pumpkin pie mix")

½ cup brown sugar

½ tsp. ground ginger

½ tsp. ground cinnamon

½ tsp. freshly grated nutmeg

¼ tsp. ground allspice or cloves

¼ tsp. salt

Combine the graham cracker crumbs and melted butter in a bowl. Mix the ingredients well to make sure all the crumbs are coated with butter. Press the crumbs onto the bottom and sides of a 9" pie pan. Chill the crust at least 30 minutes, or bake the crust 10 minutes in a preheated 350°F oven. Cool the crust before filling. Mix the ice cream, pumpkin, brown sugar, ginger, cinnamon, nutmeg, allspice or cloves, and salt in a bowl. Pour the filling into the chilled crust. Freeze the pie at least 30 minutes or until it is firm.

Second Thoughts

Instead of using graham cracker crumbs, you can make this crust with ground gingersnaps or chocolate wafer crumbs.

How to Make Whipped Cream

After you make fresh homemade whipped cream, you can use it on practically every dessert from apple pie to chocolate cake to ice cream sundaes. It's quick and easy to make.

Level: Easy

Yield: 2 cups

Can be done completely ahead

1 cup heavy cream (preferably not ultra pasteurized) or whipping cream

1 tsp. granulated sugar

Put the bowl and the beaters in the refrigerator for 10 minutes. It is best to use a hand-held or electric mixer with a whisk attachment. Start beating the cream at slow speed, and then gradually increase the speed, adding the sugar after the cream has thickened slightly. Beat the cream only until the mixture stands in soft peaks. Do not let the mixture curdle by beating it too long.

Second Thoughts

You can vary the flavor by adding the following ingredients to the whipped cream as you beat it:

➤ 1 tsp. vanilla extract

➤ 1 TB. flavored brandy

➤ 2 tsp. instant coffee powder dissolved in some of the cream

Mom's Best Peanut Butter Cookies

No one can resist these. They're the kind of cookies that disappear from the cookie jar. If you freeze these, you can eat them straight out of the freezer.

Level: Easy

Yield: about 8 dozen

Can be done completely ahead

2½ cups all-purpose flour

2 tsp. baking soda

1 tsp. salt

1 cup white sugar

1 cup packed brown sugar

1 cup peanut butter

1 cup vegetable shortening

2 large eggs

Preheat the oven to 350°F. Lightly grease a cookie sheet. Combine the flour, baking soda, salt, white sugar, and brown sugar in a large bowl and beat them with a handheld or electric mixer set at moderate speed about 1 minute, or until the mixture is uniform and ingredients evenly distributed. Add the peanut butter, shortening, and eggs and beat the mixture about 2 minutes, starting at low speed, and then gradually switching to moderately high speed until a uniform dough forms. Take off pieces of dough and shape them into balls about 1½ inch in diameter. Flatten the balls between your palms. Place the cookies on the prepared sheet, leaving an inch of space between them. Press the top of each cookie with the flat, bottom side of a fork, and then press again to make a crisscross design on top of each cookie. Bake 16–20 minutes or until cookies are richly browned and crispy. You can freeze these cookies for 6 months.

Gingersnaps

These cookies are gently spicy and are especially good when the weather turns colder.

Level: Intermediate

Yield: about 6 dozen

Can be done completely ahead

1 cup vegetable shortening

1 cup sugar

1 large egg

¼ cup molasses

2 cups all-purpose flour

1 TB. baking soda

¼ tsp. salt

1 tsp. ground cinnamon

¾ tsp. powdered ginger

¾ tsp. ground cloves

⅛ tsp. freshly grated nutmeg

3 TB. additional sugar for rolling cookies

continues

continued

Preheat the oven to 350°F. Combine the shortening and 1 cup of sugar in a large bowl and beat them with a handheld or electric mixer set at moderate speed 1–2 minutes or until the mixture is light and fluffy. Scrape the sides of the bowl with a rubber spatula. Add the egg and molasses and beat the ingredients to blend them. Scrape the sides of the bowl again. Add the flour, baking soda, salt, cinnamon, ginger, cloves, and nutmeg. Beat the ingredients 1–2 minutes or until the mixture is smooth and uniform. Take off pieces of dough and shape them into balls about 1" in diameter. Roll the balls in the additional sugar. Press gently on the balls to flatten the tops very slightly. Place the balls on a cookie sheet, leaving an inch of space between them. Bake 12 minutes or until cookies are flat and crispy looking with thin cracks on the surface. You can freeze these cookies for 6 months.

Fannies

When we were growing up, we thought everyone called these cookies "Fannies." Little did we know that this was one version of a recipe for classic butter cookies. This particular recipe came from the recipe files of one of our ancestors whose name happened to be Fanny.

Level: Intermediate

Yield: about 5 dozen

Can be done completely ahead

½ lb. butter, cut into 2" chunks

½ cup sugar

2 cups all-purpose flour

2 egg yolks

½ tsp. salt

1 tsp. vanilla extract

1 can or jar of apricot *lekvar*, butter, or cake filling, or use jam or preserves

Preheat the oven to 350°F. Combine the butter and sugar in a large bowl and beat them with a handheld or electric mixer set at moderate speed about 1 minute, or until the mixture is light and fluffy. Add the flour and mix at moderate speed 1–2 minutes, or until it is almost incorporated. Add the egg yolks, salt, and vanilla extract. Mix the ingredients 2 minutes, or until a uniform dough forms. (You may have to scrape the sides of the bowl and the beater with a rubber spatula.) Take off pieces of dough and shape them into balls about 1" in diameter. Flatten the balls between your palms. Press each circle with your thumb to make an indentation in the center. Place the cookies on a cookie sheet, leaving an inch of space between them. Fill the thumb print spaces with a small amount of the apricot lekvar, or apricot preserves (you'll use about ½ cup in all). Bake about 25 minutes or until the cookies are golden brown. You can freeze these cookies for 6 months.

What Is It?

Lekvar is a sweet fruit spread that's thicker than jam. You can use it in cookies or spread it between cake layers.

Lemon Bars

These are slightly tangy, slightly sweet cookies that are exceptionally tasty with tea.

Level: Intermediate

Yield: 30 cookies

Can be done completely ahead

Dough
1¾ cups all-purpose flour
½ cup confectioner's sugar
1 cup butter or margarine,
    cut into small chunks

Topping
4 large eggs
1½ cups sugar
6 TB. fresh lemon juice

¼ cup all-purpose flour
½ tsp. baking powder

Preheat the oven to 350°F. Combine the flour and confectioner's sugar in a bowl. Using your fingers, a pastry blender, or two knives, work the butter into the flour mixture until the ingredients resemble crumbs. If you use a food processor, add the ingredients to the work bowl and pulse the ingredients 15–20 times, or until the mixture resembles coarse meal. Press the crumbs onto the bottom of a 9" × 13" baking pan. Bake about 25 minutes or until the dough has browned lightly. Remove the dough from the oven.

Combine the eggs, sugar, lemon juice, flour, and baking powder in a bowl. Beat the ingredients with a handheld or electric mixer set at moderate speed for 1–2 minutes or until the mixture is creamy looking and uniformly colored. Pour the mixture over the partially baked dough. Bake 20–22 minutes or until the surface has browned lightly. Let the dessert cool in the pan. Cut the cookies into bars with 5 cuts on the long side of the baking pan (making 6 strips) and 4 cuts on the short side (making 5 strips). You can freeze these cookies for 6 months.

Beverages

Most of us don't think of making beverages as "cooking." But you do cook some beverages—hot chocolate, for example. More importantly, drinks of some sort go hand and hand with food. You might serve cocktails with hors d'oeuvres before dinner, make iced tea to sip with the lunch, or prepare coffee after a feast. The point is, making beverages is one of the skills you learn as you master cooking techniques. Fortunately, most are quick and easy to prepare.

Spiced Apple Iced Tea

This version is a little jazzier than most.

Level: Easy

Yield: 2 servings

Can be done completely ahead

2 tea bags	1 (3") piece of cinnamon stick
1 TB. brown sugar	1 strip orange or lemon peel, 2" long, 1" wide
½ apple, sliced (no need to peel it)	2 slices fresh ginger root (optional)
4 cloves	2 cups boiling water

Place the tea bags, brown sugar, apple slices, cloves, cinnamon stick, orange peel, and ginger root in a pitcher. Pour the boiling water over them and let the mixture steep at least 30 minutes. To make iced tea, strain the liquid after it has cooled, and pour it into glasses filled with ice cubes.

Lemonade

If you've never tasted homemade lemonade, you're in for a treat.

Level: Intermediate

Yield: about one quart lemonade base, enough for 12–18 drinks, depending on the size of the glass

Can be done completely ahead

1½ cups water
1½ cups sugar
1 lemon peel, grated
1½ cups freshly squeezed lemon juice, about 6–7 large lemons
ice cubes
cold water or club soda

Combine the water and sugar in a saucepan and bring to a boil over high heat. Lower the heat slightly and cook the liquid for 3 minutes. Remove the pan from the heat and stir in the lemon peel and juice. Refrigerate the liquid for at least 1 hour. Strain into a storage container. To make lemonade, fill a glass ⅓ full with the lemon-flavored liquid, add a few ice cubes and enough water or club soda to fill the glass, and stir.

Sweet Lassi

This is a light, refreshing, and exceptionally thirst-quenching beverage from India.

Level: Easy

Yield: 1 serving

Cannot be done ahead

1 cup plain yogurt
1 TB. sugar
3 ice cubes
3 TB. ice water
2 TB. milk or cream (any kind)

Place all the ingredients in a blender jar (or the work bowl of a food processor). Blend at high speed 30 seconds, or until the drink is well blended and frothy.

Second Thoughts

You can create all sorts of lassi flavors by adding fruit. Depending on the fruit and your taste buds, you may need to increase the sugar. Try these variations:

➤ Add ¼ cup sliced strawberries

➤ Add ⅓ cup cut-up mango

➤ Add ¼ cup blueberries

➤ Add ½ banana

Strawberry Lemon Shake

This makes a wonderful warm-weather treat you can serve at a cookout. For a lower fat version, use skim milk and frozen yogurt.

Level: Easy

Yield: 2 servings

Cannot be done ahead

¾ cup sliced strawberries

1 TB. sugar

1¼ cups strawberry ice cream

⅓ cup lemon sherbet

½ cup milk (skim, low-fat, or whole)

Combine the ingredients in a blender jar (or the work bowl of a food processor). Blend at high speed 30 seconds, or until the drink is well blended and thick.

Spiced Coffee Shake

Coffee drinking has become a national pastime in recent years. This thick, cold shake combines coffee with some warm spices, which means you can enjoy it in any kind of weather.

Level: Easy

Yield: 2 servings

*Can be done up to the * in the instructions*

2 tsp. brown sugar

2 (2") cinnamon sticks

4 whole cloves

4 whole allspice

2 strips orange peel, 2" long, 1" wide

1½ cups extra strong hot coffee

1 cup coffee ice cream

½ cup milk (skim, low-fat, or whole)

Combine the brown sugar, cinnamon sticks, cloves, allspice, and orange peel in a pitcher and pour the hot coffee over them. Let the ingredients rest at least 1 hour. Strain the liquid.

* Put the liquid into a blender jar (or the work bowl of a food processor). Add the ice cream and milk. Blend at high speed 30 seconds, or until the drink is well blended and thick.

Marshmallowed Hot Chocolate

Oh, this is so good when you come in from the cold!

Level: Easy

Yield: 2 servings

Can be done completely ahead

2 cups milk (skim, low-fat, or whole)

6 marshmallows

3 TB. unsweetened cocoa powder

2 TB. sugar

pinch of salt

3 TB. very hot water

¾ tsp. vanilla extract

Heat the milk and marshmallows in a saucepan over moderate heat for 5–6 minutes or until the milk is hot, bubbles appear around the edges of the pan, and the marshmallows have almost melted. Mix the cocoa powder, sugar, and salt in a small bowl. Add the hot water and stir the mixture to form a smooth paste. Add about ¼ cup of the hot milk to the cocoa mixture, stir the mixture, and pour the mixture back into the pan. Heat the mixture until it almost comes to a boil (you will see bubbles forming more rapidly). Remove the pan from the heat. Add the vanilla extract and stir.

Kitchen Clue

This has a much better texture if you transfer the liquid to a blender and whirl it a few seconds until it becomes frothy. Or, froth the liquid in the saucepan, using a hand blender. Leave out the marshmallows if you don't like your hot chocolate so sweet.

Raspberry-Champagne Punch

This is a beautiful punch, worthy of almost any celebration.

Level: Easy

Yield: 8–10 servings

Cannot be done ahead

1 pint raspberry sherbet
⅓ cup frozen lemonade concentrate
1 (⅘ quart) bottle chilled rosé wine

1 (⅘ quart) bottle chilled champagne
1 pint fresh raspberries

Stir the sherbet, lemonade concentrate, and a cup of the rosé wine for 2–3 minutes, or until the sherbet has softened. Place the mixture in a punch bowl and stir in the remaining rosé wine and the champagne. Add the raspberries and serve.

Three Classic Cocktails

These are the most enduring cocktails; they never go out of style.

Level: Easy

Yield: each makes one serving

Cannot be done ahead

continues

continued

Dry Martini

ice cubes

⅙ part dry vermouth

⅚ part gin or vodka

one pitted or pimiento-stuffed green olive per cocktail

Put ice cubes into a cocktail glass. Add the vermouth and the gin or vodka in the proportions given. Stir. Add anolive. You may make several of these at one time in a cocktail shaker.

Bloody Mary

3 oz. tomato juice

1 jigger vodka, (1½ oz. or 3 TB.)

½ tsp. lemon juice

½ tsp. Worcestershire sauce

⅛ tsp. hot pepper sauce

ice cubes (optional)

freshly ground black pepper

a celery stick for garnish

Combine the tomato juice, vodka, lemon juice, Worcestershire sauce, and hot pepper sauce in a glass. Add ice cubes if desired. Sprinkle the cocktail with some freshly ground pepper and garnish with the celery stick. You may make several of these at one time in a cocktail shaker.

Margarita

1 jigger tequila (1½ oz. or 3 TB.)

½ oz. triple sec, or any orange-flavored liqueur (1 TB.)

1 oz. fresh lime juice (2 TB.)

ice cubes

lime quarter

salt, preferably Kosher (coarse) salt

Combine the tequila, triple sec, and lime juice with some ice cubes in a cocktail shaker. Shake vigorously to combine the ingredients. Moisten the rim of a cocktail glass with the lime quarter, then press the rim into some salt. Pour the beverage into the salted glass.

Second Thoughts

Some people prefer their martini with a cocktail onion, a twist of lemon, or a tiny amount of chopped jalapeño pepper rather than the traditional martini olive. You can find cocktail onions in jars near the olives in your supermarket. You may create new versions of the martini if you like, substituting various brandies for the vermouth or adding crushed fresh ginger, raspberries, strawberries, and so on, to the cocktail shaker (strain into the cocktail glass).

Second Thoughts

You can give the popular Bloody Mary a little more oomph if you use V-8 juice or clam-flavored tomato juice.

Mulled Wine

Mulled wine tastes and smells wonderful on a cold, wintry day.

Level: Intermediate

Yield: 6 servings

Can be done completely ahead

1 (750 ml) bottle of red burgundy
    wine (about 3 cups)

½ cup water

¼ cup sugar

⅓ cup currants or dark raisins

⅓ cup golden raisins

½ orange

½ lemon

2 (3") pieces of cinnamon stick

8 cloves

1 tsp. whole allspice

1 sliced orange for garnish

continues

continued

Combine the wine, water, sugar, currants, golden raisins, half orange, half lemon, cinnamon sticks, cloves, and allspice in a stainless steel, enameled, or other *nonreactive saucepan*. Simmer for 10 minutes. Strain the liquid into a chafing dish or other heated serving vessel. (Alternatively, you may combine the cinnamon sticks, cloves, nutmeg, and allspice in a small muslin pouch or a piece of cheesecloth tied with kitchen string or a bag tie, and immerse the bag into the liquid, removing the bag to strain the brew.) Garnish the beverage with a few extra orange slices.

What Is It?

You need a **nonreactive saucepan** because the acid in the wine could corrode metals that react with acid. Stainless steel, glass, ceramic, and porcelain are nonreactive materials that will not corrode.

Mulled Cider

People think of mulled cider as a winter drink, but it's delicious anytime and is especially suitable for parties as a good alternative to alcoholic beverages.

Level: Intermediate

Yield: 8–10 servings

Can be done completely ahead

2 quarts apple cider

½ cup brown sugar

2 (3") pieces of cinnamon stick

1 dozen whole allspice

1 dozen cloves

6 black peppercorns

1 TB. crystallized ginger or a small chunk of peeled ginger root

peel of half an orange

1 orange studded with 12 whole cloves for garnish (optional)

Combine the cider and sugar in a saucepan. Cook over moderate heat 3–4 minutes, stirring frequently, or until the sugar has dissolved. Combine the remaining ingredients in a small muslin pouch or a piece of cheesecloth tied with kitchen string or a bag tie. Immerse the bag into the liquid and simmer the ingredients 25 minutes. Remove the bag. (Alternatively, you may add the seasonings to the liquid and strain them out when you're ready to pour the brew into the chafing dish.) Pour the cider into a chafing dish or other heated serving vessel. Garnish the beverage by immersing the clove-studded orange into the cider.

Index

F

G

P–Q

Recipe Index